"The scope of our art is to give wings to the soul. . . ."

GREGORY OF NAZIANZUS

THE SCOPE OF OUR ART

The Vocation of the Theological Teacher

Edited by

L. Gregory Jones and Stephanie Paulsell

WILLIAM B. EERDMANS PUBLISHING COMPANY
GRAND RAPIDS, MICHIGAN / CAMBRIDGE, U.K.

Wm. B. Eerdmans Publishing Co.
255 Jefferson Ave. S.E., Grand Rapids, Michigan 49503 /
P.O. Box 163, Cambridge CB3 9PU U.K.

Printed in the United States of America

06 05 04 03 02   7 6 5 4 3 2

Library of Congress Cataloging-in-Publication Data

The scope of our art : the vocation of the theological teacher /
edited by L. Gregory Jones and Stephanie Paulsell.
p.   cm.
Includes bibliographical references.
ISBN 0-8028-4958-X (pbk. : alk. paper)
1. Christian education — Teacher training.   I. Jones, L. Gregory.
II. Paulsell, Stephanie, 1962-
BV1533 .S36   2002
230'.071'1 — dc21

2001040534

www.eerdmans.com

Contents

CONTENTS

THEOLOGICAL TEACHERS IN THEIR CLASSROOMS

THEOLOGICAL TEACHERS IN THEIR SCHOOLS

Introduction

IN THE SUMMER OF 1997, seventeen theological teachers and scholars gathered at the Wabash Center for Teaching and Learning in Theology and Religion to begin a conversation about vocation. Some of us were tenured professors; some of us were deans; others of us had been in our first jobs for only a few years. Some of us taught in undergraduate colleges, some in free-standing seminaries, some in university divinity schools. We were Catholic and Protestant, some formed in liberal traditions, others in conservative ones. We had attended a variety of graduate schools, and were each, to some degree, stamped by our school's distinctive ethos. We represented a wide range of disciplines: theology, history, ethics, philosophy of religions, religion and literature, biblical studies, spirituality. Our pedagogical practices were diverse, as were our understandings of our task as theological teachers. And from our very first conversations, it was clear that there were profound theological differences among us.

Sound like a recipe for disaster? It might have been. But held within the gracious hospitality of the Wabash Center, with time for conversation and time for rest, and lots of good meals together, we found that in spite of all that might divide us, we were bound together by this: a love of our work, a conviction that it was what we were meant to do with our lives, and a belief that the way we practiced our vocation mattered. We were all looking for alternatives to religious cultures that often mistrust intellectual work as isolating, irrelevant, and corrosive of the spirit, and to academic cultures in which intellectual work is a commodity to be traded for employment, for tenure, for promotion, for a better job than the one we have. We were all intrigued by the idea of exploring the spiritual dimension of the work that we were daily engaged in as teachers and scholars, readers and writers. Several questions immediately arrested our attention: What is the relationship between academic and spiritual formation? What difference might it make in our teaching and research if we understood the work of reading, writing, teaching, and learning as potentially religious practices? How ought the relationship between an individual's vocation and an institution's mission be understood? How does one's sense of vocation help one negotiate a path through the demands of the several constituencies that make claims on the theological teacher? Could the way we practice our vocation draw our students into a livelier consideration of their own?

Although we had questions in common, it was clear that terms like "vocation," "spiritual formation," and "mission" would be highly contested among us. And so we began our work together autobiographically, each participant preparing for our first meeting a short narrative of the formative experiences on which his or her vocation was balanced. We told stories of books and questions that had refused to let us go, of great teachers who had invited us into conversations that were at once ancient and very much alive, and of languages whose unfamiliar vocabulary and grammar made us see the world fresh. As these stories accumulated, we learned which experiences undergirded each other's intellectual positions, which passions had given shape to our angles of vision, which deep joys and real griefs had led us to devote our lives to theological scholarship and teaching. In our conversations over the next three years, we found ourselves unable to pigeonhole one another, unable to label and dismiss each other's intellectual commitments because we had come to know each other's positions first as complicated and three-dimensional, born of real experiences, real questions, real life. This made an enormous difference in our work together. Our knowledge of one another and our knowledge of what had led us to embrace the work of theological teaching made us more patient than we might otherwise have been, more willing to listen, more willing to try on perspectives with which we were not immediately comfortable.

This does not mean that all our disagreements were solved. Far from it. We tried early on, for example, to come up with a working definition of "vocation" to which we might all give our assent. This was, shall we say, somewhat less successful than our shared autobiographical work. The word "vocation" possessed different valences for different members of our group. Among those who had grown up with the word, some embraced it as a rich source of meaning while others wanted to keep a safe distance from it, associating it with oppressively narrow ideas about how one might live one's life. For others, "vocation" was not a word they had ever used to understand or describe their life work, and they were curious about how the word had been used by others. For some, "vocation" had a distinctively theological cast; for others not. Some came at their understanding of vocation from the perspective of a particular church body; others approached it from a more academic perspective.

Rather than producing a systematic definition of "vocation," we decided to draw upon our diverse perspectives in a way that did not smooth out the differences among them. We began writing essays for one another on aspects of what we understood to be our "vocation," which eventually became the essays in this book. Many understandings of the theological teacher's vocation emerged in these essays. For Clark Gilpin, it is a "vibrant attachment to 'public thoughts'" that makes scholarly work a vocation. For Paul Griffiths, it is a vibrant attachment to "particularly Christian intellectual habits." Paul Wadell sees his vocation as a theological teacher as helping his students "to grow captivated with God." Susan Simonaitis believes the vocation of the theological teacher is to initiate students into "the difficult discipline of genuine conversation" through the interrogation of complex texts constructed by humans in response to the sacred. Bonnie Miller-McLemore and Rosemary Skinner Keller insist on an understanding of vocation that includes all aspects of one's life, not just one's professional life. And Gordon Smith feels that something important is lost when we consider an individual's vocation apart from the mission of the institution within which that individual lives and works.

In the midst of these various understandings of vocation, however, several common touchstones emerged. We had all been influenced, it seemed, by Simone Weil's work on attention, especially in relation to intellectual work. All of us were intrigued by her claim that academic study can hone our capacity for attention, making us better able to be present to God and to our suffering neighbor. We all felt that the cultivation of attention in our teaching and our learning, our reading and our writing, our relationships with colleagues and our administrative work was crucial to the practice of our vocation. Mindfulness, generosity, hospitality, and discipline also emerged as common themes in our essays.

So what we offer you here is not a systematic treatment of the vocation of theological teachers and scholars. Rather, we hope to invite you into a living, breathing conversation about that vocation. We hope to open enough space within the question of the vocation of the theological teacher that you will find a place to consider your own. We hope to offer portraits of vocations lived out every day, in the tasks, large and small, that make up the theological teacher's life. We found in the writing of these essays that we became more attentive to the formative power of those tasks: we became more mindful of the contemplative dimension of reading and writing, more engaged by the holy work of teaching, better able to see in the details of our administrative work the precious scaffolding of the communities within which we enact our commitments. We hope that reading these essays may have the same effect for you.

The essays we wrote for one another clustered around three distinct themes: study, teaching, and institutional life. We began to imagine the three sections of the book as reports from three locations of the theological teacher's life: the desk, the classroom, and the school. The boundaries of these locations are fluid, of course, as the essays themselves attest. But we found it helpful to write from these particular locations, and we hope you will find the structure helpful as you consider in what ways and in what places your own vocation is enacted.

The first section, "The Formation of the Theological Teacher," takes as its starting point Clark Gilpin's spacious rendering of the phrase "academic disciplines" to refer not only to our specialized fields of study but also the disciplined formative practices of our vocation. Essays in the first section explore the formative power of graduate education, vocational kinship with other teachers and scholars, the spiritual disciplines of reading and writing, and the tension between traditional contemplative models and the material conditions under which our vocations are lived out.

The second section, "Theological Teachers in Their Classrooms," focuses on our work as teachers and features four essays that propose four models for the teaching vocation: as conversation, as a ministry of hope, as the cultivation of wisdom in a complex world, and as ceaseless prayer. Within these essays, you will find teachers in action, putting their theological and pedagogical commitments into practice through "generative lectures" and reading groups, through conversation and compassionate listening, and through the constant struggle to understand the world of their students and to open paths between what theological teachers have to offer and what students need and desire.

The third section, "Theological Teachers in Their Schools," attempts to address the question of the relationship between an individual's vocation and an institution's mission. Using the *Rule of St. Benedict*, Claire Mathews McGinnis reflects on stability in academic life, while Frederick Norris turns to the Cappadocian theologians to reflect on doing theology "in the outback." Greg Jones offers reflections from his experience of the tension between the teaching vocation and the vocation of the administrator. Leanne Van Dyk and Gordon T. Smith contextualize the tensions and congruencies between individual and institutional vocations by examining how this relationship is negotiated in their schools as the missions of their institutions evolve.

You will find, in these diverse reflections, many ways to understand the vocation of theological teachers. There are many important agreements among these essays and many spirited disagreements. But all are in *conversation* with one another. Although we could not all agree on one final definition of "vocation," we all sighed a deep sigh of recognition when Frederick Norris retrieved from the writings of his beloved Gregory Nazianzen an image of the vocation of the theological teacher and scholar. "The scope of our art," Gregory wrote, "is to give wings to the soul." We hope that this account of the scope of our art is rich enough to inspire reflection on the scope of yours.

The work of many people made possible the extraordinary conversation that continues, we hope, in this book. We are deeply grateful to the Lilly Endowment, which funded this work through its support of the Wabash Center for Teaching and Learning in Theology and Religion and the Catholic Theological Union Project on the Vocation of Theological Educators. Craig Dykstra, the Vice President for Religion at the Endowment, let us know that the work we were doing was close to his own heart and offered thoughtful counsel along the way. Raymond Williams and Lucinda Huffaker of the Wabash Center were the best of hosts, offering the resources of the Wabash Center and their own keen questions and observations to our work together. Donald Senior, C.P., the President of Catholic Theological Union, welcomed and supported the CTU Project from the very beginning and helped shape many of the questions that the Wabash Center Consultation on Vocation took up.

We are also grateful to two members of our group who were unable, due to pressing personal and professional commitments, to contribute essays to this volume, but whose presence in our ongoing conversation was crucial. Beverly Gaventa of Princeton Theological Seminary maintained a spirited defense of academic specialization throughout our discussions that gave all of us a fresh perspective on our research. Phillis Sheppard of DePaul University taught us what she had learned through her research into African-American women's religious experience, that listening is one of the spiritual disciplines of the theological teacher, a discipline we ignore at our peril.

We would also like to thank the families and communities who made it possible for us to spend a week together for three summers in a row. This book would not exist without them.

Finally, we would like to thank our colleagues in theological education, those who teach in colleges and seminaries, divinity schools and Sunday schools, in classrooms, in pulpits, in homes. With gratitude, we dedicate this book to them. Paul Wadell writes in his essay, "If teaching is to be a ministry of hope and of joy, it requires the companionship of friends who care about what we care about and care about us caring for it." We have been privileged to find such friendship among the colleagues with whom we have studied and taught, and we were fortunate to find it in each other. It is such friendship that we wish, through this book, to extend to you.

FORMATIVE PRACTICES OF THE
THEOLOGICAL TEACHER'S VOCATION

The Formation of the Scholar

W. CLARK GILPIN

DELIVERING THE PHI BETA KAPPA address at Harvard in August 1837, Ralph Waldo Emerson enunciated high aspirations for "the American Scholar," who "raises himself from private considerations, and breathes and lives on public and illustrious thoughts. He is the world's eye." In what follows, I will elaborate Emerson's image of the American scholar by proposing that this vibrant attachment to "public thoughts" is the dimension of scholarly work that makes it a vocation. Now, as in 1837, it is a difficult vocational aspiration, since the active passion for thinking too frequently becomes constricted, such that the scholar "tends to become a mere thinker, or, still worse, the parrot of other men's thinking." Now, as in 1837, it challenges institutions of higher education with the daunting responsibility to foster intellectual creativity, failing which, "our American colleges will recede in their public importance."[1] In my elaboration of Emerson, the academy and the individual scholar, alike, are called to a vocation of lively "public thoughts."

The more specific purpose of this chapter is to assay the contribution of graduate education to the vocation of scholarship in our time. I focus my attention on education and scholarly vocation in the academic fields of theology and religion, but I do so mindful that analogous questions are

---

1. Ralph Waldo Emerson, *Essays and Lectures,* ed. Joel Porte (New York: Literary Classics of the United States, 1983), pp. 63, 54, 59.

present and actively discussed across the humanities and social sciences. I ask how Ph.D. programs in the various specialized fields that comprise the academic study of religion ought to prepare a person to pursue the interlocking, direct responsibilities of the scholar — research and teaching — at colleges, universities, and theological seminaries. And, I ask how such a preparation invites the graduate student to think about the scholarly career as a persistent and consistent expression of his or her orientation toward life as a whole, that is, as a vocation.

My reflections on doctoral education in religion are divided into three parts. In the first, I focus on the North American cultural context of graduate research and suggest how broad cultural questions about religion influence the questions that students pursue in their specialized research. In the second, I consider the curriculum of doctoral education in religion, thinking of the curriculum both as a process through which a student deepens her "broad cultural questions about religion" into a specialized inquiry and also as a framework that relates specialized questions to a more comprehensive investigation of religion as a field of study. In the third, I suggest that the term "academic disciplines" may connote not only "specialized fields of study" but also "disciplined intellectual capacities" that are cultivated in the process of graduate education. These intellectual disciplines of scholarship, I will indicate in conclusion, are pivotal to the formation of the scholar.

The Cultural Context of Graduate Research

Perhaps the most familiar criticism leveled against the specialized nature of the research doctorate is its insularity. Rarefied research, it is said, pursues topics that have little consequence beyond the immediate field of specialization. There is some truth to this criticism. With the massive expansion of American higher education since World War II, much that passes for scholarship has been reduced to the status of an "inter-office memorandum." By this, I mean that sufficiently large numbers of people are now engaged in research and teaching in various areas of study that they themselves constitute a sufficient audience for a journal article or monograph without regard to any wider publics. The "business" of higher education supports its own internal communication and the academic argot in which that communication occurs. Recent critics of graduate theological education, for example, have charged that standards and priorities for the Ph.D. degree are dominated by highly specialized academic disciplines, firmly institutionalized in academic professional societies such as the American Academy of Religion, the American Society of Church History, or the Society of Biblical Literature. These scholarly "guilds," as they are often termed, cultivate criteria for excellence and forms of inquiry that are widely judged to have impeded the capacity of scholars to address the religious issues facing churches and other salient publics. Furthermore, by emphasizing the independence of discrete fields of inquiry rather than the comprehensive aims of theological education as a whole, specialized disciplines are thought to have fragmented and thereby deformed the theological curriculum as an instrument for clergy education. Left unaddressed, this insularity of doctoral education indeed disrupts the common idea that a vocation is work that addresses a society's needs, including the need for critique, and thereby enriches the commonweal.

The question of *how* doctoral education ought to be related to the wider society raises a second problem, which may be illustrated from an article in the March 30, 1998, *New Yorker* about Michael Lynton, the recently appointed chief executive officer of Penguin Books. With reference to Lynton and other major publishing executives, the article asserts that "in big publishing, books are increasingly being regarded less as discrete properties than as one vital link in a media food chain that begins with an idea, takes early shape as a magazine article, gets fleshed out between book covers, gains bigger life on a movie or TV screen, and enters the hereafter as a videocassette or the inspiration for a toy."[2] As a provider of information, the intellectual constantly participates in a "commerce of ideas" that reductively homogenizes those ideas in a socially affirmative market consensus. Although few academics either hope or fear that their books will inspire new toys, we are, as a group, far too seldom challenged to state how our scholarship explores, tests, and sometimes resists the boundaries of the culture in which it occurs. A vigorous concept of vocation will include a professional ethic that guides the conduct and orders the social relations of the scholar.

These two criticisms of doctoral education in the United States and their implications for an adequate concept of the scholarly vocation raise,

2. Robert S. Boynton, "The Hollywood Way," *The New Yorker* 48 (March 30, 1998): 48-56.

for me, fundamental questions about the responsibility of the intellectual in contemporary society and about the publics to whom we are accountable as we pursue our work. My own concern with these issues of public accountability leads me to measure doctoral education in religion by the extent to which it produces scholars who are able to enrich the public's ability to understand and evaluate the roles that religion plays — for good and for ill — in common civic life. Further, I want to ask whether interdisciplinary and comparative interpretations of religion might offer critical resources for understanding and responsibly practicing any particular religious tradition. In pursuing this inquiry into graduate education, I do not wish to disparage or diminish specialized research but, instead, to reconsider and accentuate the reciprocal relations of specialized knowledge with the wider culture. Nor, by orienting scholarship toward public understanding and common civic life, do I intend to diminish its connections to particular religious communities but rather to consider those communities as parts, albeit important parts, of civil society. Similarly, by making religion the encompassing subject of doctoral education, I am not excluding theology from Ph.D. programs but conceiving theology as one element in the academic study of religion. I want, in other words, an approach to specialized doctoral education in religion that presses faculty and graduate students to reflect on the wider human significance of the intellectual work to which they have devoted themselves. In short, this essay explores how specialized doctoral education in religion can shape a public vocation for the scholar, one that makes a substantial, even critical, intellectual contribution to religious communities and civic culture.

Students beginning Ph.D. programs in religion, like many thoughtful citizens today, are both fascinated and perplexed by life in a society of extensive and diverse religious beliefs and practices. Although various forms of Christianity still predominate in this religious mix, the older image of the Protestant mainstream as the American host culture is seriously unsettled by the practical and intellectual recognition of the many cultures that constitute "American religion." Daily life in contemporary culture impresses graduate student and citizen alike with a series of questions about religion. What are these religious traditions? How have the various world traditions and their multiple denominations come into existence? Beyond such seemingly defined religious neighbors as Sikhs, Korean Presbyterians, Polish Catholics, and Reform Jews, how do we even begin to understand less clearly bounded appeals to religious community such as "new age spirituality" or "the African-American religious experience"? What implicit or explicit claims do these religious groups make about the nature and conduct of human life? About gender, race, or labor? What have been their characteristic cultural productions in art, literature, or scientific discovery? Do the religions help us to respond to the difficult moral and intellectual problems that face individuals and the society as a whole, in such fields as medicine, law, education, or family policy? Can we clarify and understand more fully the points of agreement or disagreement among these various religious communities, such that this understanding can shape our perspective toward the common good and the contribution of religion to that good?

My own conversations with contemporary students strongly suggest that public questions such as these provide the background ideas that directly or indirectly motivated them to pursue graduate study in religion. During their studies, these broader public or cultural questions about religion continue to influence the issues and topics of their formal academic research. In important ways that are often not immediately evident to the student, these broad, frequently vague, sometimes misplaced public questions about religion are gradually shaped into the more specific historical, exegetical, and theological questions the student will pursue through courses and, eventually, a doctoral dissertation. I believe that the human significance and scope of specialized research can be dramatically enhanced if students are challenged throughout their doctoral programs to understand this complex interaction between public questions and academic questions about religion.

From this perspective, the educational process of courses and examinations that culminates in writing a specialized Ph.D. dissertation should include reflection on the reasons that have motivated a student to select and pursue a particular topic. The process would raise questions about the importance of the topic: its importance to the student, its importance to the educational purposes of colleges, universities, and theological seminaries, its importance to churches and to civil society. The process would invite the student to explore living religious traditions and cultural forms as the matrix from which his or her specialized research has emerged. It would encourage the student to consider ways in which his or her specialized research might illuminate religion and culture for other inquisitive persons, be they college students, clergy, or citizens in other walks of life.

The graduate study of religion will not proceed very fruitfully, I think, unless we constantly struggle to ascertain the tacit influences of the cultural context in which we are pursuing it. The questions that scholars pose about even the most distant religions in time and space are nonetheless questions posed by scholars, in a particular historical context, expressing the particular interests and pre-understandings that they bring to their research. The achievement of modern historians of Christianity, for example, in recovering and interpreting the religion of African-American slaves or the writings of medieval women mystics has, in no small measure, been prompted by contemporary cultural concerns. Of course, the fact that such retrievals have proven necessary is equally an illustration of cultural influences on scholarship. The selection and pursuit of a research topic thus inescapably bears an ethical component, to which doctoral education must help students become attentive. The challenge of publicly engaged scholarship is not, therefore, devising ways to "apply" scholarship to matters of cultural consequence. Rather, culturally attentive scholarship attempts to achieve some self-critical understanding of the pre-existing connection between our scholarly inquiries and what I have called the current, broader cultural questions concerning religion. One mark of excellence in doctoral education is the presence of pedagogical strategies that cultivate a student's capacity for reflexive understanding of the way her scholarly questions participate in public questions with wider human import.

The Curricular Process

These observations about the reciprocal relations between public questions and scholarly questions about religion have important consequences for interpreting the general aim and structure of the curriculum of doctoral studies. In broadest strokes, the general purpose of a doctoral curriculum is easily stated. It is designed to lead a student into gradually increasing competence in the subject matter and methods of inquiry that characterize a specialized field of study. At the same time, it is designed to interpret the importance of that specialization to some larger orbit of studies. Thus, the scholar writing a history of Christianity and politics in colonial Rhode Island is ideally expected to be able not only to offer a fresh reading of that particular topic but also to explain its importance to the larger history of Christianity and, in turn, to the academic study of religion as a whole. These general purposes of any doctoral curriculum are substantially complicated by the fact that, like the scholarly interests of individual faculty and students, the curriculum too is being reshaped by its reciprocal relations to public questions of religion, although this reshaping usually occurs at a slower rate and elements of earlier curricula usually persist within new forms. Consequently, graduate programs in religion today look very different from those of an earlier period.

My own experience, first as a graduate student at the University of Chicago in the early seventies and then as a faculty member in the early nineties, provides a useful illustrative contrast that suggests how background public questions about religion tacitly shape doctoral education in a given era. Looking back on the 1970s, the organizing question of the curriculum at the Divinity School of the University of Chicago seems to have been the plausibility of religious belief in the context of secular modernity. This generally tacit question became explicit in the two required course sequences for M.A. students: "Western Religious Traditions" and "Religious Thought and the Modern World." It also appeared as the organizing principle of what we then called the "dialogical fields" of Ph.D. specialization: "Religion and Literature," "Religion and Psychological Studies," and "Ethics and Society," in which the Christian tradition was related, even correlated, to some domain of modern knowledge or culture. Even the study of world religions bore the stamp of this underlying question. Mircea Eliade's best-known book, *The Myth of the Eternal Return* (ET, 1954), for example, was organized around the contrast between "archaic man" and "modern man," and it concluded by asking whether the modern historical consciousness, "the terror of history," had rendered religious expression impossible.

Although I will not develop a descriptive interpretation here, I would be prepared to argue that this general question about "faith and the secular" was tightly related to the public questions about religion that dominated the Divinity School's principal constituency in liberal or mainstream Protestantism at mid-century. Although this question has not disappeared from the Divinity School today, it is now overshadowed by the current set of questions around religious pluralism discussed in the preceding section of this chapter. These more recent public questions about religion tend to assume not so much religion's gradual eclipse by secularity but rather its evident, even troubling, vitality. In a world of finite resources, how do the various religions interpret the conduct of human life, and do their interpretations contribute to a possibility that all may flourish?

9

The shift from questions about secularity to questions about pluralism seems to me to lie close beneath the surface of the reorganization of the faculty at the Divinity School during 1992-93. This reorganization created three academic committees of the faculty: the Committee on Historical Studies in Religious Traditions, the Committee on Constructive Studies in Religion, and the Committee on Religion and the Human Sciences. As a process of inquiry, this reorganization presupposes a more religiously diverse faculty and student body than had been present twenty-five years earlier. Although questions about faith and secularity have not disappeared, they are currently overshadowed by investigation of the multiple religious interpretations of the world and of human conduct. So, for example, the required M.A. course sequence today revolves around three topics: the role of narrative in religious communities; comparative study of the role of the exodus narrative in Judaism and Christianity; and the implications of narrative for theology and ethics.

I tend to think about the three committees of the current Chicago faculty by beginning with the one of which I am a member, the Committee on Historical Studies in Religious Traditions. It seems improbable that anybody could understand religion in general without trying to understand at least one religion in particular. It is also difficult to imagine that anybody could understand religion without understanding the chronological development of a single tradition, its endurance in time and space. The Committee on Historical Studies in Religious Traditions includes those members of the faculty — historians — who seek to understand the continuities and contexts of particular traditions. Right now, it focuses primarily on biblical studies, the history of Christianity, and the history of Judaism; but of course, in principle, this focus could be expanded to include, for example, a scholar whose specialty is the historical development of Islam or of the religious traditions of China. The point is that this committee is composed of scholars who want to understand the development of individual traditions.

In various ways, this historical study of religious traditions raises a whole set of constructive or normative questions about the nature and conduct of human life. Each of these traditions makes claims of what it is to be properly human. A second faculty committee, the Committee on Constructive Studies in Religion, inquires into claims regarding "the truth about life" that appear in the religious traditions, appraising their internal coherence, their relations to alternative interpretations of reality, and their diagnostic or transformative power with respect to human life. Within this committee are specialists in theology, ethics, and the philosophy of religions.

Third, since religions come to expression within cultures and social institutions, scholars may investigate religions in their relationships to culture and society. To do so, they employ the methods of the humanities and social sciences in order to accentuate the cultural embeddedness of religious traditions. Furthermore, to speak interchangeably, as I have been doing, of *religion* and *the religions* necessarily raises a whole set of comparative questions: What is it that makes the religions in some sense a single category, and how can we think about what we refer to as myth, ritual, sacred text, or religious leadership in cross-cultural and comparative ways? These questions about the cultural embeddedness of religious traditions and about the comparison of religions across cultural boundaries are the particular purview of the Committee on Religion and the Human Sciences. It includes faculty members who work in religion and literature, in the psychology and sociology of religions, and in the history of religions.

It is useful to imagine the curriculum of doctoral education as a process with a series of multiple phases or moments that together comprise the comprehensive process of studying religion. Each phase pursues a part, but only a part, of the subject. Reorganization of the Chicago faculty in 1992-93 assumed that the adequate study of religion requires all three moments or phases of inquiry that these three committees represent. The student or faculty member who was, so to speak, a renaissance person would have to be able to attend in some depth to all three dimensions in order to give a full account of the study of religion. Being mortal, all tend to specialize in one of the three but are mindful of the approaches and the interests of the others. We expect our students to take examinations that move them out of their own bailiwick into one of the others, and we think that any approach to the study of religion that entirely left out one of the three areas of scholarship represented by the faculty committees would fail to grasp the complexity and profundity of the subject we study.

A second mark of excellence in doctoral education is a curricular process that enables students to understand their respective specialties as phases in a comprehensive enterprise. The model currently in place at the University of Chicago includes historical understanding of multiple religious traditions, theological and ethical appraisal of the conduct of life informed by those traditions, and a culturally specific sensibility for comparative interpretation of the religions. As I have tried to suggest, however, the particular organization of the operational elements of religious studies into a curricular process will not only vary from school to school but from era to era. Participation in the more comprehensive curricular enterprise is thus important to the pursuit of specialization, but the student must also be encouraged to think about how the curricular structure itself is a historical construction, gradually shifting in dialogue with contemporary public questions concerning religion. Throughout, the vocation of the scholar is a vulnerable, socially conditioned enterprise in which individual scholarly passions are played out within a curriculum of historically contingent academic disciplines.

The Academic Disciplines of Doctoral Education

Academic specialization has frequently been characterized as a fragmenting and debilitating force in theological education, and Edward Farley has warned that "specialism" is the heart of the problem for graduate education in religion. Increasingly specialized research, Farley warns, threatens to turn doctoral studies into an aggregate of independent academic disciplines that obscures the coherence of the subject matter, isolates the student from scholarship in contiguous fields, and preempts the formative or transformative purposes of education that are intended to orient the life and career of the scholar in humanizing, moral, and interpersonal ways.[3]

Specialized scholarship presents serious difficulties, and Farley and others have carefully explored them. In addition to Farley's cogent criticisms, I would also say that "specialism" is boring, primarily because it too often simply accepts the questions and terminology of a specialized discipline and thereby robs the scholar of independent voice and fresh formulation of issues. The question facing doctoral education is whether study in specialized disciplines can cultivate a depth of understanding that generates intellectual scope and communicative power. At the risk of seeming to have latched onto a panacea, I would propose that the effort to achieve a self-critical understanding of the connection of individual scholarly ques-

---

3. See especially Edward Farley, *Theologia: The Fragmentation and Unity of Theological Education* (Philadelphia: Fortress, 1983) and *The Fragility of Knowledge: Theological Education in the Church and University* (Philadelphia: Fortress, 1988).

tions to prior, background public questions of religion is the invigorating heart of doctoral education.

To cultivate this capacity for recognizing the reciprocal relations between scholarly questions and public questions, I believe that doctoral education should develop strategies for inviting students to explore the public scope of their research projects. This would include opportunities for conversation with informed citizens and professionals from other fields, whose expertise might contribute alternative perspectives on the formative stages of dissertation research, in order that dissertation writers might better recognize the scope and import of the questions they are pursuing. This would include supervised teaching experiences that engage students with diverse audiences, in order to cultivate student capacity for accessible, substantive dialogue about their work. Such public engagement would encourage graduate students to think about the social assumptions that shape their research as well as its broader social implications, which might not have been initially evident to them. It will encourage them to consider from the outset how they plan to communicate with appropriate audiences about their research.

There could be, of course, two immediate objections to these or similar educational strategies of public dialogue. On the one hand, they might appear to measure the importance of scholarship by its capacity for popularization. On the other hand, they might seem to reduce the value of research to its significance for public policy decisions. I would answer that any scholar who has not self-critically appraised the governing reasons that motivate a particular academic inquiry risks becoming little more than the instrument of tacit societal values or a conventional academic agenda. When doctoral students critically examine the public questions in which their scholarship participates, I believe it will increase the intellectual power and profundity of their work, by providing opportunities for recognizing the reasons and motivations for their own research. I further believe that when citizens are invited to explore civic life from the vantage point of serious scholarship on religion, fresh and revised perspectives on culture and the common good may emerge. These dialogues of students with public groups thus have the possibility of representing in microcosm the more general social dialogue between scholarly and public questions of religion.

But, beyond valuable strategies of public dialogue around student scholarship, I believe we must also entrust the scholarly enterprise with the solitary attentiveness espoused by Emerson. In this regard, the proposal to connect scholarship to public questions assumes that sustained academic specialization gradually trains thought into a distinctive viewpoint on those public questions. The devoted practice of specialization thereby develops a resistance to cultural questions in the process of engaging them.

To indicate how this is so, I must enlarge the connotation of the phrase "academic disciplines," in order to refer not simply to specialized fields of study but also, and equally, to the disciplined formative practices through which the scholar pursues his or her work. As will be evident in later chapters of this book, these formative practices are precisely the everyday activities of scholarly labor: writing, reading, teaching. Insofar as these labors become the formative practices — the academic disciplines — of the scholar's vocation, they should exert a steady pressure on the scholar to articulate the wider human significance of the work to which she has devoted herself. To return to Emerson's formulation, academic disciplines are the formative practices by which the scholar "raises himself from private considerations, and breathes and lives on public and illustrious thoughts." In short, academic disciplines should also be understood as formative practices, and doctoral education requires strategies that would cultivate this dimension of specialized inquiry.

Since the earlier sections of this chapter have emphasized the influence on scholarship of broad cultural themes and questions, this characterization of academic disciplines takes the other side, by emphasizing with Emerson the active, shaping power of the scholar's point of view. Through attentiveness to nature, through reading, through daily action in the world, Emerson thought that the scholar's proper mode of appropriation was not to receive, merely, but to "transmute." Hence, he made it his dictum that "one must be an inventor to read well."[4] And this creative, "inventive" reading had as its purpose the creation of newly attentive, reciprocal relations with the life world. The "self-trust" that Emerson espoused as the cardinal virtue of the scholar, indeed, placed a premium on the solitary labors of thought and study. But through disciplined inwardness, Emerson the scholar believed he was performing the imaginative labor of conceiving a new vocation for himself and, perhaps, a new society in which this vocation might have meaning. Whatever contribution the intellectual might make to the common good was a contribution that dared to begin,

4. Emerson, *Essays and Lectures*, p. 59.

though not to end, with independent thought. In solitude, the American scholar "learns, that in going down into the secrets of his own mind, he has descended into the secrets of all minds. . . . The poet, in utter solitude remembering his spontaneous thoughts and recording them, is found to have recorded that, which men in crowded cities find true for them also."[5]

The resistance required for distinctively informed critique of public questions entails, as Pierre Hadot has argued for classical philosophy, a set of spiritual exercises that would discipline the intellectual's participation in everyday life in such a way as to provide an alternative perspective on it. In *Philosophy as a Way of Life,* Hadot describes the classical philosopher as one who

> must live this life every day, in this world in which he feels himself a stranger, and in which others perceive him to be one as well. And it is precisely in this daily life that he must seek to attain that way of life which is utterly foreign to the everyday world. The result is a perpetual conflict between the philosopher's effort to see things as they are from the standpoint of universal nature and the conventional vision of things underlying human society, a conflict between the life one should live and the customs and conventions of daily life.[6]

In summary of this point, I would say that a third mark of excellence in doctoral education is the presence of pedagogical strategies that cultivate specialized inquiry as a distinctively informed critical stance toward the public questions of religion.

When, therefore, Emerson declared that the scholar "is the eye of the world," his intent was not to presume a special privilege for scholarly expertise. To the contrary, his point was a point about the discipline required of scholarship if it is authentically to be a vocation. He thought, as do I, that we are too often content to see the world through the eye of "private consideration," whether that private consideration be thought of as specifically academic conventions and status or more broadly understood social and economic privileges. Rather, by contrasting private consideration with the eye of the world, he sought, amidst the undeniable power of conven-

---

5. Emerson, *Essays and Lectures,* pp. 63, 64.

6. Pierre Hadot, *Philosophy as a Way of Life: Spiritual Exercises from Socrates to Foucault,* ed. Arnold I. Davidson, trans. Michael Chase (Oxford: Blackwell, 1995), p. 58.

15

tion and privilege, amidst the historicity of the seers and the seen, to engage, like the classical philosophers, in the perpetual conflict between the "effort to see things as they are from the standpoint of universal nature and the conventional vision of things underlying human society, a conflict between the life one should live and the customs and conventions of daily life." This is the vocation.

Writing as a Spiritual Discipline

STEPHANIE PAULSELL

IMAGINE YOURSELF IN A ROOM where a young woman is sitting at a table before a blank page. Or perhaps she's standing at a desk; the year is 1286, and our vision can't be completely clear from such a distance. But imagine that you can see that she holds a goose quill pen in one hand and a knife for sharpening it and scraping away mistakes in the other. These tools rest easily in her hands because she is a member of an order dedicated to the production of manuscripts, and she uses them every day. She is a Carthusian nun, and like her Carthusian brothers and sisters, she believes that the contemplative and active dimensions of the Christian life can be united in the work of the scribe. Copying the works of others protects the solitude of the monastic cell from more intrusive forms of ministry. But it also allows silent monks and nuns to "preach," as the Carthusians liked to put it, "with their hands." It allows them to reach across the boundaries of geography and time to be in intimate communion with people they will never meet, but whom they hope to lead to God. The tools and the work of the scribe are very familiar to this woman, but the work she plans to do on this day is not. Today she does not take up her pen as a copyist.

If you can draw a little closer to this woman, you'll see that her eyes are rimmed with shadows, for she has not slept or eaten well for several days. She is, in fact, reeling in the aftermath of an intense experience of God's presence, an experience for which she is profoundly grateful, but which has left her exhausted and ill. Several days earlier, the words of lam-

17

entation in a pre-Lenten liturgy had made her anxious about her salvation, an anxiety she attempted to resolve through further meditation on Scripture. Her meditation led her to prayer, in the midst of which God came to her, full of sweetness, and she felt herself changed and renewed. But the God known by this woman is a God who writes, an author whose chosen parchment is the human heart. Her own heart is now congested with God's writing and overburdened with the response to it that is taking shape within her. She believes she will die if she cannot relieve her wounded heart, but she is afraid of losing what her heart contains. And so, knowing that she is about to depart from her role as a scribe, she puts her pen to the page and begins to write, probably for the first time, without a text from which to copy.

She writes in Latin, the language of the liturgy with which her life is permeated and the literature that nourishes her prayer, although she breaks into the vernacular now and then when she cannot make Latin words say what she wants them to say. And as she writes, not only is her festering heart soothed, but she finds that the act of writing brings her to another experience of God, an experience of God working in her. She acknowledges that it is impossible to find accurate words to describe divinity, but her pen nevertheless gathers up images for God as it moves across the page: mother, father, brother, friend; creator, judge, blessed food; true refreshment, precious stone; mirror into which the angels peer; medicine, physician, health itself; fragrant rose; life of the soul.

Now imagine time passing, and one century giving way to another. Imagine meeting the same woman, older now, at her desk again. If you can come close enough to look over her shoulder, you'll see that she is composing a letter this time, not in Latin, but in the vernacular of her correspondent. Latin is no longer the language of her growing body of writings; she now writes most often in her native Francoprovençal. She knows enough French, however, to maintain a correspondence with friends and fellow religious who do not share her dialect.

As she writes, we see that she is still preoccupied with the way a word can wound a heart, can inscribe itself so deeply that it swells and festers there. She tells her correspondent a story about a woman who is deeply vulnerable to the power of words. Hearing the word "vehement" in pious conversation, it becomes lodged in her heart, and she can think of nothing else. She believes that if she could only understand the word, she would find relief from the pressure it is creating inside her. Someone tells her that "vehement" means "strong," but that doesn't help. Finally, she prays to God to teach her the word's meaning and remove it from her heart.

Before she can finish her prayer, God answers her in such a way that she seems to be standing in a desert. She sees before her a dry and dying tree at the foot of a solitary mountain. The leaves on its drooping branches are inscribed with the names of the five senses. "Sight" is written on the leaves of the first branch, "hearing" on the leaves of the second, "taste" on the third, "smell" on the fourth, "touch" on the fifth. A large circle, like the round bottom of a barrel, rests on top of the tree, keeping out everything the tree needs to flourish — the sun, the rain, the dew.

The woman gazes at the tree, and then lifts her eyes to the mountain. She sees a great stream rushing from the mountain toward the tree with such strength that the tree is uprooted and replanted upside down. With its top in the ground, the roots of the tree turn upwards, its branches reach toward the sky, its once dry leaves become green and lush.

Suddenly a door opens, and the woman looks up from her writing. There's a problem in the fields, or in the kitchen, or with one of the sisters. She's the prioress of the community now, so such matters are her responsibility. She puts down her pen and leaves the room. We can't see how the letter ends, whether the vision has brought healing to the woman with "vehement" written on her heart. The vision itself, however, suggests that when the woman makes herself available to God's own vehement presence, the stifling, oppressive weight of the word will be lifted. For the vehement river of God restores not only the five physical senses, but reaches even deeper, to a place where expression and understanding are intertwined. The woman in the letter is wounded by a word because she cannot understand it. The woman writing the letter seems to say that it is in the work of expression, in the struggle to unite human and divine creativity, that understanding begins.

* * *

This portrait of a medieval woman writing is of a woman named Marguerite d'Oingt, a Carthusian nun in southern France, who died in 1310. I read her collected works[1] for the first time in 1987, in my first years of lan-

---

1. Marguerite d'Oingt, *Les oeuvres de Marguerite d'Oingt,* ed. Antonin Duraffour, Pierre Gardette, and Paulette Durdilly. Publications de l'institut de linguistique roman de Lyon 21 (Paris: Société d'édition "Les belles lettres," 1965).

guage study. Writing in three languages, she posed an almost insurmountable obstacle to my fledgling language skills: I would spend hours over a sentence, over a phrase, trying to figure out what she was saying. I felt like I was standing outside an unfamiliar house with dirty windows, and slowly wiping away the grime until I could see what was inside. What I've described above is what I found: the story of a woman who sought God through the practice of writing, who wrote to understand God and language and the world around her, a writer whose every word was a response to what God had written in her heart.

The rest of the way through my graduate studies, Marguerite was my constant companion, not just as the subject of my dissertation, but also as a challenge to me as a writer. Marguerite worked hard to forge an authorial identity in the midst of a culture that often mistrusted women's writing, and she pushed me to embrace the identity of writer as well. Writing matters, she seemed to say. On days when cleaning my apartment seemed preferable to writing my dissertation, she goaded me. Do your work, she said. Writing is your work. Finishing a degree or getting a grade is the least of it. Write to learn, to understand, to communicate with another, to seek what is real and true.

For Marguerite, writing was a spiritual discipline, one of the ways she sought to deepen her relationship with God. As a theological teacher, I've tried to let Marguerite's voice penetrate the often competing commitments of my vocation to remind me why writing is important. So many things conspire to obscure writing's potential to be for us a spiritual discipline. Because writing is the currency we trade for tenure, for promotion, for a better job, the usual terrors of sitting down to a blank page are multiplied many times over. We must produce to advance. Many departments require that faculty list the number of pages of each book and article listed on their vitae, as if the accumulation of pages were a good in itself.

In recent years, many thoughtful voices in theological education have sought to question the academy's commodification of writing and its embrace of publications as the central criterion for advancement. The critique of these practices, however, has unfortunately sometimes led to the conviction that writing is the opposite of teaching. The teacher who writes is imagined as one forever turning away — turning from students, colleagues, and responsibilities, in order to sit alone in a room and write. New graduates on the job market are imagined as mercenaries who don't care where they teach as long as they have time to do their research and writing.[2] The constant murmur of faculty complaint that there is no time for writing is heard as an inability to shake free of the sticky hegemony of graduate education, a reluctance to embrace wholeheartedly the vocation of teacher.

Of course, having to write in order to stay employed does force us to embrace the discipline of writing when we might otherwise never make time for it. And the critique of those who seem to disappear into their writing, leaving no energy for the classroom or for work with colleagues, does remind us that the vocation of the theological teacher is made up not only of the work we do alone but the work we do together. But neither of these ways of articulating the relationship of writing to our vocation offers any clue as to how writing might be embraced as part of our spiritual formation and the formation of our students. Indeed, the twin problems of the commodification of writing and the suspicion of writing in theological education obscure the ways in which writing might be practiced as a creative, meditative, intellectual activity that might gradually change our lives. In this essay, I want to suggest some ways in which writing might be embraced as such an activity, a discipline within which we might meet God.

The Difficulties of Writing

Making writing an integral part of the vocation of the theological teacher is not easy, and not only because there is so little time in our day for it. Writing is frequently unbearable — not only because of the work it must do on behalf of our careers, but because it is so difficult, because we are not always able to find the right words, because language is never quite under our control. Marguerite d'Oingt shifted back and forth between languages, trying to say what she meant. Anyone who has ever tried to express something one is interiorly convinced of in spoken or written words can identify with Augustine's complaint: "I am saddened that my language cannot suffice to my heart."[3]

Writing theologically, writing words about God, presents even more

2. Barbara Wheeler, "The Faculty Members of the Future: How Are They Being Shaped?" *Christian Century* 115 (1998), p. 109.
3. St. Augustine, *De catechezandis rudibus,* in *Patrologia Latina* 40:310-48.

21

difficulties. When ancient and medieval Christian writers tried to describe the difficulties of writing theologically, they often quoted Psalm 115:11: *omnis homo mendax.* Everyone is a liar. Augustine, one of the most persistent worriers over language, laments the fact that there is no way of speaking and writing of God that is completely true. One can never speak fast enough to say Father, Son, and Holy Spirit at the same time, and no matter how carefully one writes, Father, Son, and Holy Spirit always occupy their places separately on the page.[4] For Augustine, writing is but a poor human remedy for the way spoken syllables strike the air and immediately pass away. We try to catch them with our pen, but even after we fasten them to the page, they refuse to say precisely what we had hoped.

But of course these worries over the inadequacy of language never stopped Augustine from writing. Indeed, in response to the dilemma he seemed to write more and more. He came at the same ideas over and over, recasting them in different forms, putting them in conversation with different texts, burnishing them with his pen until they glowed.

For writers like Marguerite d'Oingt and Augustine, writing required a combination of audacity and humility (more audacity, perhaps, for Marguerite; more humility for Augustine). Audacity, for attempting to write anything of God at all; humility, because all one's attempts will have to be revised and, even then, will never be wholly satisfactory.

It is precisely this need for both audacity and humility in approaching the blank page that opens a space for writing to become for us one of the spiritual disciplines from which our life as theological teachers might take its shape. We need the audacity to believe that our writing matters, to stick with a difficult task, to live a life that makes room for the discipline of writing. We also need the humility to know that our writing must always be under revision, to do slow, painstaking work with no immediate external rewards, to be willing to seek and receive the critical response of others. Allowing writing to focus our attention, we may have our capacity for attention honed and increased.

---

4. Augustine, *De trinitate,* ed. W. J. Mountain, Corpus Christianorum Series Latina (Turnhout, Belgium: Brepols, 1968), IV.21.30.

Writing and Attention

Simone Weil famously wrote that academic work, when pursued with the love of God as its end and practiced as a set of tasks that require us to be rigorously attentive to what is other than ourselves, is nearly sacramental because it increases our capacity for attention. Without attention, she insists, we can neither pray nor be present to those who suffer. Every effort put forth in learning languages, solving mathematical problems, or grappling with ideas in reading and writing could bear fruit, she argues, in prayer and in our relationships with others. For Weil, academic work done not for some external reward but out of a desire for a deeper life with God and others, is a pearl of great price, worthy of the sacrifice of our time and resources to pursue.[5]

Writing is an academic task that can sharpen our capacity for attention, but in a slightly different way from learning a language or solving a mathematical problem. Those activities require us to enter into a logic wholly outside of ourselves, a grammar not our own. Writing can also require us to enter into unfamiliar ways of thinking, depending upon what we are writing about, but it also requires us to make choices from within a wider array than if we are struggling to translate from Latin into English, or to untie the knots of a mathematical problem. When we write, we must constantly make choices: this word, instead of that one; this form, this voice, this tone. Weil says that there is "a way of waiting, when we are writing, for the right word to come of itself at the end of our pen, while we merely reject all inadequate words."[6] But how do we know the right word when it comes? On what basis do we make our choice?

We are only able to recognize a word as the right one if we are attending closely to the words with which we are working, to what they mean, to how they sound, to what is evoked when one is placed against another. We only know the right word if we have a feel for what we are writing and for whom we are writing. We only know the right word if we have been living with our ideas in our reading and our teaching, our conversation and our meditation.

5. Simone Weil, "Reflections on the Right Use of School Studies with a View to the Love of God," *Waiting for God*, trans. Emma Craufurd (New York: G. P. Putnam's Sons, 1951), pp. 105-16.

6. Weil, "Reflections," p. 113.

Weil's image of the writer waiting for the right word to spill out of her pen makes it sound as if a first draft can be a final draft. But that is hardly ever the case — and in my case, never. I am comforted in this matter by Botticelli's image of Augustine in his cell. In his painting, Botticelli imagined Augustine at his desk, writing. But there are no angels whispering the right word into his ears, no ghostly hand guiding his. Instead there is a floor littered with broken quills and, best of all, crumpled bits of paper, signs of Augustine's having to abandon a draft and start again, of having to try again and again to work out in writing something true about God. And although Augustine most likely dictated his writings to a scribe, Botticelli is right about one thing: there are traces in his writing of his having gone over and over his words, trying to get it right.

Sometimes the most difficult thing about writing is staying with it as the wads of paper accumulate around us. For most of us, writing is slow, daily work. I do have one friend who reads and reads and reads and reads, and then, over a weekend, can produce a chapter that is rigorously argued, brilliantly articulated: a thing of beauty. But this kind of virtuosity is rare, I think. So disciplined is her mind and so exhaustive is her reading — she reads absolutely everything — that the constant conversation between books and ideas that shapes her life allows her writing to unscroll inside of her long before her fingers touch the computer keys.

I have often wished I could write this way. But the truth is, I write in order to do what my friend does through reading and thinking: to figure things out. A minister with whom I once worked used to explain church rituals to me like this: we do not do these things because we know exactly what they mean. We do them in order to find out what they mean. That is what writing is for me. Writing can be a kind of reading, a kind of thinking. A way of receiving and considering the work of others, a way of discovering what we think about particular questions. A way of articulating what we think in a way that invites others into the process of reading, thinking, and articulating.

So it matters what words we choose, what voice we speak in, what tone we take. It matters both for the quality of our own thought, and for the quality of our invitation to our readers. The intellectual and aesthetic choices we make when we write are also moral, spiritual choices that can hold open a door for another to enter, or pull that door shut; that can sharpen our thinking or allow it to recline on a comfortable bed of jargon; that can form us in generosity and humility or in condescension and disdain.

With so much at stake, no wonder revision is such an indispensable part of writing. Even my friend, who writes a first draft so quickly and so well, painstakingly revises until she can hardly bear to look at her words one more time. It is revision that leads Kathleen Norris to call writing a way of life that requires "continual conversion."

> . . . no matter how much I've written or published, I always return to the blank page; and . . . to the blankness within, the fears, laziness, and cowardice that, without fail, will mess up whatever I'm currently writing and, in turn, require me to revise it. The spiritual dimension of this process is humility, not a quality often associated with writers, but lurking there, in our nagging sense of the need to revise.[7]

When we revise our writing, we listen for the false notes, we watch for signs of an incomplete train of thought, we read with an eye for our own failures. While it is deeply pleasurable to improve a piece of writing, it is not always easy to contemplate our paragraphs of cluttered thinking and blurry sentences. It is even more difficult to submit our writing to another — a colleague, a spouse, a friend — and ask them to show us our mistakes. But that is where we have the choicest opportunity to sharpen the faculty of attention that Simone Weil describes. For we have to hold our writing lightly in those moments: we have at the same time to be convinced of its importance and willing to change it radically or even to crumple it up and toss it out. We have to care about it enough to make it better while at the same time cultivating a detachment toward it. The combination of loving attention with detachment is a spiritual discipline of long-standing in many religious traditions. We have an opportunity, in a small way, to cultivate it through our writing.

All of this, of course, takes time. And who has an excess of time? Certainly not the theological teacher, who must respond to students and colleagues, church and academy, community and, oftentimes, family. For the theological teacher, writing cannot happen in our spare time, for we have none. Writing must be made a part of the daily practice of our vocation, like grading papers, sitting on committees, teaching classes. If we are going to write, we have to learn to live a life that has room for writing.

Annie Dillard notes that "a work in progress quickly becomes feral. It

---

7. Kathleen Norris, "Degenerates," *Ploughshares* (Fall 1994), pp. 116-17.

reverts to a wild state overnight."[8] Part of shaping a life that has room for writing is to learn to write every day — a simple lesson, but one I am constantly having to relearn. Like any spiritual discipline, we must practice it regularly in order for it to do its work on us, to form us in attention, to draw us more deeply into the life of the world. If we do not tend our writing daily, we are always starting over, always gearing up for it. When we write daily, even in small snatches of time, we come each day to a more or less well-tended garden: we know where things are planted, we see where we might prune and trim, we sense where we need to dig more deeply. If we visit our writing only on the weekends or holidays, we have to cut our way through brambles and weeds, trying to recover the seed of our idea.

Of course, it is so much easier for me to write this than to practice it. I am a beginner at the spiritual discipline of writing; I am always beginning again, always recommitting myself to the task. Marguerite d'Oingt complains in her letters that the work of running the monastery keeps her from writing all she would like to write as well as she would like. But she kept at it, starting over and over, first in one language, then in another, trying to practice writing as a way of learning something about God and her life with God, trying to find a place within God's creativity for her own. Our goals are, perhaps, more modest: to explicate a complicated text, to narrate a historical moment that sheds light on our contemporary situation, to argue for a theological position. But in the ordinary, daily work of explication, of narration and argument, we learn to hold in our attention both what we study and what we think about what we study, what it means for us and what it might mean for others. Choosing our words with care each day, we nourish the soil of our vocation and perhaps, on occasion, catch a glimpse of a creativity that makes our choices possible.

Writing and Community

In the dichotomized conversations we so often have in theological education about teaching and writing, writing is often portrayed as isolated, isolating work. We write only to please our respective guilds, according to some. Our writing diverts our attention from our classroom, from the life of our institution. It is only in our teaching and our work among our col-

---

8. Annie Dillard, *The Writing Life* (New York: Harper and Row, 1989), p. 52.

leagues that we live in relationship; in writing, we separate ourselves from the community.

Certainly it is possible to practice writing as a way to distance ourselves from our lives as teachers and colleagues. But if we practice writing as a spiritual discipline, our writing ought to deepen our life in community. This does not mean we will not need to apply for sabbatical grants, to ask our institutions for time off to complete sustained writing projects. This does not mean that we will not need to protect part of every day for writing. It means that, in our writing, our engagement with the world will not stop at the boundaries of our own lives.

Some of the richest descriptions of how writing leads us into the life of the world can be found among the most cloistered of people. Medieval monks often thought of writing, by which they meant not the production of original manuscripts, but the copying of the manuscripts of others, as manual labor, as indeed it was in an age when all writing was done by hand. For the Carthusians, the order of which Marguerite d'Oingt was a part, writing was understood as silent, manual labor that performs great works in hiddenness. Writing gave the Carthusians an active form of ministry; through writing, cloistered monks and nuns moved about in the world, traveling wherever their books and letters traveled, offering nourishment to persons they would never meet.

Practicing writing as a spiritual discipline means holding potential readers, and the other writers with whom we think and write, in our hearts. Writing is work we do alone, certainly: we sit before a blank screen, a blank page, and slowly begin to arrange words on it. But writing is also work we do with others: like medieval copyists, we have before us, in our memories and imaginations if not before us on our desks, the work of others. We respond to that work, argue with it, reshape it to help us construct our own argument. And we write towards others, reaching out to them from the scaffolding of our words. When we write with attention, we write in and for community.

Before I got swept into medieval studies by the thought of being able to recover neglected women's writing, I had hoped to study Virginia Woolf. What interested me about Woolf was this: that for her, writing seemed to be a spiritual discipline, a practice that helped her explore what she believed was really real. Although not a theist, Woolf does write of something just beyond her grasp, something she senses even in the midst of her profound depressions, something she seeks when she writes in her

27

diary, "it is not oneself, but something in the universe that one's left with . . . one sees a fin passing far out."[9]

Virginia Woolf believed that we are all wadded in by the cotton wool of nonbeing which is occasionally punctured by what she calls moments of being that hit with the force of a sledgehammer. It is her own susceptibility to these moments of being that Woolf believes made her a writer. She has a revelation, often painful, of some real thing behind appearances and, she writes, "I make it real by putting it into words. It is only by putting it into words," she continues, "that it has lost its power to hurt me; it gives me, perhaps because by doing so I take away the pain, a great delight to put the severed parts together. Perhaps this is the strongest pleasure known to me. It is the rapture I get when in writing I seem to be discovering what belongs to what."[10] Her daily practice of writing gives birth to what she calls her "philosophy," which she articulates in the rhythm of a creed. She believes, she writes, "that behind the cotton wool is hidden a pattern; that we — I mean all human beings — are connected with this; that the whole world is a work of art; that we are parts of the work of art. *Hamlet* or a Beethoven quartet is the truth about this vast mass that we call the world. But there is no Shakespeare, there is no Beethoven; certainly and emphatically there is no God; we are the words; we are the music; we are the thing itself."[11] This philosophy drives her vocation as a writer. "I prove this now," she writes in her memoir, "by spending the morning writing, when I might be walking, running a shop or learning to do something that will be useful if war comes. I feel that by writing I am doing what is far more necessary than anything else."[12]

Doing what is far more necessary than anything else — isn't that what we want to discover, isn't that what we want to shape our lives and our vocations as theological teachers? Those moments in our classrooms when we seem to reach our students in a way that matters, when they find their voices and engage the material we offer with passion, when they come alive to all the ways what they study could shape their ministries — those are moments when we know we are doing something necessary. It is

9. *The Diary of Virginia Woolf,* Volume 3, 1925-1930, ed. Anne Olivier Bell (New York: Harcourt Brace Jovanovich, 1980), p. 113.

10. Virginia Woolf, "A Sketch of the Past," *Moments of Being,* 2nd ed. (San Diego: Harcourt Brace Jovanovich, 1985), p. 72.

11. Woolf, "A Sketch of the Past," p. 72.

12. Woolf, "A Sketch of the Past," p. 73.

perhaps more difficult to know how necessary our writing is: no eyes look back into our eyes, no one breaks in with questions, no one interrupts to take our thinking to another level. We don't always know who will read our writing; sometimes we don't know if it will be read at all. Practicing writing as a spiritual discipline requires acts of faith and imagination: we must care about our readers, no matter how anonymous they are. We must, like Woolf, discover in our writing how to reunite what has been severed, to connect what seems disparate, to create out of a diversity of material and perspective some new thing. Writers are lovers, Woolf suggests in *To the Lighthouse*. "There might be lovers whose gift it was to choose out the elements of things and place them together and so, giving them a wholeness not theirs in life, make of some scene, or meeting of people (all now gone and separate), one of those globed compacted things over which thought lingers and love plays."[13]

To write in such a way as to invite both thought and love is to write on behalf of others. It is to practice writing as a spiritual discipline that has the good of others at its heart. It is to write in a way that exposes one's hopes and motivations, that betrays one's love. It is to write in language that invites rather than excludes, in forms that are full of doors through which a reader might walk. To write this way requires time and a certain measure of solitude. But it also requires that each writing project begin and end with others, both those near at hand, and those we may never know, but to whom and for whom we write.

Teaching Writing as a Spiritual Discipline

How might we teach our students to embrace writing as a spiritual discipline? Can only our best students, our best writers, do so? Certainly not. All a student needs is the desire to sharpen his or her attention through attending to words and the desire to write towards others. Some students will write more proficiently than others, but all can write with attention.

In order to invite our students into this discipline, we will have to ask them to write more than a final paper at the end of the course. We will have to encourage the kind of daily writing we aspire to ourselves. This can

13. Virginia Woolf, *To the Lighthouse* (New York: Harcourt Brace and World, 1927), p. 286.

be done in many ways: short papers, journals, in-class writing assignments, reviews of the writing of others can all accustom students to daily writing and, hopefully, introduce them to the pleasure of it. Asking students to explore the same idea in several forms — in an academic paper and a sermon, for example — can show students how different forms give rise to different thoughts, how it is possible to learn through writing. Showing students how to read and critique each other's writing can further sharpen their attention to words and to others and help shape not only generous writers but generous-spirited readers as well.

We should also be willing to talk with students about our own writing, the frustrations and excitements we experience in writing. We should model writing as a way of reading, a way of receiving the world that turns what we read and experience over and over in the crucible of language until we learn something new and say something meaningful.

Writing is too difficult, and too potentially transformative, for us to write out of motives other than love and generosity. This does not mean we should not write critically, or polemically, or prophetically. But it means we should write in a way that betrays what we care most deeply about, a way that betrays our love.

For the contemporary American novelist Carole Maso, the act of fixing words on a page is itself an act of love. Every moment of life, she writes, is a precious, disappearing thing. To which one says when one writes, "Stay a little." To which one says when one writes, "I love you."[14]

Our students' years in school are an irreplaceable chance for them to grow intimate with language, to find a voice that's true, to write in a way that betrays their love. If we speak of this in our classrooms, it will bear fruit in our students' ministries: in their scholarship, in their sermons, in their liturgies and prayers. We should teach them, and teach ourselves, that if we write from any other motive than to find out what belongs to what, or to heal and reunite, or to reach across boundaries, or to seek communion with others, or to respond to what is written on our hearts, or to peel back the cotton wool of nonbeing, or to seek the real behind appearances, or to illuminate invisible connections, or to open a path between solitude and community, or to find God, then writing will not change us. Nor will we know the rapture Virginia Woolf speaks of, or the deep understanding Marguerite d'Oingt describes. The very best writing emerges from gener-

14. Carole Maso, "An Essay," *American Poetry Review* 24, no. 2 (March/April 1995): 27.

osity, the desire to meet and nourish another. No matter how inadequate our words may seem to us, in our struggle to find the right ones, we make room for others to find words of their own.

Reading as a Spiritual Discipline

PAUL J. GRIFFITHS

"For the Christian philosopher, reading should be an encouragement, not busy-work; it should nourish good desires, not kill them."[1]

Reading and the Theological School

SUPPOSE WE UNDERSTAND a theological school as John Webster does: "A theological school is a place where Scripture and the classics of theological response to Scripture are read in common to the end of the formation of Christian intellectual habits."[2] This is reasonable and straightforward, especially in the view, clarified and defended in the rest of the essay from which the quotation is taken, that reading of this sort is primary or basic for theological education: without such reading no theological formation can occur, and with it all things are possible.[3] This is not to say that only

---

1. Hugh of St. Victor, *Didascalicon,* v.7 ("Christiano philosopho lectio exhortatio debet esse, non occupatio, et bona desideria pascere, non necare").

2. J. Webster, "Reading Theology," *Toronto Journal of Theology* 13, no. 1 (1997): 53-63, at 61. See also his inaugural lecture as Lady Margaret Professor of Divinity at Oxford, "Theological Theology" (Oxford, 1998).

3. "Formation" is generally to be preferred to "education" as a word for what does (or ought to) go on in a (Christian) theological school because it emphasizes that Christians are

"Scripture and the classics of theological response to it" ought to be read in theological schools; but it is to say that any other reading done in such places ought to be subservient to and framed by that sort of reading, and that reading Scripture and the classics of theological response to it is the kind of activity whose presence and centrality mark off a theological school from other kinds of school.

To say that a theological school is a place defined by reading ought immediately to raise the question of what it is to read. But this question doesn't naturally occur to those teaching and learning in theological schools at the beginning of the third millennium. This is because those of us in such settings, professionally literate as we are, think we know both what reading is and how to do it. But these thoughts are mistaken: most of us have little or no idea of what reading is, have never given its history much thought, and do not teach or learn in institutions where instruction in it has a place.

"Reading" has come, in late-capitalist democracies at the end of the twentieth century, to denote a particular technical skill: the skill of interpreting written language, of making sound and meaning from scratch marks or squiggles on paper. This is what we learned at school; this is what is endlessly and mechanically tested (in SAT, ACT, ESL, GRE, LSAT, GMAT, MCAT, and so endlessly and acronymically on through the products of the educational-testing bureaucracy) by assessing the fledgling reader's ability to extract information from passages of prose. This skill is essentially a technique with a single modality, though many gradations. In this it is like, say, running: in both cases, the gradations have to do with speed (or, better, dispatch). Once you have learned the basic techniques used for decoding the squiggles of written language (the alphabet or the ideographs, the fundamental rules of grammar and syntax, a working vocabulary), all that remains if you want to improve is to perform the semi-magical feat of extracting meaning from squiggles with more dispatch and less hesitation. And, moreover, your effectiveness as a reader tends to be measured precisely in terms of the speed with which you can perform. Similarly, once you have learned the basic physical techniques required for running, all that remains is to learn to run faster, and the faster you can run the better runner you are.

---

made, not born, and that their Christian-ness must be given them rather than educed (drawn out) from them.

Teachers in theological schools are professionally literate: our livelihood depends in part upon our firm possession of the skill described in the preceding paragraph. Our students, too, are usually approximately literate in this sense. This is why we (and they) think we know what reading is and how to do it. We think we know these things because we have assimilated and reduced reading to literacy, and we know perfectly well what the latter is — or at least we know it well enough not to think it necessary to give theoretical thought to it, much less to teach it or to advocate its teaching as a central element in the theological formation that is the job of a theological school. But "reading" need not mean mere "literacy." Lectio, for instance, as understood in the Latin-writing West, certainly did not mean this: when Augustine heard the words "tolle, lege" what he understood by the command to read may have required literacy (though I doubt it), but certainly wasn't reducible to it. When Christians from Augustine to Calvin and beyond have advocated close and repeated scriptural reading as an essential part of the Christian life they have typically not thought that they were advocating the application of the skills of literacy to the written text of Scripture. George Herbert, for instance, wrote of Scripture: "Oh Book! infinite sweetnesse! let my heart/Suck ev'ry letter and a hony gain."[4] But you can suck perfectly well without being literate (perhaps all the better for not being literate). So why have we come to identify reading with literacy?

Briefly, and much too superficially, the chief reasons why this identification has become standard are economic and political. Since the eighteenth century, economists and intellectual historians have thought that there are close conceptual and causal connections between the possession of a medium of economic exchange (usually coinage), which permits large-scale and translocal trade, and the possession of a medium of intellectual exchange (usually letters, litterae, whence literacy), which permits large-scale and translocal intellectual commerce. Gibbon, for example, says that "both these institutions" (he means coinage and alphabets), "by giving a more active energy to the powers and passions of human nature, have contributed to multiply the objects they were designed to represent."[5] He also suggests that those polities in possession of the one have usually

---

4. These are the opening lines of Herbert's "The H. Scriptures I," cited from C. A. Patrides, ed., *The English Poems of George Herbert* (London: Dent, 1974), p. 76.
5. E. Gibbon, *The Decline and Fall of the Roman Empire*, ed. H. Trevor-Roper (New York: Knopf, 1993; first pub. 1776-1788), vol. 1, p. 245.

come to possess the other, and that civilization is found wherever both are present, while in the absence of one or the other we find only a "herd of savages incapable of knowledge or reflection."[6] Gibbon's rhetoric isn't one I would choose, and I don't know whether he's right about the conceptual and causal connections; but that he thought there were such connections and that many of his successors have repeated the idea are matters of import for understanding how we, teachers and students of theology at the end of the second millennium, think about literacy and reading.

One result is that theorists have typically homologized their thought about the economic and political order with their thought about the intellectual and spiritual order: the same tropes crop up on both sides of the divide, and they enter deeply into the culture at all levels. This means (painting now with a very broad brush) that as mass production became possible by way of technological innovation, and speculative investment became possible by way (principally) of the invention of that quasi-person, the limited-liability corporation, thought about reading became dominated by tropes of mass production, speed of throughput, and return on investment: lectio devolved into literacy. It is not accidental in this connection that the aspiration to universal adult literacy is strongest precisely in those states most committed to (and furthest along the path of) late-capitalist democracy.

It's important to be aware how recent that aspiration is (no nation gave clear voice to it until the nineteenth century), and how odd it would have seemed in, say, thirteenth-century Europe, or even in the nascent nation states of the sixteenth and seventeenth centuries. Even now, no state has achieved it, even if it is construed moderately as basic reading literacy in one language. The Scandinavian countries probably came closest in the mid-twentieth century, but there, as everywhere, literacy rates are now declining. The United States has never been remotely close to achieving universal adult literacy. It is very probable that as the forms of economic life that gave sense to the aspiration for universal adult literacy pass away, the aspiration will also cease to be lively.

Furthermore, this history is not inevitable. We need not be entirely subject to it in our thinking about theological formation, which is to say that we do not need to think that when John Webster speaks of reading Scripture and the classics of theological response to it, he is really speaking

6. Gibbon, *Decline and Fall*, vol. 1, p. 243.

of the application of the skill of literacy to these materials. We can, instead, begin to think as Christians about what it means to read; and if we do, we begin to find that there is a rich tradition of thought and practice to draw upon, a tradition that calls into question both the reduction of reading to literacy and the metaphors of the market by which that reduction is almost always informed. If we do begin to rethink our attitudes to reading in this way, we will be turning our attention to the Christian past as though it might have something to teach us about what intellectual work is and how best to do it, and thus also about how best to form in our students and ourselves the habits proper to such work. And this is a procedure that we, those engaged in theological formation, ought generally to follow when thinking about what such formation is and how best to nurture it and encourage its development. This is because we have a vocation to form Christian intellectual habits in our students (or at least to be of some causal significance in such formation, a qualification made necessary by the fact that the principal agent in theological formation is always God), and to be thoughtlessly subject to orthodoxies and orthopraxies on the matter of learning and teaching that have nothing to do with Christianity is unlikely to help us in fulfilling that vocation. Resisting such orthodoxies and orthopraxies is best achieved by making Christian thought and practice about these matters our point of first theoretical and practical refuge.

A full corrective would require a thorough study of the Christian theory and practice of reading and a set of recommendations on the basis of such a study as to how best to teach and practice reading in theological schools. I can't offer all that here; what I shall do instead is present impressionistic sketches of three ways of understanding and practicing reading, vignettes of what it would be like to teach and practice reading as, first, an academic; second, a Proustian; and third, a Victorine. The aim of these vignettes is not exhaustiveness (there are other modes of reading, and those I sketch will have to be treated very summarily); it is only to show that there is no single way to read, and to point to the question of choice among the possibilities by doing so.

Academic Reading

This mode of reading has been adumbrated in what I've said to this point. It's the standard mode of reading for us all, the mode in which you, the reader of the book in which this essay appears, are almost certainly now reading. Technical mastery and consumption-for-use are its governing tropes. Max Weber will be my main representative of this position, especially in what he says about the academic life in his 1918 lecture "Wissenschaft als Beruf" (Science as a Vocation).[7]

Ideal academic readers about to read will have prepared themselves as technicians. They will have mastered the necessary linguistic skills to read what it is they want to read (Latin for Aquinas, Greek for Chrysostom, Sanskrit for Vasubandhu, and so on). They will, again ideally, have read everything the author they're reading had read, and, indeed, everything of any possible relevance to the understanding of their chosen work. This will be a minimal preparation (bear in mind that I write of ideal academic readers here; actual ones rarely manage anything approaching this). Fuller preparation will depend upon decisions as to just what is hoped for from the act of reading: different purposes will require mastery of different skills and bodies of knowledge. If, for example, you read a body of manuscripts with the goal of establishing a critically edited text, you'll need to have different skills and different kinds of knowledge than you would were you to read a printed edition with the goal of understanding its rhetoric, conceptual structure, or use of imagery. In general, academic readers prepare themselves as technicians with the skills needed to prosecute whatever task they have in mind.

Academic readers typically show a deep concern with reading just what the author of whatever they're reading wrote. They want the *ipsissima verba* set down in a bounded and fixed text, an authoritative object to be mastered and used. The ideal type, perhaps, is the printed edition with full apparatus criticus. The academic reader applies the skills of literacy to this object, and does so in solitude and silence. The eye, trained to the skill of sucking up lines and paragraphs of print, delivers its visual input to the brain, where meaning is made. The object read, the printed text, remains always before the reader; its reassuring continued presence means that reading can be rapid, for the text is there to be consulted again should anything be forgotten or misconstrued. The printed text, designed as it is for

7. Max Weber, "Science as a Vocation," in H. H. Gerth and C. Wright Mills, ed. and trans., *From Max Weber: Essays in Sociology* (New York: Oxford University Press, 1946), pp. 129-56. First delivered as a lecture, "Wissenschaft als Beruf," at Munich University, 1918. German in Weber, *Gesammelte Aufsätze zur Wissenschaftslehre* (Tübingen: J. C. B. Mohr, 1951; 1st ed. 1922), pp. 566-97.

easy and repeated reference, lies passively on the desk as a permanent possibility of rereading. The reader-technician flicks the pages back and forth
to find in it what will serve her purposes as she reads and refers, using her
technical tools to find what she needs. She values, above all else, speed and
clarity about the purposes of her reading.

This mode of reading establishes a certain kind of relation between
reader and text read. It is, above all, a relation in which the reader is the
agent and the text the patient; the text lies supine before the reader, await-
ing the exercise of intention and desire that only the reader can bring. The
application of technical skill to an object is always like this; it is an instrument in the service of an end other than itself, an action that occurs principally within the sphere of technique and its derivative, technology. When
the right technique has been used for the purpose at hand, the act of reading is exhausted and the object read irrelevant; the book, at that point, is
put back on the shelf. There is no moral relation between book and reader
for the academic reader; anything at all can be done with the book that
serves the reader's purposes. What the work being read claims, its topic
and goals, bear no intrinsic relation to what academic readers do and the
purposes for which they do it: the academic reader (in his ideal type, at
least) can as happily read a work on the methods of making papyrus rolls
from the reed *cyperus papyrus* as one on how best to love God, and remain
equally unaffected, morally, by each.

What, then, are the purposes of the academic reader? Max Weber is
helpful here, providing as he does an understanding of such a reader's vocation that is subtle and nuanced. Fundamental to his argument, and to
the family of views it represents, is the attempt systematically to separate
fact from value, and to identify the former with what can be arrived at by
empirical procedures. Dealing with facts as an analytical thinker is what
characterizes the work of the academic reader, the reader in search of
Wissenschaft.[8]

Such readers engage in specialized intellectual work: they focus on a
tightly defined question within a delimited field. Specialization is necessary because mastery is the goal: academic readers ought to know everything that is relevant to their question. Imagery of mastery and domination is threaded throughout Weber's essay. Academic readers work in a
disenchanted world, a world in which there are no occult or mysterious

8. Weber, "Science," p. 139.

forces, or at least none of relevance to the work of the academic reader. What there is in the world, for academic readers, is just and only what can be mastered and understood by technical means: "Technical means and calculations perform the service. This above all is what intellectualization means," as Weber says.[9] This is reading whose principal tools are the concept deployed in coercive argument and the repeatable experiment. Academic readers should want to demonstrate by argument and prove by experiment (Weber of course acknowledges the differences between what "experiment" might mean in physics and what it might mean in history, but thinks nonetheless that there is sufficient commonality between the two to make it reasonable to use the same term). They are committed to explanation and analysis using only what is derivable from broadly empirical methods, which means at least that academic readers can appeal to no supernatural factors while they're acting as such (this means at least that an intellectual cannot appeal to the agency of God while doing intellectual work). Finally, the academic reader's quest for Wissenschaft is an activity intimately linked to the idea of progress: academic readers know that the results at which they arrive will be superseded, just as these results superseded earlier ones.

Academic reading is, then, not aimed at and does not lead to God, or true art, or effective happiness, or moral transformation. It does not provide answers to questions of value (in, e.g., aesthetics, medicine, jurisprudence, religion); it answers only questions of fact. Academic readers must never adopt a position on questions of value, at least not while practicing their craft. Adopting a position in the academic lecture hall or in the pages of an academic book on such questions is to abandon the work of the academic reader; this is a strong theme in Weber's essay.

The positive benefits of academic reading as presented by Weber are, first, that it can teach students to recognize and deal with facts inconvenient for their party position. Weber takes this to be a moral benefit. Second, the practice of such reading aids technology, which Weber understands to be the means of controlling and ordering things; it does this principally by fostering habits of thought that make the development and use of technology possible. Third, it aims at (and sometimes achieves) clarity in seeing the assumptions and implications of any position — but most especially on questions of value. It will show those who do take po-

9. Weber, "Science," p. 147.

sitions on questions of value (on, say, the desirability of worshiping God or advocating democracy) what they are assuming by taking such a position. This is the "final service that science as such can render to the aim of clarity."[10]

So much for academic reading. You, the reader of this essay, almost certainly know from inside what this mode of reading is like. If you possess a graduate degree or are working toward one, it's just what you'll have learned or be learning to do, and this is true whether or not you have studied in a theological school. But it is not the only way to read a book. I turn now to another possibility, that of the Proustian reader.

Proustian Reading

For my sketch of this mode of reading, I'll draw principally upon Marcel Proust's essay "Sur la lecture" (On Reading), composed between 1900 and 1905 to serve as preface to a French version (partly made by Proust) of John Ruskin's *Sesame and Lilies*.[11]

Proustian readers read in order to be incited to reverie, to be pushed by the catalyst of reading into the internal depths of memory and aesthetic sensibility. Reading is productive of sensual, aesthetic, and (often) properly sexual pleasure, as Proust says it is "a pleasure at once ardent and restful (*jouissance à la fois ardente et rassise*) . . . during it, a thousand poetical sensations and a thousand sensations of undifferentiated well-being well rapidly up from the depths of our good health to interfuse the reader's reverie with a pleasure as sweet and golden as honey."[12] Reading is like lovemaking. Lovers are ardent and restful; the pleasures they get from the caresses and play of love, from jouissance, are intense and manifold, but typically not precisely differentiated or demarcated.[13] The pleasurable rev-

10. Weber, "Science," p. 151.
11. I've used the version of Proust's essay that appeared in the seventh edition of J. Ruskin, *Sésame et les Lys: Des trésors des rois, des jardins des reines* (Paris, n.d., but probably the 1920s), pp. 7-58. I've consulted the English version by J. Sturrock, in M. Proust, *On Reading* (London, 1994), with profit, but all translations are mine. Sturrock gives further information about the somewhat complicated composition and publishing history of "Sur la lecture."
12. Proust, "Lecture," p. 25 n. 2.
13. Proust, "Lecture," p. 26.

eries of foreplay and of postorgasmic ease are, for them, as sweet as honey, as golden as sunlight refracted through stained glass (both favorite Proustian images).[14]

But the book read, for the Proustian reader, unlike the lover, is not an active partner in the reader's jouissance, matching kiss for kiss and caress for caress; it is, instead, a catalyst for the reader's solitary pleasures, an instrument that draws pleasures from within the reader, and that exhausts its function when these pleasures have been catalyzed into being. This means that Proustian readers are not much interested in the content of what they read. They are more concerned with the inner work it prompts them to do. Proust makes this point most strikingly when he speaks of childhood reading; when he recalls this, he does not think of what was in the books he read, but rather of the inner life of the child who read them. It is important to the Proustian reader to separate the act of reading and the work it catalyzes from the content of what is read; the latter is unimportant; the former all-important. Reading, on this view, is an element in the reader's continuing work of self-creation: it evokes memory, decorates the mottled screen of the reader's mind with increasing density and complexity, and permits the pointed refinement of the reader's aesthetic sensibility.

What Proustian readers most want to read, then (and here the contrast with the academic reader's desire for the bounded text and the ipsissima verba is very striking), are books whose elegance of style and subtlety of aesthetic insight can intoxicate them into developing feelings and aesthetic insights that go beyond what is in the books. "It is," says Proust, "at the moment when they [books] have said to us all they can say that they bring to birth in us a feeling of which they have yet said nothing (le sentiment qu'ils ne nous encore rien dit)."[15]

This view of the benefits of reading leads Proustian readers also to be aware of its limitations. It can be a curative discipline for those whose weakness of will prevents them from developing the habits of perception that permit penetration beneath the surface of things to the profound inner regions of the self; it can, that is, be a useful exterior stimulus. But it can never be more than that. Proust mentions with approval Emerson's

14. For a very useful discussion of this image in Proust, see Mieke Bal, *The Mottled Screen: Reading Proust Visually* (Stanford: Stanford University Press, 1997), pp. 13-65.

15. Proust, "Lecture," p. 33.

habit of reading a few pages of Plato each day before beginning his own work, and Dante's of doing the same with Virgil.[16] But reading of this sort is done without deep interest in what Plato or Virgil say; it is done, instead, as the apprentice dancer might watch the expert's pirouettes, with the goal of absorbing (and in absorbing, transforming) the technique of the expert. Emerson and Dante, on this view, did not make the mistake of thinking that their reading could give them access to truth in the form of "a material thing deposited between the pages of books, like honey entirely prepared by others."[17] They knew, as all good Proustian readers know, that the real work of reading has nothing to do with what's on the page read. Reading is a preparation for no longer needing to read, a preliminary training to be abandoned when the sensibilities of the reader are sufficiently finely tuned. Proust says:

> Original minds are able to subordinate reading to their own personal activity. For them, it is no more than the most noble of distractions, and certainly the most ennobling, because only reading and knowledge are able to make a well-mannered mind (seuls, la lecture et le savoir donnent les "belles manières" de l'esprit). We can develop our sensibility and intelligence only inside ourselves, in the depths of our spiritual lives (dans les profondeurs de notre vie spirituelle); but our minds are fashioned by reading, which is contact with other minds.[18]

Again, the person in charge is the reader; what is read is an important (but finally contingent) tool for self-development.

Proustian readers, then, understand reading as an instrument in the service of a goal other than itself; in this they are like academic readers, but the goal, of course, is different. What Proustians want to read also differs from what academic readers want to read; the former want anything that intimates or evokes a more profound and finely tuned aesthetic sensibility; they show no interest whatever in ipsissima verba or critical editions, in the scientific questions of the Weberian intellectual, or, indeed, in remembering or placing any intrinsic value upon what they read. Proustians want to be ravished by their reading; Weberians want technical mastery of a dis-

16. Proust, "Lecture," pp. 35-36.
17. Proust, "Lecture," p. 38.
18. Proust, "Lecture," p. 50.

cipline from theirs. For both, though, the reader is the one in charge and the text, the thing read, the servant of the reader. Relations of dominance are one way.

Victorine Reading

For a sketch of this third mode, I draw mostly upon Hugh of St. Victor's analysis of reading in his work *Didascalicon: De studio legendi (A Handbook of Learning: On the Pursuit of Reading)*, composed in Latin at the Abbey of St. Victor in Paris sometime in the 1120s.[19]

Victorine readers begin by locating the work they're planning to read. There are two fundamental possibilities: one is that the work belongs to the arts *(artes)*; the other is that it belongs to the "writings that should be called divine" *(scripturae divinae appellandae sint)*,[20] which is to say, to the canon of Scripture. Every work belongs to one of these two categories, and none belongs to both. Since, for Victorines, scriptural works have deeply different properties from all others, different methods of reading will be appropriate for works in each group, and this is why it is important to know, before you begin reading, where the work you're planning to read belongs. Hugh of St. Victor has this to say about the difference between the two groups:

> The writings of the philosophers *(philosophorum scripturae)* are like white-painted walls of clay *(quasi luteus paries dealbatus):* they have a surface radiance of eloquence. While they present the appearance of truth, they do so by mixing it with falsehood, concealing, as it were, the clay of error with an overlay of color. By contrast, divine eloquence *(divina eloquia)* is best likened to a honeycomb *(favus):* while it seems

19. I've used T. Offergeld's *Hugo von Sankt Viktor: Studienbuch* (Freiburg: Herder, 1997) for the Latin text of Hugh's work, and have consulted J. Taylor's English version found in his *The Didascalicon of Hugh of St. Victor* (New York: Columbia University Press, 1991). All translations from the *Didascalicon* are my own, and references to it are given by book and chapter (ii.9, e.g.). Both Offergeld and Taylor give much useful information about the *Didascalicon* in general, and about particular points in it, and on this I have frequently and gratefully drawn. I have, in addition, consulted I. Illich's *In the Vineyard of the Text: A Commentary to Hugh's Didascalicon* (Chicago: University of Chicago Press, 1993) with considerable profit.

20. Hugh, *Didascalicon*, preface.

dry because of the simplicity of its language, it is in fact full of sweetness inside. It alone is found to be free from the infection of falsehood.[21]

Victorines do not, however, think that nonscriptural works are to be ignored. That they always contain error means that they have to be read carefully, but not that they should be left alone. Intellectual and spiritual benefit can be had from these whited sepulchers. But how to get it? There is an ordered program here. Victorines begin their reading of nonscriptural works by analyzing them grammatically, syntactically, and semantically; this, of course, requires deployment of the appropriate linguistic skills, as was also true for the academic reader. The next step is to study, analytically, the central topic of the work read, and of the order of thought proper to its understanding and exposition. Here too we are on much the same ground as the academic reader (and in a very different place from the Proustian reader). Next, the memory must be used to order and compile (*colliger* is the favorite verb here) extracts that illustrate the analytical outline made in the second stage; these extracts are to be memorized verbatim and stored in the "treasure-chest of the memory" (*arcula memoriae*), from where they can later be ruminated at leisure. And, finally, in connection with this chewing-over of memorized extracts in the context of an ordered (and also memorized) analytical outline of the work read, the Victorine reader engages in deeper analytical thought about the implications of the work read.

Even in the case of nonscriptural works Victorine readers are concerned to establish a moral as well as a memorial relation with what they read. The emphasis upon storage in the memory already suggests this; but it becomes abundantly clear when Hugh emphasizes the need for humility before what is read, and for an eagerness to read and learn that permits sacrifice of ease and luxury on the part of the reader.[22] The reader's mind becomes conformed to what she reads as a result of this assumption of humility before the work read; and this means in turn that, for Victorines, even the reading of nonscriptural works is an instrument that contributes to the reader's wisdom and that permits advance toward divine wisdom.[23]

For Victorines, all nonscriptural reading is framed by and ordered to

---

21. Hugh, *Didascalicon*, iv.1.
22. Hugh, *Didascalicon*, iii.13.
23. Hugh quotes Boethius at some length on this, *Didascalicon*, i.2.

scriptural reading. But scriptural reading, like nonscriptural, may be done well or badly, and Hugh emphasizes this by providing a division of those who read Scripture into three kinds.[24] There are those who seek knowledge through such reading for fame and honor — Hugh would likely place most academic readers into this category, and he says that such readers are to be pitied; there are those who read for aesthetic delight (the Proustians, perhaps) — these, says Hugh, have praiseworthy but insufficient motives; and then there are those who read because they want to understand better the hidden things of God *(secreta Dei)* — and these are the ones whose motives are in order. For them, all the methods used for reading nonscriptural works ought be used (grammatical and syntactical analysis, systematic outlining, memorial storage), but these must then be supplemented by attention to (and repeated reading in light of) the various levels of meaning possessed by Scripture, levels not to be found elsewhere. Victorine theorizing about these levels is a complicated matter which I can't treat here; all that needs to be said is that the theory is a complex one, that its application is always constrained by what the Church teaches, and that learning to apply it properly is a matter that requires much training.[25]

Victorine readers, then, read with the knowledge and love of God always before them as the point and purpose of their reading. They also have a canonical view of reading, a view that sees the set of things to be read as divided into two basic categories: the canon, the reading of which is essential and primary; and everything else. The canon is deep and inexhaustible; everything else, while useful, is shallow and can be used up. Everything noncanonical (nonscriptural) is to be read in the light of what is canonical. This division, for Victorines, is not a matter of preference on the part of the reader. It is, rather, a matter of what the universe is like; a Victorine reader's universe is configured very differently from either an academic's or a Proustian's. A Victorine's reading also requires the specification of limits on the meaning and use of what is read (whether scriptural or not) as part of the process of instruction in how to read; there is always explicit constraint by authority. Finally, Victorine reading requires the es-

24. Hugh, *Didascalicon*, v.10.

25. Hugh distinguishes three levels of meaning and seven hermeneutical principles (*Didascalicon*, v.2, v.4). A detailed analysis of this kind of view may be had from Henri de Lubac's *Medieval Exegesis*, vol. 1: *The Four Senses of Scripture*, trans. Mark Sebanc (Grand Rapids: Eerdmans 1998; the four-volume French original — *Éxégèse Mediévale* — was published between 1959 and 1963.

tablishment of a set of moral relations between reader and work read. These moral relations make the work read the chief agent, and the reader a subordinate agent, to be conformed to the text. The differences here with both Proustians and academics are deep.

Reading Choices

The worlds in which our three kinds of readers live and move and do their reading are very different. These differences require some choices. The reading practices of a Proustian are, in fundamental respects, noncompossible with those of both the academic and the Victorine. This is to say that you can't be a serious Proustian reader and a serious Victorine or academic reader. Proustians and academics, for instance, do not share the canonical view of reading advocated by Victorines; neither Victorines nor academics can countenance the Proustian insouciance about the importance of textual particularity and textual memory. This is not to say that there are no commonalities among the three. A Victorine reader preparing for the study of a work of philosophy will do many things that an academic reader will do preparing for the study of the same work (though Proustians will find such technical preparation largely irrelevant); and a Proustian interested in the formation of sensibility by reading will have something in common with a Victorine's interest in the conformity of the reader's mind to God ideally produced by reading. But in spite of these small-scale similarities, the three kinds of reading are, understood as complete programs, quite incompatible one with another.

Realization of this returns us to our beginning. It provides us, theological teachers and learners, with some forced options. The history of academic institutions in the West presses upon those who teach and learn in theological schools at the beginning of the third millennium a particular view of what reading is and is for. It makes one choice about how to read and teach reading — the academic choice — seem natural and obvious. But in fact it is neither. Treating it as if it were is to lose, by default, without the loss fully coming to consciousness, other possibilities. Reading may be a transformative spiritual discipline. It is so, I think, for both Proustians and Victorines. Reading for Christians must be understood as a transformative spiritual discipline if it is to remain Christian, to be properly articulated with the Christian life. This, in my judgment, should make Christians look

46

again at the history of Christian thought about and practice of reading (of which the Victorine option is an important instance), and in so looking, think again about choices made about how reading is done and taught. If we Christians don't do this, we'll remain subject to decisions about these fundamentally important matters given to us by those who have no interest in or understanding of what Christian formation is. The result will be that the formation of Christian intellectual habits, which is the proper and primary task of a theological school, will remain a task left undone.

Contemplation in the Midst of Chaos:
Contesting the Maceration of
the Theological Teacher

BONNIE J. MILLER-McLEMORE

THE LIFE TO WHICH I feel vocationally called sometimes feels like a complete mess — despite or perhaps because of the good fortune of a good teaching position and a spouse who shares the care of our home and three sons. Take this summer, for example. The tasks I have agreed to do will never fit around the national and international conferences I have scheduled, the relentless pace of kids' camp, church, friends, and sports activities, my husband's own travel and work calendar, the basic necessities of maintaining a home, and the vacation we should all take to recover. Heaven forbid anything out of the ordinary, such as illness or accident. When I talk with colleagues who have more students to teach, more articles to write, more meetings to attend, and less help from their partners, I realize one thing: I am not the only one deeply distracted by life's multiple details and demands — the child I have just dropped off at school with his poster board, the assigned book I have not read for tomorrow's class, the

I would like to thank the Wabash Center for its gracious hospitality, the facilitators Stephanie Paulsell and Greg Jones who wisely guided a wonderful collaborative project, and all the participants in the consultation, all their insights and humor, without whom this essay would not have come to fruition.

newsletter I have brought along in the car to skim at stoplights. That so many of us have acquired an expertise in perpetual overextension and distractibility gives me pause.

Like contemporary life in general, academic life has fallen captive to the syndrome of escalating demands. A widely acclaimed study by Juliet Schor, *The Overworked American,* documents a national trend toward longer work hours.[1] Despite widespread assumptions about the ease of a tenured teaching life, academics do not escape the predilection to overwork. Some professors argue that they face the "same pressures and conflicts as other workers, as well as some particular to academic life."[2] Moreover, problems of overextension and what one study calls the "intensification of work" are heightened for populations still underrepresented in the academy — women in general, women and men with primary family responsibilities, and minorities.[3] Indeed, many of those who ought to shape new horizons of higher education are the very people who find themselves overcommitted and without the usual assumed support systems.

While a fast-paced, stress-filled life is not good for anyone, it raises particular problems for those who teach theology and religion, especially those who hope to form students for ministry. In general, scholarship and good teaching require periods of quiet study and serious thought. Theological teaching and scholarship for the sake of the church require a contemplative mode that deepens understanding and wisdom. What, indeed, are we really teaching students through our hurried lives?

In this essay, I want to explore what I see as one of the serious challenges of today's teaching context — the cacophony of demands. I believe this problem ultimately undermines even the best efforts to restore the teaching of theology and religion as a religious vocation. Discussion of the work pace of the theological teacher becomes especially critical as recent efforts to improve teaching gain momentum. There is the real danger that the need to produce a substantial "teaching portfolio," for example, will become yet one more hurdle that, contrary to its overt intention, preoccu-

1. Juliet B. Schor, *The Overworked American: The Unexpected Decline of Leisure* (New York: Basic, 1991).

2. Mara Holt and Leon Anderson, "The Way We Work Now," *Profession 1998* (an annual publication of the Modern Language Association), pp. 131-42.

3. Jennifer Gore, "Unsettling Academic/Feminist Identity," in *Everyday Knowledge and Uncommon Truths: Women of the Academy,* ed. Linda K. Christian-Smith and Kristine S. Kellor (Boulder, Colo.: Westview Press, 1999), p. 17 (17-23).

pies new faculty, raises anxieties, and drains energy rather than fosters improved teaching. Even the support of outside institutions can inadvertently subvert the very goal of enriching teaching by generating yet another seminar or meeting to attend. While I do not mean to discount the many benefits of supplemental programs and funding, I do believe that the escalation of expectations merits discussion. As one of my friends and colleagues admitted, many of us need time and space rather than money. Yet these qualities and, indeed, an enhancement of the teaching environment itself are elements that outside agencies have more trouble giving away.

These observations lead me to ask two kinds of questions: How might I understand my ragged attempts to follow my vocation as pastoral theologian, mother, teacher, speaker, researcher and author, wife, mentor, advisor, and counselor as religious practice? More generally, how might one understand religious contemplation in the midst of vocational chaos? Are alternative models of contemplation necessary? Second and as important, do personal and public understandings of successful theological teaching need reconsideration? My thesis is twofold: on the one hand, the oversight and dismissal of material conditions — the messiness of daily life — in the definition of ideal spirituality has left us with a limited model for understanding theological teaching as a religious vocation. On the other hand, reigning models of academic life often promote distorted norms of success. In short, the conflict for many scholars of theology between the professional demands of teaching, publishing, and advising and the ideal of contemplative life espoused by Christian faith traditions suggests the need for qualifications on both sides. Theological teachers would do well to reconsider models of contemplation *and* to challenge prevailing academic expectations.

I raise both questions and retain a double thesis because these problems go hand in hand. This essay, however, focuses primarily on the first half of my proposition, the need for qualifications in models of spirituality. Although I begin with a phenomenological depiction of the current chaos of academic life, my main interest as I move from chaos to contemplation to contemplation in the midst of chaos is a reconsideration of ideals of contemplation. The appeal to reorder the hectic patterns of the teaching life arises more indirectly and is a deserving topic to which I hope to return. In the meantime, my attempt to reclaim alternative avenues of religious experience will draw upon what I consider to be some parallels between the chaos of parenting and the practice of teaching.

Chaos

In attempting to challenge academic expectations and imagine new models of teaching in the midst of multiple demands, it is important to identify several pitfalls. On many, many accounts the teaching profession affords the luxury of introspective time that most jobs do not. Teaching does not entail hard physical labor or harsh working conditions. Faculty often have immense freedom to determine the subject of courses and research and the timing of work and classes. Faculty have considerable flexibility in daily schedules and sabbaticals from regular work. In general, there are many, many people who work to sustain life under less fortunate circumstances with far more demanding and poorer paying jobs. The professors, students, and ministers to whom I address my remarks do not face anything like the political chaos encountered by those threatened by the chaos of poverty, arrest, torture, and killing in more dire contexts. Faculty then ought to be wary of the hubris of claiming that we are overworked while other people clean our houses and harvest our grapes. We should also be wary of the hubris of sporting a "busier-than-thou" sentiment, following the all-too-popular U.S. trend toward brandishing one's busyness, as if the number of speaking engagements or editorial appointments earns a heavenly reward. Finally, academics must take care not to become unjustifiably plaintive in the face of abundance. For the most part, the problem is not a destructive dilemma of good versus bad; rather the problem is one of plenitude and competing goods. We are fortunate, people can justifiably contend, to have such a "problem."

Nevertheless, despite these caveats, my own experience still tells me that there is something terribly wrong with the routine pace of life in schools of theology and religion. A dormitory on the college campus where I did my undergraduate study has an engraved stone plate over an entrance that reads, "The end of learning is gracious living." Unfortunately, a better description of the harried lives of many academics is "graceless living." Contrary to stereotypes that professors work only the six or twelve hours they spend in class and contrary to polemical claims that professors waste resources, those in the academy now experience their own peculiar form of a wider social phenomenon. The problems of an accelerated pace of life assume a distinctive shape in academic life where scholars are called to ponder, ruminate, pause, and create. Teaching requires a high degree of consciousness, intentionality, and discernment. The practices of

51

reading, writing, and gaining a voice in the wider public (described in the preceding chapters) require slow time and open space. Teachers of theology, one might assume, are especially called to contemplate and engage life's deepest mysteries and meanings.

In the study of theology and religion, this problem is complicated by several interrelated realities. Many teachers of theology encounter a deep separation between the practice of faith and life in the academy. Many have undergone graduate education in which developing one's intellect seems to imply abandoning or at least temporarily suspending one's religious convictions. A general disquietude surrounds those of us who see our vocation as helping students know and love God in an academic culture in which we are trained to keep quiet about our faith.[4] Within many institutions of theological education, it is hard to shake the dominant liberal Protestant view of religious formation and spiritual fervor as secondary to cognitive knowledge and intellect. While such a position justifiably rejects the parochial assertion of piety over intellect sometimes operative in more conservative institutions, it has obscured the essential interconnections between faith and knowledge. Finally, the hardening of the boundaries between religious and theological studies has also partly served to fortify the study of religion as a more or less detached cerebral enterprise.

These patterns form a backdrop for the heart of my concern, the conflict between the incessant claims upon us and the ideal of teaching as a religious vocation. Several decades ago theologian Joseph Sittler wrote an essay called "The Maceration of the Minister." Although focused on ministry and slightly nostalgic for the good old days of the pastor in his study (male identity assumed), his comments still have relevance for theological education today. In fact, his concern about the overextended minister underscores the analogy between problems of the teacher of ministry stu-

---

4. Several books have appeared in the last decade pertaining to this problem: Mark Schwehn, *Exiles from Eden: Religion and the Academic Vocation in America* (New York: Oxford University Press, 1993); Douglas Sloan, *Faith and Knowledge: Mainline Protestantism and American Higher Education* (Louisville: Westminster/John Knox, 1994); Conrad Cherry, *Hurrying toward Zion: Universities, Divinity Schools, and American Protestantism* (Bloomington, Ind.: Indiana University Press, 1995); George M. Marsden, *The Outrageous Idea of Christian Scholarship* (New York: Oxford University Press, 1997); and James Burtchaell, *The Dying of the Light: The Disengagement of Colleges and Universities from Their Christian Churches* (Grand Rapids: Eerdmans, 1998).

dents and problems of parish ministry itself. Ministers and teachers face some of the same dilemmas of time and space. Teachers therefore have a heightened responsibility, one might say, to attend to this problem.

A preacher at heart, Sittler begins by declaring that "Someone ought to speak up against what I call the maceration of the minister." Only "maceration" can capture what he sees as the brutal "chopping into small pieces" of the minister's focus, time, vision, sense of vocation, and "contemplative acreage."[5] He protests pointless parish "busyness" as contrary to the genuine vocation of Christian ministry, not from the angle of a psychologist with tricks of time management but from the vantage point of a practical theologian dedicated to the preservation of a congregation's soul.

The study of God's Word no longer holds an intrinsic place. Instead the pastor's study becomes an "office" and the message is "simplified," "reduced," and essentially "*managed* in terms of its instrumental usefulness for immediate goals" of advancing the programs of the congregation.[6]

What are the causes of the problem? Sittler identifies three: the bureaucratization of the parish, the worldly banality of denominational organization, and the collapse of a sense of ministerial identity. Parish life has fallen into a Weberian "iron cage" in which the holy is systematized and the spiritual charismas are ordered, mass produced, and certified. In such a context, ministers lose a sense of the awesome task to which they are called, trading a vocation for a profession and ordination to an office for running an office. The result is a "sense of vocational guilt" that "no diminution of hours or other rearrangements of outer life" can decisively affect.[7] On several scores, analogous observations might be made about theological education today.

What then might be done? Sittler's instructions are not detailed or programmatic. This would go against the grain of the normative shift for which he calls. Instead he advocates a centering of heart and mind, a "tightening and clarification" of the minister's vocation, a grappling with the seriousness of life and gospel.

He calls first upon professors themselves. Theological teachers "ought to be more courageous, critical and noisy advocates for our stu-

5. Joseph Sittler, "The Maceration of the Minister," *Christian Century*, June 10, 1959, p. 698 (698-701).

6. Sittler, "The Maceration of the Minister," p. 698, emphasis in the text.

7. Sittler, "The Maceration of the Minister," p. 700.

dents, more concerned protectors of their reflective future."[8] Here he displays an amazing confidence in schools of theology. He assumes, wrongly as it turned out, that they will escape the very iron cage of productivity, time management, and accreditation procedures that he saw destroying religious life. He assumed that schools preserved an environment of study ("unhurried reflection and honest work") that he found lacking in churches. When I used his late-1950s essay in a class on pastoral care in the late-1980s, I felt the distance of years and the duplicity of recommending a life that neither I nor the school modeled. Perhaps at the time he wrote, professors were successfully resisting the "numbers game" of books assigned, pages read, papers written, students taught, evaluations tabulated, and articles published. Unfortunately, many of the problems Sittler describes have now spread to schools of theology themselves. Professors are in little position to act as advocates of reflective time. Indeed, we are just as often guilty of the reverse by both example and class requirements.

In Sittler's analysis, however, the responsibility extends to parish, denominational officers, and finally to individual ministers. On this last front he makes his only concrete suggestion, the "ordering of one's study." Between the lines is a longing for the days when ministers spent hours, not minutes, studying Scripture and reading widely rather than comparing estimates on resurfacing the parking lot or organizing a stewardship campaign to pay for it. Although partly sardonic and occasionally idealistic, his point is well taken: we have lost our way amid increasing demands. More is not necessarily better.

While awareness of overwork has increased in recent years, Mara Holt and Leon Anderson argue for more analysis of this problem in the academic context. Like Sittler, they describe factors of maceration, identify three causes, and suggest changes. The increase in work hours documented by Schor is compounded by the academic temptation to allow work to flow well beyond the normal eight-to-five schedule into nighttime and weekend reading and writing, library and bookstore browsing, coffee shop, phone, and e-mail conversations. More significantly, faculty feel pressures to work harder because demands have expanded both chronologically and geographically. Professors plan courses in three-year sequences, promise lectures a year or more in advance, and make national and even international commitments, often without adequate knowledge of future circum-

---

8. Sittler, "The Maceration of the Minister," p. 700.

stances. Demands, such as routine administrative paperwork, accreditation and assessment procedures, and service on an ever-growing number of editorial boards, have also proliferated. Technologies of progress backfire: "Electronic communication, touted as a timesaver, has meant the development of new electronic journals, e-mail, the listserv, the World Wide Web, and the constant need to update one's computer skills, including computer-assisted instructions."[9] While acknowledging the time saved by computers, most people have also cursed the time lost in repairing, retooling, and simply keeping abreast of the latest developments, including those with ramifications for teaching. Finally, many professors struggle to adjudicate the many and sometimes different work roles and "role switches" of teacher, researcher, advisor, and administrator, to name a few.[10] While individual demands are manageable, the cumulative effect leads to "role overload" and increases the risk of failure.

What do Holt and Anderson identify as the sources of the current crisis? They name three: the proletarianization of academic labor, technology under the sway of capitalism and bureaucracy, and competitive individualism. The rise in adjunct teaching and a coinciding increase in the administrative demands made on full-time faculty exemplify the first factor. Also characteristic of the assault on working conditions is the "speeding up" of academic research. Even Ph.D. students flock to academic meetings to present papers, sometimes prematurely and without adequate research but perceiving a need to publish before seeking a job. Second, as indicated above, technology has tended to increase rather than decrease workloads. Finally, the academic "superstar" system rewards those who secure minimal teaching and service responsibilities. Publication is prized at the cost of other crucial activities that preserve the teaching environment, just as modern conceptions of work have rendered domestic work invisible.

In this latter observation, Holt and Anderson allude to an important connection between the devalued status of household work and the secondary status of teaching. Teaching is, in a way, the domestic labor of the household of the academy. No one really wants to do it, or if they actually like doing it, they seldom admit it or share their sense of enjoyment and effectiveness with others. Tenure committees and academic program reviews

---

9. Holt and Anderson, "The Way We Work Now," p. 133.

10. See Shirley Fisher, *Stress in Academic Life: The Mental Assembly Line* (Bristol: Open University Press, 1994).

often act as if publications alone sustain institutions. The work that actually does do so is often hidden, holds less value, and is seldom a cause for pay increase or promotion. It comes as no surprise, then, that many of us feel as though we must get our teaching out of the way so we can do our "real work."

Holt and Anderson conclude by making a countercultural appeal for a "less driven and competitive academic culture that valorizes the need for unharried time for creative intellectual work." Reflective leisure and time away from work provide the "mental space for free play essential for the cultivation of critical creativity."[11]

In the end, however, Holt and Anderson admit there are "no easy answers." Like Sittler, they call for a normative change rather than spell out practical ways to reach it. On both accounts, the intent seems more to break the silence than to pose workable solutions. One wonders, however, if these rhetorical attacks tend to avoid concrete details precisely because the work habits and routine expectations of academic culture, especially those related to hiring, tenure, and promotion, are the last and hardest behaviors to change.

In their depiction, Holt and Anderson do not acknowledge that for many faculty, especially for teachers in theology, a commingling of work and play, labor and leisure, is natural and even inherent in the definition of vocation. Following a vocation requires more than learning a specific task and completing it. Recognizing one's vocation means recognizing a way to use one's full life for the glory of God. When one enjoys one's work and finds it meaningful, it is hard to draw an artificial boundary between "work" and "nonwork." In a way, the very idea of vocation can easily lead one down the rosy path to trouble, workaholically and otherwise.

Oddly enough, Holt and Anderson's claim for leisure and creative personal space is even more difficult to justify within schools of theology, where anything that smacks of selfishness is suspect and religious values exalt a certain measure of self-sacrifice. Creative research and teaching, however, cannot happen without a certain amount of self-indulgence and even loafing in the best sense. Reducing the amount of work expected of students and professors alike might have the unexpected consequence of enriching academic life. The institution in which I first taught preserved each Friday as a day free from classes and meetings. While the implications

11. Holt and Anderson, "The Way We Work Now," pp. 137, 138.

for the life of the seminary would be hard to quantify, time away from classroom and meetings and the preservation of time for study and congregational work sent a strong message about the proper pace of life in theological education. Similarly, institutions that hope to solve financial problems and expand opportunities for theological education by offering evening and weekend classes and summer intensives should think twice about the consequences for the lives of those who teach and learn in the extra hours around the edges. While many students must work and need courses during non-business hours, institutional leaders must compensate by recognizing that a good education can no longer be organized as if the student population has few outside commitments.

Holt and Anderson do not consider the relevance of a wider ideological critique. Evaluations of the vocation of teaching have fallen under the sword of the prevalent and insidious market-driven cultural assumption that one's worth is measured by how hard one works. This commodification of life leaves little space for anything that seems like "nonwork" or, heaven forbid, for the gift of a vocation that is pleasurable and even effortless at times. That is, there is no space or tolerance today for a non-busy work life. Under the reign of capitalism, even leisure becomes hard work.[12] The best bargain is good education at a low price: more students in class and fewer faculty on full-time salary and benefits, thus less money spent by the institution. A professor's value then rests on how many students she lectures, how many books she publishes, how many administrative jobs she completes. Who cares about quality of education in such a scenario, much less the overworking of professors? It is odd that few people seem to worry that genuine education may slowly vanish if increasingly measured according to market prices.

One day a few years ago I accompanied my seven-year-old on a field trip to the science museum. After our return to school at noon, he pleaded, "Please stay for lunch." When I said, "I have work to do — how will I get it done?" he replied succinctly, "work faster." I certainly knew how to do that. "Work faster," however, is not just the story of my life. It is a problem with far wider causes and consequences. I did stay for lunch. I was glad I did. But why do we so often feel we need to justify moments away from "work" as worthy rather than claiming their validity as essential to the gracious teaching life?

12. See Cindy Aron, *Working at Play: A History of Vacation in the United States* (New York: Oxford University Press, 1999).

Does theological teaching as a religious vocation require a certain quality of life that is sometimes difficult to realize mid-semester amid competing fidelities to multiple vocational commitments? Does the way theological educators live, the pace of our lives, convey inadvertently harmful messages about living in faith to those who must be able to approach the ultimate and lead others there? In both cases, I believe the answer is yes. In the way we live our lives, theological educators have grossly underestimated the holy ground on which we tread.

Contemplation

Part of the problem is the model of contemplation that has defined spirituality. Contemplation and chaos are admittedly strange words. Contemplation is often equated with silence and serenity. If I were to ask one of my sons about the term "contemplation," he would likely raise his fingers, imitating movie images of meditating Zen masters. When I have told people the title of this essay, I have watched with interest the common assumption that I am writing about something monks do in solitary settings involving mystical experiences. Gauged by these understandings, most of us do not engage frequently in contemplation.

This, however, is only one of several understandings. Contemplation is also defined by the dictionary as the "act of considering with attention: study" or the "act of regarding steadily." In this sense, we all engage in contemplation with greater and lesser intentionality, dexterity, and practice. As Paul Wadell asserts in his chapter in this volume, contemplation as a steady "fixing of one's attention" can alter our customary ways of seeing, allowing us to see hope where before we have seen only despair.[13] Practical theologian Mary C. Boys describes contemplation as an activity essential to the "grace of teaching" which involves attending carefully without exploiting the object of thought, fostering awareness, and cultivating wonder.[14] In a word, contemplation as attentiveness, focus, and equanimity is a word worth redeeming. It is a word that certainly captures good parenting, and it is also a word essential to teaching theology. Teachers must not just

13. See p. 124 in this volume.
14. Mary C. Boys, "The Grace of Teaching," *Trinity/Special Issue Lilly Fellows Program in Humanities and the Arts* (Summer 1996): 14.

think; they must contemplate. In its fullness, contemplation is a word that captures an important quality of human life and the human-divine relationship.

Likewise, chaos. Just the other day, I picked up an essay that associated chaos entirely with absolute evil and violence.[15] Now there certainly are some aspects of chaos that are evil and destructive. Yet not all chaos is destructive. The first story of creation depicts God creating out of chaos, pointing at least indirectly to potential fecundity as well as the abyss. Recent explorations in physics reveal that the universe does not seem to be governed by inexorable laws that order the smallest particle to the most distant planet and allow for causal predictions of future changes. Instead, chaos theory indicates that the universe is more appropriately understood as standing on the border between chaos and order with order emerging spontaneously and as a result of infinitesimally small uncertainties in a complex system of interrelationships between motions. As Ian Barbour writes, "disorder is often the precondition for the appearance of a new form of order." There may be "a deeper order within apparent randomness."[16]

Chaos is, it seems, a part of life, analogous to Paul Tillich's claim that anxiety is part of created being and not merely an evil consequence of the fall. Even if we cannot make any such absolute ontological claims about chaos, we might as well admit that we are not going to get rid of it. In the classroom as in the home, we only tame chaos. We do not ultimately dispel it. Typical questions on student evaluations ignore this. They ask how well the class was "organized" and usually overlook the constructive role of disorder in making space for the emergence of fresh insights and inspirations. Indeed, sometimes the pressing questions that emerge in class should subvert the carefully laid plans of the syllabus and lecture schedule.

As becomes apparent in this effort to offer rough definitions, I am not completely happy with the going use of either of these terms. The ideal of contemplation and the problem of chaos deserve more careful thought. Further reflection, I contend, warrants the redemption of chaos and a spirituality that appears out of disruption, interruption, and confusion. Life's busyness is not an utterly secular wasteland; limited perceptions of spiritu-

---

15. Elaine V. Emeth, "Lessons from the Holocaust: Living Faithfully in the Midst of Chaos," *Weavings: A Journal of the Christian Spiritual Life* 13, no. 2 (March/April 1998): 16-26.

16. Ian G. Barbour, *Religion and Science: Historical and Contemporary Issues* (New York: HarperSanFrancisco, 1997), pp. 183-84.

ality have hidden the possibility of God's presence in the clutter and mess. Meaning can emerge *in* the chaos.

Unfortunately, however, conventional models of spirituality and contemplation have often made it difficult, if not impossible, to conceive the sometimes frenzied activity of today's teaching life as a religious practice and vocation. This is nicely exemplified in the model developed by Henry Nouwen, a Catholic priest, teacher, and author who wrote profusely on the spiritual life, his own in a variety of contexts and that of others. He remains one of the great spiritual guides and writers of the late twentieth century. I only use one of his works as an example of a common problem with understandings of spirituality and not as an adequate assessment of his many and varied contributions. He, in fact, might agree with the heart of my complaint; one of his books, *The Genesee Diary,* a journal of his seven-month stay in the Abbey of the Genesee in upstate New York, records some of his struggles with the problems this essay addresses.[17]

Nonetheless, in *The Way of the Heart,* Nouwen falls into a common trap. Here he draws upon the *Sayings of the Desert Fathers* and a story about Abba Arsenius to suggest three means to remain full of zeal for the Word of God: solitude, silence, and prayer. "The words *flee, be silent* and *pray* summarize the spirituality of the desert. . . . 'these are the sources of sinlessness,'" says Arsenius.[18] These three keep the world from shaping us in its image. Solitude or aloneness with God reminds us of our brokenness and transforms compulsive conformity into compassion. Silence is primarily a quality of heart that redirects the heart to the proper perspective from which to speak. Silence and solitude lead to prayer. Prayers containing simple words, voiced silently and persistently, open us up to God's presence. Praying is not thinking about God or speaking with God; the latter misleads us into expecting answers and the former taxes our minds. Rather, praying is "standing in the presence of God with the mind in the heart."[19]

When I first read Nouwen's book, I had three children six years and under. Silence and solitude were rare commodities. They can become rare commodities in the teaching life. While Nouwen notes that "there were

17. Henri J. M. Nouwen, *The Genesee Diary: Report from a Trappist Monastery* (New York: Image Books, 1981).

18. Benedicta Ward, trans., *The Sayings of the Desert Fathers* (London & Oxford: Mowbrays, 1975), p. 8, cited by Henry Nouwen, *The Way of the Heart* (New York: Ballentine, 1981), p. 4. emphasis in text.

19. Nouwen, *The Way of the Heart,* p. 59.

Mothers, too," he does not mean biological mothers.[20] As a result, in this context he fails to account for the place of intimate relationships in the formation of compassion even though his last book, *The Sabbatical Journey*, makes it clear that relationships with others remained one of the most important parts of his life.[21] He leaves readers to figure out for themselves how they find solitude in a life that demands their presence with others, how to practice silence with children learning to speak, and how to distinguish between a good silence and the voiceless silence of those who do not possess the means or the power to speak or to control the words most remembered in the academy and public at large.

Certainly, there are spiritual traditions that point to the holiness of the everyday. Ignatius of Loyola, the sixteenth-century founder of the Society of Jesus, created a tradition combining contemplation with action that has been reclaimed in recent years.[22] Close to the core of Martin Luther's Protestant Reformation theology stands the rejection of the idea that only those in cloistered religious life can exercise the priesthood of belief. Luther himself found God in daily life, even in the stench of diaper changing.[23] Even earlier, in the chaos surrounding the fall of Rome in the fifth century, St. Benedict created a monastic order that incorporated cloistered and corporate life. Recently Catholic religious and lay persons have drawn on this tradition to "distill wisdom from the daily," as Joan Chittister titles her book on the retrieval of the Rule of St. Benedict.[24] I do not doubt that indirectly this current in the tradition shapes my present protest.

Nonetheless, I am still called to protest, precisely as another small tributary of this stream. For, despite these many efforts in the Christian tradition, a bias against the outer forms of spirituality in bodily, familial,

---

20. Nouwen, *The Way of the Heart*, p. 3.

21. See Henri J. M. Nouwen, *Sabbatical Journey: The Diary of His Final Year* (New York: Crossroad, 1998).

22. Ignatius of Loyola, *The Spiritual Exercises of St. Ignatius*, trans. Louis J. Puhl, S.J. (Chicago: Loyola University Press, 1951); see also Paul Begheyn, S.J., and Kenneth Bogart, S.J., "A Bibliography on St. Ignatius' *Spiritual Exercises*," *Studies in the Spirituality of Jesuits* 23 (May 1991): 1-68.

23. Martin Luther, "The Estate of Marriage," in *Luther's Works*, ed. Walther I. Brandt and general ed. Helmut T. Lehmann (Philadelphia: Muhlenberg Press, 1962), pp. 13-49.

24. Joan Chittister, OSB, *Wisdom Distilled from the Daily: Living the Rule of St. Benedict Today* (San Francisco: Harper & Row, 1990); see also Esther de Waal, *Seeking God: The Way of St. Benedict* (Collegeville, Minn.: Liturgical Press, 1984), and *Living with Contradiction: An Introduction to Benedictine Spirituality* (Harrisburg, Penn.: Morehouse, 1989).

and communal life and the prejudice toward spirituality as something that pertains to the inner or interior life remains. Perhaps more than a retrieval is necessary. A more radical reorientation may be in order.

For many centuries, propagation was considered lower than celibacy and contemplation. Spiritual desire for communion with God ranked far above relational desire for human attachment and love. Spiritual hunger and sexual longing were often regarded as mutually exclusive. A dichotomy emerged between inner spirituality and outer worldliness.

In such a schema, the path of spirituality and the path of pedagogical life collide. Others have made a similar critique, turning to the parenting life to make an analogous point. Wendy M. Wright, a historian of Christian spirituality, has attempted to articulate systematically the nature of "family spirituality." While a deep appreciation for the vision of life and the understanding of prayer in historical figures such as Bernard of Clairvaux and Teresa of Avila guides her work, she argues that their view of contemplative life holds little in common with her own reality:

> Few of the great remembered prayers of our tradition were married. Few had children. They spoke of a God who was encountered one-on-one in the silence and solitude of a hermit's cell or the mobility of unattached apostolic life. They modeled a type of human loving that was not bonded to one person or group of persons but extended to all dispassionately. The majority of them radically cut ties with families, and often they strenuously resisted matrimony, holding it to be incompatible with ardent devotion to God. Many of them believed that to attain spiritual heights one had to subdue or transcend the body. Frequently they taught that following Christ required a life of voluntary poverty. . . . And they generally spoke of the spiritual life as a journey, a going away to somewhere else, a ladder ascending from earth to heaven, or a pilgrimage to destinations far beyond earth's (and family's) purview.[25]

On each account, Wright notes the cognitive dissonance between traditional portrayals of contemplation and the realities of her life — marriage,

---

25. Wendy M. Wright, "Living the Already But Not Yet: The Spiritual life of the American Catholic Family," *Warren Lecture Series in Catholic Studies*, No. 25, University of Tulsa, March 21, 1993, pp. 2-3. See also chapter 7, esp. pp. 155-58, of my book, *Also a Mother: Work and Family as Theological Dilemma* (Nashville: Abingdon, 1994).

children, the daily grind of family activities, passionate attachment to particular people, sexuality and embodiment, homemaking and ownership.

Certainly parenthood became a religious vocation in the Reformation. Over the past few centuries, however, the mother as the "Angel in the House" has secured her sanctification through maintaining the domestic rectitude of family members while largely sacrificing her own needs. The father's vocation as protector and provider became progressively equated with economic support and relational distance. These understandings of maternal and paternal vocation are highly ambiguous and problematic. Today, for better and for worse, being a mother or being a father is often seen by the general public as largely irrelevant to spiritual practice. Moreover, it is Catholics more than Protestants who have made overt efforts to reclaim the spirituality of everyday life.[26]

There is an interesting analogy between resistance to the idea of women writers and resistance to the spirituality of domestic chaos. People have trouble, observes Ursula Le Guin, picturing the woman writing, particularly the mother writing with children. "The Victorian script calls for a clear choice — either books or babies," not both.[27] The conventional contemplative script, I contend, also calls for a choice — either silence or chaos, not both. Many people today have trouble imagining an engrossed and active mother, or scholar for that matter, praying and meditating as she labors. To identify the busyness of motherhood or teacherhood as contemplative acts challenges classic dualisms between

26. See, for example, Thomas Merton, *Contemplation in a World of Action* (Garden City, N.Y.: Image Books, 1973); Parker Palmer, *The Active Life: A Spirituality of Work, Creativity, and Caring* (San Francisco: HarperSanFrancisco: 1990). Wendy M. Wright, *Sacred Dwelling: A Spirituality of Family Life* (Leavenworth, Kans.: Forest of Peace Publishing, 1994); Carol Lee Flinders, *At the Root of This Longing: Reconciling a Spiritual Hunger and a Feminist Thirst* (San Francisco: Harper and Row, 1997); Chittister, OSB, *Wisdom Distilled from the Daily*; de Waal, *Seeking God* and *Living with Contradiction*. Of course, Protestants have also made recent contributions, sometimes in close dialogue with the Catholic monastic traditions: Marjorie Thompson, *Family, the Forming Center: A Vision of the Role of Family in Spiritual Formation* (Nashville: Upper Room, 1989); Ernest Boyer, *A Way in the World: Family Life as Spiritual Discipline* (San Francisco: Harper & Row, 1984); and Kathleen Norris, *The Quotidian Mysteries: Laundry, Liturgy, and "Women's Work"* (New York: Paulist, 1998).

27. Ursula K. Le Guin, *Dancing at the Edge of the World: Thoughts on Words, Women, Places* (New York: Harper & Row, 1989), p. 218. See also Alicia Ostriker, *Writing Like a Woman*, Michigan Poet on Poetry Series (Ann Arbor: University of Michigan Press, 1983), p. 126.

flesh and spirit and between spiritual practices and philosophical theories.[28] Such identification forces us to recognize the ways in which we have excluded a large portion of lived reality from our thinking about contemplation.

Class privilege has also shaped ideals of study and contemplation. Many scholars spent long hours in uninterrupted study with most of their daily needs provided by others, whether wives, daughters, secretaries, or domestic servants. In a scene in "Shadowlands," one glimpses the comfortable scholarly life of C. S. Lewis, similar to other prominent men of his day, where his housemaid serves him tea in the quiet of his study. The temporal concerns of the world loom as a distraction from which one ought to protect oneself rather than as a realm of knowledge from which one might learn. This dualism of spiritual and material values, partly based on class prerogatives, runs deeper than many might suppose.

Historically, the severance of art from housework and family responsibility has been based on an ethic of self-sacrifice. In this heroic ethic, the "artist must sacrifice himself to his art."[29] Le Guin uncovers an alternative ethic of responsibility that reconnects the artistic vocation and the vocation of domestic work. She demonstrates the differences between these two ethics by comparing the creative processes of Joseph Conrad and Louisa May Alcott. This comparison between Conrad and Alcott, I believe, also illustrates two different approaches to the contemplative life. And it has implications for all those with multiple worldly demands. Like Jo March in *Little Women* writing on a trunk in the garret, her desk an old tin kitchen table, Alcott creates in a vortex, a creative whirlwind. She is a participant, surrounded by the steady inquiry of her family about her well-being and their interaction and care. By contrast, Conrad wrestles, struggles alone, and seeks mastery, a hero rising above the depersonalized "tireless affection" that supports him.

Does not the "sinlessness" for which Arsenius strives become more difficult the deeper one is immersed in relationship to others? And "to have and bring up kids is to be about as immersed in life as one can be," Rachel Blau Du Plessis suggests.[30] How does one escape conformity to

28. For a critical examination of philosphy as involving spiritual exercises, see Pierre Hadot, *Philosophy as a Way of Life: Spiritual Exercises from Socrates to Foucault*, ed. with an introduction by Arnold I. Davidson, translated by Michael Chase (Cambridge: Blackwell, 1995).

29. Le Guin, *Dancing at the Edge of the World*, p. 222.

30. Rachel Blau Du Plessis, *Writing Beyond the Ending: Narrative Strategies of Twenti-*

the world while living in the middle of its chaos rather than by fleeing to the desert? I believe that the former is just as hard, if not harder, than the latter.

Let me clarify: I am not renouncing the benefits of rest, solitude, silence, and retreat to the hills and the desert. Far from it. Such spiritual activities have real importance to a committed religious life. Those burdened by distractions especially know the importance of these often lost spiritual practices. Rather, far from renouncing spiritual disciplines of long-standing value, I want to stretch the understanding of silence and solitude to encompass fresh realities. I want to reconnect silence and solitude to their companion practices.[31] What, if anything, can we learn from the rigors of life with children that might have applicability to the lives that many people live, including those who teach in schools of theology and religion? Conventional reflection on contemplation, I believe, has missed an opportunity to discover how the practices of parenting *and* teaching offer other ways to think about spiritual practices.

Contemplation in the Midst of Chaos

Are there alternative models of contemplation with which we might begin to understand the theological teaching life in all its fullness? Is prayer possible in the midst of the cacophony of academic demands when prayer has so often been understood as requiring silence and a serene attitude? Might a reconceptualization of the contemplative stance allow theological teachers to envision and live out their vocation as religious in the midst of chaos and conflicting demands? Are there disciplines of the active life that might serve as a counterpart to or oscillation point with the traditional disciplines of the contemplative life?

If flight, silence, and prayer characterize the religiosity of the desert, what characterizes the spirituality of the home and the academy? As companions to (1) solitude and (2) silence, I propose that contemplation in the

---

eth-Century Women Writers (Bloomington: Indiana University Press, 1985), p. 101, cited by Le Guin, *Dancing at the Edge of the World*, p. 235.

31. Marjorie Thompson says it well when she writes, "The contrast is not between contemplation and action or prayer and service, but between attention and distraction" (*Leading from the Center*, Spring Newsletter of The General Board of Discipleship of the United Methodist Church, 1999, p. 2).

midst of chaos also rests on (1) relational connection and (2) "authentic conversation" as sources of sustenance and transformation and as avenues to the sacred.[32] Fleeing a communally oriented society in which identity rested upon social status allowed the Desert Fathers to reach new self-understandings. Inversely, in an individualistic society in which identity has become a near solipsistic activity, the initiation of genuine connection, the responsibility for dependent lives, and the creation of community and civil society contain corollary disclosive power.

I first read Nouwen's complaints about wordiness while watching one of my sons, not much over a year old, play with words as he took a bath and I guarded him from going under. Words opened up worlds for him; they became sources of self-knowledge, meaning, and relationship. They allowed him to begin to conceptualize different orders of reflection and gave him the power to name and share his experience. While certainly "words lead to sin" (as the Desert Fathers say) and silence "keeps us pilgrims,"[33] silence can also lead to stagnation and words can build a home. That is, seeing a child grasp the power of language or participating with children in weaving family traditions of story, song, and prayer confirms the place of conversation alongside silence and connection alongside solitude as vital sources of spiritual centeredness. It is, moreover, in communities of conversation as much as in solitude and silence that we discern the gospel message. Our individual readings of sacred texts were never meant to stand on their own. They must be abetted, amplified, corrected, and amended by the insights and inspirations of others.

Nouwen claims that the "goal of our life is not people. It is God."[34] But can these two be separated so simply? Far better to ask, how can we enhance our capacity to meet God in and through others who are dependent upon our charity and wisdom for their well-being? Beside the rich encounter with our nothingness in solitude, encounters with child, student, and even text can also turn our hearts to utter dependence on God and the cultivation of compassion. If compassion requires an "inner disposition to go with others to the place where they are weak, vulnerable, lonely, and

32. See David Tracy, *The Analogical Imagination: Christian Theology and the Culture of Pluralism* (New York: Crossroad, 1981), p. 101. For further analysis, see Hans-Georg Gadamer, *Dialogue and Dialectic: Eight Hermeneutical Studies on Plato* (New Haven: Yale University Press, 1980) and *Truth and Method* (New York: Seabury, 1975), pp. 325-41.

33. Nouwen, *The Way of the Heart*, pp. 35, 37.

34. Nouwen, *The Way of the Heart*, p. 26.

broken" as Nouwen proposes,[35] intimate participation in raising children provides ample opportunities to practice this, even if the parental role and the insidious, relentless nature of children's demands tempt one toward impatience, callousness, and judgment. When one practices compassion daily in the minutia of care, one has an opportunity for a change of heart that can be generalized outward. When compassion in intimate relationship comes up short, as it most inevitably will, family life teaches repeatedly the needs for self-scrutiny and penitence. For some parents, the birth and care of a child enable them to begin to see "each person as someone else's child." This can foster a "fierce, inarticulate urge to protect the vulnerable" and to protest the "misery we inflict on each other" in a more personal and direct way.[36] One smiles at the tumult of children in restaurants or on airplanes instead of scowling. Or one sees in the pettiness of one's daily family conflicts with partner and children thousands of places where one's utter fallibility calls for the arduous turning around of repentance and reconciliation.

Thomas Breidental contends that wise householding is a Christian vocation and discipline, a "Christian spiritual path" or the "nexus of disciplines."[37] "Paul is fond of calling the church a household, a temple of God, a commonwealth — all images drawn from the Hebrew scriptures, and all suggesting that the kingdom of heaven is a crowded place, thronged with worshippers and noisy not only with the sound of prayer but with conversation."[38] The whirlwind of activity that sweeps through my home can be incredibly disorienting. Yet householding with children offers untold opportunities for the rigorous practice of several virtues: restraint, patience, perseverance, endurance in fidelity, persistence in the pursuit of one's vocational passion, humility in the face of foibles mirrored back perfectly by one's child, receptivity to self and other, and, perhaps most difficult, loving another for their own sake, despite the distortions of the unavoidable identification and overinvestment in one's children. One is de-centered into imagining the world of another. Many of the attitudes needed for parenting also characterize the daily rhythms of teaching — respect for

---

35. Nouwen, *The Way of the Heart*, p. 20.

36. Camille S. Williams, "Sparrows and Lilies," *First Things*, August/September 1993, p. 12.

37. Thomas E. Breidental, *Christian Households: The Sanctification of Nearness* (Boston, Mass.: Cowley, 1997), pp. 2, 56, 92.

38. Breidental, *Christian Households*, pp. 5-6.

finitude and ignorance, awareness of mystery, receptivity to surprise and idiosyncrasy, delicate balancing of intense involvement and proper distancing.

Just as the opposition between silence and speech in models of spirituality is a false dichotomy, exclusive use of the metaphor of pilgrimage for spiritual development, detached from its companion metaphor of home and homemaking, is problematic. The spirituality of vocation has often been understood in terms of being called, "presumably from another place toward which we are to move in response." Pointing out the limits of this model or of any single model, Sharon Daloz Parks suggests cultivating the vocation and practice of homemaking or the building of "a space where souls can thrive and dream — secure, protected, related, nourished and whole."[39]

Similarly, Le Guin argues that babies and books are not only compatible but there is some benefit to their reconnection. Margaret Oliphant, a previously disregarded author who had six children, "seems to feel that she profited, that her writing profited, from the difficult, obscure, chancy connection between the art work and the emotional/manual/managerial complex of skills and tasks called 'housework,' and that to sever that connection would put the writing itself at risk, would make it, in her word, unnatural."[40] Having and caring for a child actually breaks down the dichotomy between solitude and relational life. Alicia Ostriker states simply, "The advantage of motherhood for a woman artist is that it puts her in immediate and inescapable contact with the sources of life, death, beauty, growth, corruption."[41] Might the same be true for those who teach theology? Might something of its chaos be reclaimed as source of life? Rather than thinking one must give up prayer or turn it over to others when one births a baby or teaches a class, perhaps prayer becomes something different in the midst of this new flurry of activity and demand.

If we can reclaim the material spirituality within the language of homemaking, I believe that we will begin to pave the way for reestablishing the world-maintaining activities of teaching, such as reading, writing, and creating collegial communities, as rich spiritual disciplines. The almost

39. Sharon Daloz Parks, "Home and Pilgrimage: Companion Metaphors for Personal and Social Transformation," *Soundings* 72, no. 2-3 (Summer/Fall 1989): 304 (297-315).

40. Le Guin, *Dancing at the Edge of the World*, p. 222.

41. Ostriker, *Writing Like a Woman*, p. 131, cited by Le Guin, p. 228.

impossible discipline of writing from the heart is transposed into a "monastic exercise, a divine office; it is zen sitting; it is a kind of yoga."[42] Careful reflective reading becomes, as it was for Augustine, "nothing short of
salvific."[43] If reading and writing involve certain kinds of conversion experiences, then teaching in the spiritually centered classroom has "something
in common with the ancient craft of spiritual guidance." In the centered
classroom, the teacher draws out the knowledge of the participants and
creates a space for the interplay between verbal witness and silent meditation.[44] Recognizing that "it takes a long time to take in a few words" and
that students are "relentlessly overstimulated" by the bombardment of life
and school today, this may mean that the professor talks less, listens more,
assigns fewer and shorter texts, reads aloud in class, starts class softly
rather than with a "bang," uses in-class writing as a means of focusing attention, and invites the wisdom of the less extroverted who do not speak
under the conditions of most classrooms.

In his consideration of prayer, the third component of desert spirituality, Nouwen at least asks "how can we, who are not monks and do not
live in the desert, practice the prayer of the heart?"[45] Like solitude and silence, connection and conversation can also be aimed toward the practice
of unceasing prayer. Unceasing prayer, Nouwen argues, comes through
charity toward others and through the disciplined activity of repetition
and remembrance. Our neighbor, whether child, student, or colleague,
can become our partner in unceasing prayer. Finding a place of rest amid
the cacophony of demands requires the discipline of prayer oriented
around the incidentals, the disruptions, and the routine chores. Prayer in
this context requires a rigorous attention of mind, will, and heart. Single
words and short prayers may counteract the dissipation common to the
domestic and the teaching life. Even moments of frustration, when a rush
of anger leads us to curse, hide an impulse "however darkly . . . to pray,"
Robert Morris observes, and may be turned into prayer with the "second
breath" of recognizing such instances as "occasions for spiritual prac-

---

42. Mary Rose O'Reilley, "The Centered Classroom: Meditations on Teaching and
Learning," *Weavings* 4 (Sept./Oct. 1989): 26, 30; also appeared in slightly different form in
College English 46, no. 2 (Feb. 1984) and 51, no. 2 (Feb. 1989).

43. Margaret Miles, "On Reading Augustine and on Augustine's Reading," *The Christian Century*, May 21-28, 1997, p. 510 (510-14).

44. O'Reilley, "The Centered Classroom," p. 30.

45. Nouwen, *The Way of the Heart*, p. 63.

tice."[46] Sometimes pivotal interactions foster insights (e.g., "work faster"). Wisdom somehow emerges out of the chaos itself, stops us dead in our tracks, and heightens awareness.

In the end, "charity, not silence," reminds Nouwen, "is the purpose of the spiritual life and of ministry. About this all the Desert Fathers are unanimous."[47] Care of and hospitality toward others, even when these acts interrupt monastic rituals of silence and solitude, assume priority. There are, I would add, many paths to charity besides these standard monastic routines. While I do not argue that contemplation in the midst of chaos is the ideal spiritual path, I believe we can wrestle from the chaotic life of teaching the depth of vision and wisdom that lies in that vocation, as is also the case with family life and parenting.

All this is not to say that eight days of silence in a Jesuit retreat center do not have personal appeal and an important place in the spiritual life. In fact, the ability to sustain oneself in the midst of chaos draws deeply upon what one has learned in times of solitude and sometimes depends on moments akin to monastic silence. Rather, I want to argue that silence and solitude do not exhaust the avenues of spiritual renewal and, when taken as exhaustive, render other avenues invisible and neglected. "What is needed now," Wright argues, "is a more public, shared enunciation of the texture and distinct sound of the sacred as it is refracted" in the lives of families and, by extension, in the practice of teaching.[48] She grounds her attempt to articulate a spirituality of families in a sacramental understanding of human experience as revelatory of the divine. Extending this premise to the workaday lives of those immersed in the cultivation of the minds and souls of students, the enunciation of the sacred in teaching requires a greater reckoning with the material conditions, the messiness, of the teaching life.

Nonetheless, there are hazards for those attempting to practice contemplation in the midst of teaching. One may falsely justify an overflowing calendar as a contribution to spiritual enrichment when it leads instead to depletion. One must watch all the more carefully for signs of depletion (e.g., heightened impatience; joylessness) and create pragmatic rules for holding chaos at bay (e.g., refuse invitations to speak on Sunday; accept

46. Robert C. Morris, "The Second Breath: Frustration as a Doorway to Daily Spiritual Practice," *Weavings: A Journal of the Christian Spiritual Life* 13, no. 2 (March/April 1998): 37-45.
47. Nouwen, *The Way of the Heart*, p. 47.
48. Wright, "Living the Already But Not Yet," p. 5.

out-of-town commitments only once a semester). Solitude and silence are requisite companions to connection and conversation. The ability to resist the greed of self-promotion and dependency on the affirmation of others becomes more difficult when one remains in the midst of such temptations. There is also the sheer difficulty of multiple vocations: "The difficulty of trying to be responsible, hour after hour day after day for maybe twenty *years,* for the well-being of children and the excellence of books, is immense: it involves an endless expense of energy and an impossible weighing of competing priorities."[49] While Le Guin wants to claim that intense immersion does not mean drowning — "a lot of us can swim" — the dangers of going under are well worth noting.

There are also perils of solitude and silence. The desert monastic Arsenius claims, "I have often repented of having spoken, but never of having remained silent." Such a claim for the sanctity of silence deserves a bold critique today. Many now recognize that some people and populations have wrongly remained silent before injustice and hatred and in the face of petty jokes and dramatic distortions of biblical proclamation. Silence and solitude have often hidden rather than promoted truth and justice. As I have argued elsewhere, good pastoral care and theology is often a matter of breaking silences. Indeed, "hearing into speech" is Nelle Morton's most oft-quoted phrase to depict the creation of personhood and community through giving voice to the marginalized.

Practicing Contemplation in the Midst of the Chaos of Teaching

Practicing contemplation in the midst of the chaos of the teaching life requires several considerations that may not be as readily provoked by more traditional contemplative settings. One encounters daily limits and must learn to live with finitude repeatedly. This involves living fully within the boundaries of one's decisions. What is the good that can be accomplished here and now rather than if only we were elsewhere? Embracing finitude in the chaos of teaching and parenting does not stop here, however. Living within the boundaries of one's decisions, in turn, means enduring the dread of knowing that in the midst of chaos one sometimes chooses

---

49. Le Guin, *Dancing at the Edge of the World,* p. 226, emphasis in text.

poorly or wrongly and often meets expectations partially and inadequately. One faces loss and failure continually. When pressed by multiple worthy demands, it is easy and common to fall short.

Living with finitude also means recognizing that other activities not directly related to one's work contribute to one's teaching. If theological teaching depends partly on the person of the professor, then having a child, caring for a partner or her ailing mother, working at a soup kitchen, or playing the saxophone are not the negligible activities that they have often been made out to be. As Claire Mathews McGinnis argues in her chapter in this book, we are called to regard interruptions differently, as reminders to attend to God in all things, as moments always and intrinsically touched by God.

Moreover, contemplation in the midst of the chaos of teaching demands a heightened recognition of the phases of an academic career. One cannot do everything (teaching, research, writing, administration, advising, speaking, editing) well all the time. This recognition in turn requires an appropriate appreciation for one's colleagues in the wider academic community. We do not have to do it all and can celebrate the success of others rather than experience it as competition and threat. We also depend heavily on the wider institutional community and the wisdom of its leadership to identify faculty talents and distribute wisely responsibilities for teaching, research, and administration. Arbitration of faculty expectations and "development" has, for this reason, become one of the more difficult arenas of theological leadership for deans and presidents.

Perhaps most difficult for many of us, contemplation in the midst of chaos demands learning the discipline of saying no. Making choices requires a careful, continuous reassessment of one's vocational gifts as the best vantage point from which to decide. This becomes more difficult when one feels called to multiple vocations (e.g., parent and scholar). As much as we resist the idea, we need to recognize that saying yes means saying no to other possibilities that bring "destruction and ruin" and saying no actually opens up space for the responsibilities and challenges of a larger life-affirming yes that "makes space for God."[50] For many teachers of theology, this discipline will require conquering fears that lead to the need to define productivity and success in terms that do not match one's

---

50. See M. Shawn Copeland, "Saying Yes and Saying No," in *Practicing Our Faith: A Way of Life for a Searching People,* ed. Dorothy C. Bass (San Francisco: Jossey-Bass, 1997), pp. 60, 73.

vocational call. This practice of discernment will inevitably raise profound questions about the ultimate purpose of life. This discipline may also require initiating a broader critique of the escalating demands of the teaching life, as I indicated at the beginning of this essay.

Related to the need to decline invitations and streamline work is the heightened need to attend carefully to patterns and places of study. With the multiple demands of the teaching life, the teacher has to work even harder to learn and to practice a discipline of attention that brings together piety and intellect, theory and practice. In an interview, David Tracy argues that moderns have lost a connection once present in our culture and still enduring in some other cultures between holy thinking and holy living or, in his words, between "theological and philosophical theories and spiritual exercises." "If you were an ancient Stoic," Tracy remarks, "every day you would practice certain exercises that would heighten awareness of 'my' logos and 'the' Logos. That's why Simone Weil loved the Stoics. She thought 'attention,' the ability to attend to the wider whole, was what we, her rushed contemporaries, most lacked."[51] Separating spiritual practices and theoretical reflection is a modern aberration in the history of philosophical and theological reflection.

Finally, beyond all these more or less pragmatic strategies lies a basic shift in theological conceptions of the divine that merits brief mention. Without negating the transcendence of God, contemplation in the midst of chaos relies in particular on trust in the radical immanence of God in the immediacy of one's experience. In contemplation in the midst of chaos, one awaits the sacred in unexpected and unplanned places. One of the most powerful stories in the Synoptic Gospels is that of Jesus pointing to the child in the "midst" of the disciples (Matt. 18:2). Attention to the child in our midst, Jesus seems to say, embodies a better avenue to the kingdom of heaven than a variety of more conventional spiritual or religious activities.

The redemption of chaos and the deepening of the meaning of contemplation open the way for a more complex understanding of God and Jesus' promise of peace. In chaos, God may appear as "the Uncomforter, the Truly Vulnerable One, and the Discomforter," as well as the Comforter and the Victor. God becomes less triumphant. God also becomes less quiet or passive: "God rages and weeps, shouts and pleads, commands and in-

---

51. "Reasons to Hope for Reform: An Interview with David Tracy," by William R. Burrows, *America* 173, no. 11 (October 14, 1995): 16 (12-18).

structs."[52] The tumult does not finally overpower the divine; the divine even relishes the surprising turns of the human melee. Jesus bestows peace, not as a promise of perfect serenity, but as a source of strength in the midst of turmoil. Jesus does not pledge the end of questions, anxiety, and strife but divine presence in their midst. Beyond serenity of mind, the peace of God heralds reconciliation in the midst of warring parties, including in the midst of the discord many of us feel between diverse vocational demands.

These reflections also spark a different reading of grace and contemplation. A dictionary definition describes chaos as "a state of things in which chance is supreme." While chaos can threaten sanity and survival, chaos is also a state in which the opportunity for grace reigns supreme. In medieval conceptions of the movements of religious practices, with meditation, prayer, and reading a person initiates action; with contemplation God acts. In line with a Thomistic understanding of human nature and grace, only God makes contemplation possible as an added grace. In the end, the person does not control the grace of contemplation. When meaning emerges out of chaos, it is not where one expects. Grace in chaos sometimes comes when one gives in to it; it emerges in unanticipated ways. The best one can do is live in anticipatory expectation, creating a preparatory space for meaning and fostering a way of perceiving direction in the midst of chaos. One seeks to retain the potential of chaos while reducing its destructive spin-offs and disconnections.

The reconceptualization of the contemplative stance attempted in this chapter is admittedly only a small step toward the end of helping theological teachers regain an understanding of their vocation as religious and faithful. Perhaps the more important contribution is simply bringing the question of the pace of the teaching life in theological schools into the discussion at large. While problems of overextension and overload characterize the lives of many who teach theology, these problems have seldom received the kind of analysis and response that they deserve. That the typical ministry student faces some of these same problems makes the situation even more dire. Ultimately the larger environment of academic life deserves prophetic challenge. Meanwhile, we would do well to pay better attention to human limits and to the contemplative capacities and religious dimensions of those daily, mundane activities in which we engage. There is, no doubt, space for divine presence even in the midst of the busyness of the teaching life.

52. Emeth, "Lessons from the Holocaust," pp. 18, 24.

My Vocational Kinship with the United States' First Female Theologian

ROSEMARY SKINNER KELLER

MY VOCATIONAL KINSHIP with Georgia Harkness, the first female theologian to teach in seminaries in the United States, began in the late 1980s, about fifteen years after she died in 1974. We are not related by blood ties. I never met her face-to-face. I did not even know who she was until after she had died and I began to teach at Garrett-Evangelical Seminary in 1979. However, I share a close vocational kinship with her.

The conjunction of the two words "vocational kinship" is not made in the dictionary. "Vocation" traditionally means "a regular occupation or profession: especially one for which one is specially suited or qualified," and "kin" usually is identified as "the person or persons closest in blood relationship."

"Vocational kinship" means to me a shared identity, a spiritual commitment of mutual purpose, meaning, and values, that binds persons together in such close ties that they become a family of kin. My definition expands the ways that both "vocation" and "kinship" are defined. I developed the concept of vocational kinship out of my desire to determine how Georgia Harkness and other women whom I have known through my studies in American religious history have influenced me vocationally, both personally and professionally, over the years.

"Vocation" has a religious connotation to me, though it does not necessarily mean to enter a religious order or a monastic life, as it often has been understood. Nor do I equate a vocation simply with the work one does, whether in a sacred or secular occupation, or in the public or private sphere of life, an understanding closely associated with the Protestant Reformation. In my understanding, "vocation" means the way a person responds to God with the whole of her or his life, not just through her or his work. And "kinship" can be a person or community of persons with whom one feels such affinity and intimacy that they become a self-created or self-chosen family. Because of the members' shared purposes, they may feel closer to each other than to their families of origin.

As a historian of women and religion in the United States, I have been attracted over the years to the study of autobiography and biography. I find points of identification with other women's lives; they make history personal to me and tell me much about my own life and the lives of other women and men, both contemporary and in the past. Many of the likenesses and differences in our lives transcend particular time periods.

I have experienced most deeply my vocational kinship through my American historical studies on feminists or pre-feminists, women who were pioneers, whose ventures opened new doors for women who came after them and enabled them to forge new roles for themselves and for their sisters. Their stories are filled with common experiences of trials, setbacks, breakthroughs, and new vision that create a community of ancestry and identity.

My closest vocational kinship is with Georgia Harkness. I share my understanding of vocational kinship in this essay because I hope that my kinship with her may enable other women and men to connect with foremothers and forefathers who particularly address them on their vocational journeys. Any of us may have developed vocational kinship with the historical subjects of autobiographies and biographies we have read, although we may not yet have identified our kinship in this way. I hope that my development of the idea of vocational kinship enables others to rethink the ways in which they have been motivated and inspired vocationally through a shared kinship with others.

I share my kinship with Georgia Harkness because she has been a mentor to me and to countless other women and men on their vocational journeys. Her life has affinity with the lives of women and men today and might provide spiritual and social direction to those who may read this essay, just as it has to me. I want to share my vocational kinship in two ways that I believe are significant for my own and others' lives: first, the impor-

76

tance of the particular time and place in the development of vocational kinship, and, second, the expansion of vocation beyond its exclusive identification with work to our broader life journeys.

Vocational Kinship: Time and Place

It is puzzling to me that I never heard of Georgia Harkness while I was pursuing a Master's degree in Religious Education at Yale Divinity School in 1958. Her books were not used in my classes, and I do not remember seeing them in the seminary bookstore. By that time she had published twenty-two books and a countless number of articles. She had taught in higher education for over thirty-five years, including almost twenty years in theological education, coming to Garrett Biblical Institute in 1940 and moving to Pacific School of Religion in 1950 for the final decade of her professional teaching career. By 1958, Harkness was a distinguished figure in national and international Methodist and ecumenical affairs, a modern-day social prophet who related theology to everyday life and to the issues and needs of the world. She was read widely by both laity and clergy.

However, at the height of her career in 1958, Georgia Harkness was an invisible woman at Yale Divinity School. Perhaps she was not scholarly enough. Her interests may have been too practical to qualify her as a legitimate theologian. Or, more than likely, many schools were not ready to accept a female scholar as an authority on theology in their classrooms. I do not remember any women on the YDS faculty in 1958, and there were only a handful of women teaching in all seminaries at that time.

Garrett was bold to bring Harkness onto its faculty in 1940, and she identified it as her academic home. Her legacy is imprinted on the ethos of Garrett Biblical Institute, the predecessor of Garrett-Evangelical Theological Seminary, and her influence continues to be felt there. Historically, it is a strong Protestant, United Methodist seminary in both the evangelical and liberal traditions. Harkness identified herself theologically as an evangelical liberal. She was an evangelical in terms of her personal confessional commitment to Christ, grounded in her baptism in her early teens. In her thirties, she embraced liberalism in her growing advocacy of social justice issues, notably her strong stances against militarism, racism, sexism, classism, and homophobia. These commitments would persist throughout the rest of her life.

The time and place, when and where, I came into theological education were highly formative factors in the vocational kinship I developed with Georgia Harkness. The late 1970s were a highly significant time in the history of women in ministry at Garrett-Evangelical, and it was a crucial time for me personally to join the faculty there. The ethos of the institution placed the advancement of women in ministry at the heart of its institutional priorities. This emphasis was also at the heart of Harkness's legacy.

Women had been granted "conference membership" in the Methodist Church, meaning that they could become qualified for full ordination status, in 1956. In fact, women did not begin coming to liberal Protestant seminaries in large numbers to prepare for ordination until about 1970. Harkness was one of the most pivotal persons at the General Conference of the denomination to bring the delegates to an affirmative vote on the matter. She had been working for women's ordination for over twenty years. By the 1956 Conference, she helped to mobilize women's societies in local churches throughout the United States to send thousands of petitions to the General Conference, creating a ground swell of grassroots support that powerfully motivated the delegates to make their historic affirmation of the right of women to be ordained. After the General Conference passed the resolution to ordain women, the delegates rose and gave Georgia Harkness a standing ovation, acknowledging her as the person who had done the most over the years to make ordination of women in the Methodist Church a reality.

Most female students in seminaries through the 1950s and '60s, including myself, received Master's degrees in Religious Education. In the 1970s, however, more and more women began studying for the Master of Divinity degree. A remarkable and pioneering group of women students began to come to Garrett-Evangelical to prepare for ordination in the United Methodist Church. Until the late 1970s, however, there was still only one woman on the faculty, Dorothy Jean Furnish, Professor of Christian Education, who had served valiantly as the lone woman and had earlier been a student of Harkness's there. The Board of Trustees established a Georgia Harkness Chair on the faculty and authorized President Merlyn Northfelt to seek a woman to become the first Georgia Harkness professor near the end of the '70s. These women students met with President Northfelt and strongly advocated that Rosemary Radford Ruether, then Professor of Theology at Howard Divinity School, be hired.

78

Garrett-Evangelical took a giant step in the support of women in the ministry by hiring her. She held the same title that her predecessor had held, Professor of Applied Theology. To apply theology, to make it relevant to personal and social experience, had come to be seen as an important way to teach theology that was not recognized in the 1950s. Harkness was denied the position of Professor of Systematic Theology, which focused on the theoretical exposition of theology, when she was at Garrett and became one of the first persons to chart this new field of practical theology in seminaries. For Rosemary Ruether, and for Garrett-Evangelical, it was a new day in the late 1970s.

At this same time, while still working on a Ph.D. at the University of Illinois in downtown Chicago, I taught my first course as an adjunct professor at Garrett-Evangelical Theological Seminary. As a part of my Ph.D. program in American History, I took a minor field in the History of Women. The first course I taught at Garrett was in "The History of American Women in Ministry." I went to *Notable American Women,* the three-volume biographical encyclopedia of women in America that had recently been published by Harvard University Press, and looked up all the women related to ministry. Then I went to the card catalog in the library and was astounded to find the enormous collection of old books by women related to churches.

Going into the stacks to look them up, I was shocked again to find that my white sweater had smudges on it after I perused a few old women's missionary journals. The journals were so dusty; probably few if any people had ever looked at them. These became the primary sources around which the course was built. Each student picked one woman in the history of American women in ministry whom she studied in depth, and did an oral dramatization and a written paper about her life and ministry. One of the historical figures studied was Georgia Harkness. These students knew that they were making women's history through their findings; the freshness of the course made it exciting.

After this first course and a half-time lectureship the next year, I received a tenure-track position as Assistant Professor of Religion and American Culture. Now there were three very different and highly complementary women on the faculty, to follow in the steps of Harkness and to begin a steady stream of women to be hired across the fields of the curriculum in the years to follow. The shadow of Georgia Harkness was cast upon the walls of the seminary. Her glorious hymn, "Hope of the World," which had been selected from over 200 entries to open the 1954 World Council of Churches meeting at the First Methodist Church in Evanston, Illinois, was almost always the processional or recessional hymn at graduation exercises or special chapel events.

In the mid-1980s, my vocational kinship with Harkness began to develop in earnest. I realized that she would have been 100 years old in 1991. Harkness had given all of her papers to Garrett-Evangelical. Her former colleagues and close friends, Murray and Dorothy Leiffer, who shared an office next to hers, organized and catalogued them meticulously in fourteen boxes. However, few people had ever seriously gone through these papers. Nor had I studied them in any depth. I soon realized that a biography of Harkness could not have been written without the Leiffers' careful and loving work. With my primary interest in the history of women and religion, I had a hunch when I began the project that a part of my vocation would be realized in recreating the story of Georgia Harkness for the late twentieth century. I knew enough about her to be convinced that her life needed to be recovered, and that I was the one to do it.

At about the same time, Abingdon Press invited me to write a biography of Georgia Harkness to commemorate her 100th birthday. Writing her biography was the most intimate and involving research and writing project that I have ever had, simply because we came into vocational kinship through it.

The goal that I had with Abingdon was to complete the book, *Georgia Harkness: For Such a Time as This,* so that it could be released at the 1992 General Conference of the United Methodist Church. During this intense period, I read all of her books, over forty of them, most of her countless articles, and her personal letters, sermons, speeches, and papers. At the same time, I visited the sites of her personal and professional life and interviewed many of her living relatives and a host of her remaining friends and colleagues.

Being at Garrett, and introduced to her through her academic home and the sizable collection of papers preserved by the Leiffers, gave me the courage to branch out over the entire United States in further search of the real Georgia Harkness. One of the most memorable experiences of my touring was to the site of her birth at the Harkness family farm in the Adirondack Mountains near the shore of Lake Champlain. Here I saw her gravesite and made the discovery that she was identified on her gravestone as "Georgia Harkness: Ph.D. — 1891-1974." She was the only "Ph.D." in the graveyard!

I had another wonderful personal visit spending the day with Harkness's niece and her husband, Peg and John Overholt, who were retired in Kilmarnock, Maryland. They got out albums of old family photographs, a tiny journal that Georgia had kept as a twelve-year-old child, and other old memorabilia from the family archives. Peg Overholt told me stories about her Aunt Georgia and the personal contact with her that she had never told anyone else in her life. I was humbled and awed that this woman, who had never seen me before, would confide in me and trust me. Many of the pictures, journal entries, and personal stories made their way into the book. In the midst of our day together we had crab cakes that she had made from crabs caught in the Chesapeake Bay and blueberry muffins from wild berries growing in their yard. I have never had greater hospitality extended to me than I received that day.

Harkness's professional colleagues at Garrett were either deceased or retired away from Evanston. I had a wonderful visit in 1990 with Murray and Dorothy Leiffer, who were several years into retirement in La Jolla, California. They shared that being the first female theologian at Garrett was often trying for Harkness. She would sometimes come to their office and cry, telling them that "It is hard being here." The president, Horace Greeley Smith, made it especially difficult, Murray Leiffer confided, hiring her with praise but then becoming skittish over some of her strong social stands and jealous of her growing esteem in the churches.

A number of her colleagues at the Pacific School of Religion in Berkeley were still in the area in retirement and able to be interviewed. They spoke of the full acceptance at PSR of Georgia and her housemate, Verna Miller, with whom she lived for thirty years, after they were introduced to each other by Ernest Fremont Tittle, their pastor at the Evanston First Methodist Church. Verna attended all PSR events with Georgia and took a wifely role in their relationship. They particularly noted that Verna's sense of humor was a good tonic for the more serious-natured Georgia.

In Claremont, California, where Georgia and Verna retired, I had a meaningful interview with John Cobb and his family who knew them well. I also spent a wonderful time with John Bennett, Professor of Christian Ethics and President Emeritus of Union Theological Seminary in New York City, then ninety years old and retired at Pilgrim Place. Bennett, with his hand shaking from age, served me tea. He loaned me a picture taken in

1950 of the Dun Commission of Christian Scholars on the Moral Implications of Obliteration Bombing and the use of Hydrogen Bombs for Mass Destruction. Among those pictured were Harkness, John Bennett, Reinhold Neibuhr, Paul Tillich, Angus Dun, and Robert Calhoun. The picture, which became a part of the book, was indeed worth a thousand words. Harkness was standing erect dressed very properly, as a professional woman of her time would be expected to be, with a group of men. She wore a man-tailored suit with a white shirt and sturdy tie shoes. She looked like a woman living and working in a man's world, which was the story of her life in the mid-twentieth century.

Bennett told me something else of great importance about the picture. He said that Harkness and Calhoun were the only two members of the commission who were total pacifists, opposing both first-strike and retaliation atomic bombing. Bennett, at age ninety, saw them as the true social prophets among the ten members of the Dun Commission. He said that, had he been able to conceive the destruction that atomic and hydrogen bombs would bring, he would have stood with Harkness and Calhoun.

Of all the persons whom I met or whose materials I read, the person with whom Harkness felt the closest vocational kinship was Edgar Sheffield Brightmann, Professor of Philosophy at Boston University and Harkness's doctoral advisor. She was his first Ph.D. student. In the extensive archival collection of Brightmann materials in the Mugar Library of Boston University, there were over 200 letters exchanged between Brightmann and Harkness from the 1920s, when she was writing her dissertation, until the 1950s, when she was a faculty member at Pacific School of Religion. These letters were the most revealing sources regarding the personal side of Harkness of any materials that I read. Brightmann and Harkness had esteem and affection for each other as friends and colleagues, and she opened herself freely and painfully to him at times. She wrote in detail about teaching positions that were denied her, at least in part because she was a woman, and about her controversies with Horace Greeley Smith: his denial of the professorship in Systematic Theology at Garrett and his failure to give her raises accorded to other faculty members.

The most poignant exchange among the letters came when Brightmann sent her a copy of a highly complimentary recommendation that he wrote for her in which he stated that the only negative characteristic that he saw in her was a certain "lack of feminine charm." Clearly wounded, Harkness wrote him back, telling him that he would never have stated in a recommendation for a man that he lacked qualities of masculinity. Brightmann was apologetic, but the letter had been sent and she was not offered the position.

Edgar Brightmann was a man of his time and place. Sexism was latent in his mind and way of life. Harkness, a pre-feminist, experienced sexism deeply when it was directed toward her and other women for whom she sought to open doors to the professional life of the church. We have come a long way since this letter was written in the 1950s, but we still experience vocational kinship with Brightmann and Harkness in our own time and place.

Vocational Kinship: Work and Life

I am now at a different time and place on my own vocational journey: it is almost ten years since I wrote my biography of Georgia Harkness, and I am located at Union Theological Seminary in New York City as academic dean and a member of the faculty. The concept of my vocational kinship with Georgia Harkness has come to me here only recently. However, I realize that I have been experiencing this relationship ever since I began to research and write her life story.

Before I came into vocational kinship with Harkness in the early 1990s, I began to place the nature of vocation at the heart of my teaching and my own experience. I wanted to help my students find a focus for interpreting their inward spiritual formation and their outward professional development at the heart of their own evolving vocational journeys. I began to experience more profoundly the meaning of vocation at the heart of my own spiritual journey: first, to my journey inward, my calling to a deeper personal relationship with God, and second, to my journey outward, the expression of that calling through my career as a teacher and administrator in theological education.

I felt that the meaning of vocation is insufficient when it is associated exclusively with the work one does and that it needs to be expanded to include the way one lives her or his entire life as a response to God. I remembered the words of our Puritan forefather John Cotton, founder of the First Church, Boston, who defined vocation in this way: "If thou would'st live a lively life, and have thy soule and body to prosper in thy calling, labor then to get into a good calling and therein live for the good of all." I admitted to myself that John Cotton, the Puritan patriarch with whom I, as a late twentieth-century feminist historian, did not want to identify, had some profound ideas about vocation. He understood that our vocation was to "live a lively life," a life that encompassed the prospering of one's individual "soule and body," as well as a kind of work and a kind of life that was given to the "good of all."

I also believed that my students and I needed vocational models and mentors: we needed examples of women and men who had brought together work and life in their vocations. Through my spiritual searchings, as well as through my teaching, I was naturally drawn to the reading of autobiographies and biographies. They were devotional readings for me. The life stories of women and men challenged me to live my own life as a response to God's call. I began to incorporate this biographical approach into my teaching regarding vocation and to set life stories within the contexts of the larger settings of American church and social history.

Before I came into vocational kinship with Georgia Harkness, I interpreted vocation in the same way that I believe most middle-class people do: that vocation begins when we are in college and look for an occupation or profession to pursue as a life's career. One's career continues until "retirement" when we can have "avocations" that are outside our vocation of work. The key vocational question for a young adult is *What kind of work do I want to do?*

The most basic insights that I gained from studying Harkness's life vocationally are simple but also profound. First, I came to see that the traditional equation of work with vocation is too narrow. Second, I realized that vocation is a lifelong process, a journey that begins in childhood and continues until death. Third, I decided that vocation encompasses not only our "work life" but the whole of our personal and professional life as a response to God.

I began to think about the cycles that a biographer finds in her or his subject's life, the benchmarks that help interpret continuity and change in a person's life, including birth, education, marriage, childbearing and rearing, work, career, geographical change, and death. I would like to trace this lifelong vocational journey of work and life through four periods in Georgia Harkness's experience: (1) rooted and reaching out; (2) blessing the search; (3) transformation through vocation; and (4) conceiving new life.

Rooted and Reaching Out

Harkness described her vocational roots, laid in her early childhood in the tiny hamlet of Harkness, New York, through the intertwining of her family, church, and school. Long before she had any conception of what vocation meant, those deep roots were set by her parents, Lillie and Warren Harkness, when she was three years old and they took her to church in their arms. In countless ways as a child she reached out to the church. She wanted to be baptized and become a member of the congregation during a revival service, when she was seven, but her mother insisted that she wait until she was old enough to know what she was doing. Playing the one hymn that she knew, "Trust and Obey," Georgia regularly substituted for the organist during Sunday morning services. In her early teens, she responded to God's call during another revival service when she "made her decision for Christ," was baptized and became a member of the congregation. Gold stars were beside her name over many years on the Sunday School chart, still hanging on the wall when I visited the church in 1990.

By the time she was fifty years old, Harkness had ventured far from the conservatism of her early church roots. In maturity, she identified herself as an evangelical liberal. She professed to be a highly liberal social prophet in relation to the pressing social issues of her day, including sexism, racism, militarism, classism, and homophobia, as well as an evangelical committed to personal conversion and commitment to Christ. Symbolizing the depth of her roots, she kept her membership in the tiny Harkness United Methodist Church throughout her lifetime, even though she was active in local congregations and a delegate to the General Conferences of the denomination from Illinois and California in her middle and mature years.

The beginning of Harkness's vocational journey was also rooted in her love of schoolwork, and the high quality of that work, begun in the Haddock Hall Elementary School housed on weekdays in the church building. Her parents recognized her intellectual gifts and made it possible for her to go to Cornell, the finest university in New York State, when she won a New York Regents' Scholarship for her high grades in high school. Harkness and her parents recognized her limitations, too: she described herself as "shy, green, and countrified, a social misfit" when she entered college.

I had not seriously thought of the childhood roots of vocation in my own life until I recognized them through Harkness's experience. I was an "only child," and my parents, Mary and Howard Skinner, vested high hopes in me. They were married for thirteen years before I was born in Oklahoma City, Oklahoma, and had given up on the possibility of bearing a child. I was a surprise! They wanted me to have the opportunities that had not been open to them.

An expectation that I would have some special work to do, a vocation that grew out of my talents, was a part of my upbringing. My mother wanted me to be a concert pianist, and she began piano lessons for me when I was five years old. When I was promoted to junior high school, I filled out a questionnaire asking me "what do you want to do when you grow up?" I dutifully responded: "be a concert pianist." Of course, I was not meant to be a concert pianist. I did not have the talent, the interest, or the will for it.

I excelled in high school by receiving high grades and honors and by being a leader in school activities. I was shy in developing personal relationships and I am sure that I compensated for that, as did Harkness, by throwing myself into "accomplishments" at school. The question always seemed to be coming up: "What do you want to do when you grow up?" I did not know.

However, I did know that the church was at the heart of my being since I was a small child. I was strongly grounded in the conservative, evangelical Southern Baptist denomination, a tradition with affinity to that of Harkness's congregation. The idea of a calling from God was natural to me, in my roots. My parents had been active in church life earlier in their marriage, but by the time I was born they both worked outside the home following the Depression and had drifted away from the church.

I do not know how I got started going to church by myself. However, when I was six years old, I walked six blocks every Sunday morning past Edgemere Grade School, my elementary school, to the tiny Hudson Avenue Baptist Church. I heard about God's call on my life in the hymns during the church service and in the lessons of the Girls' Sunday School Class every Sunday morning. I idolized my Sunday School teacher, Mrs. Mary James, who told me one day that I was a good listener. At that stage in my life, it had not occurred to me that it was important to be a good listener. However, she said it was important, and that was good enough for me. Perhaps she set me on my vocational course to become a teacher.

Blessing the Search

Georgia Harkness and I, along with most young people, consciously began our search for a vocation as young adults when we entered college. We were both searching for a career, a kind of work to do. Looking at her vocational journey during her college and graduate school years and recognizing the strong influence of calling upon her search for a career, I saw that same congruence in my own life. We were both blessed by the fact that our parents supported us in our pioneer desires for careers outside the home. At the deepest level, our searches were also blessed by God, and I think we realized that.

To embark on our own vocational searches of calling and career, both Harkness and I had to be released from the hold of parental expectations upon us. Mine came earlier than did hers, when I was in the eighth grade. My piano teacher, Mr. Athel Stone, told my mother "Mary, you should take piano lessons and let Rosie do her own thing." Sadly, my mother did not take piano lessons, but she let me do my own thing by giving up piano lessons and developing my interest in public speaking — another root of my later teaching career.

Harkness's release from her parents' expectations came later, during her Ph.D. program, when she felt she should come home to care for her ailing parents. Her mother told her "No," in no uncertain terms: "You have your own life to lead." Georgia continued on her search. As is true for most of us, she was not on a clear-cut vocational course. It was a circuitous journey.

Her conscious vocational search for a life's work continued from Harkness's late teens until her early thirties. While in college at Cornell, she became interested in philosophy, through Dr. William Creighton, her philosophy professor. If she dreamed of becoming a college professor, she never recorded any aspiration of pursuing a Ph.D. This was a period of blatant sexism and discrimination against women in higher education. Undoubtedly, she had no mentor who suggested the idea, even though she had high grades and was a member of Phi Beta Kappa.

We know that while in college Harkness consciously thought about a career that grew out of a calling from God. She felt accepted in the Student Volunteer Movement and it became her home while she was in college. Georgia, along with thousands of college students of her day, took its pledge: "If God wills, I will become a foreign missionary." Then, after a

87

two-year unsuccessful detour into high school teaching following college, she entered the new program in religious education at Boston University School of Theology to become a Director of Christian Education in a local church. "If I would not be a foreign missionary, this was my calling," she decided.

While on her Master's in Religious Education program, she returned to her love of philosophy and took courses under Dr. Edgar Brightmann in philosophy of religion. Though he tried to dissuade her from pursuing a Ph.D., telling her he did not think she had the "stick-to-it-ness" to do it, she summoned her courage and resolved to do it.

It astonishes me, entering college over forty years after Harkness did, how many similarities there were between our vocational searches to bring our careers together with our callings from God. By college, I had chosen a more liberal congregation of the Presbyterian denomination at the University of Oklahoma. The Presbyterians had a lot to say about vocation and calling, though in a different way than the Southern Baptists did. I was interested in philosophy of religion, as was Harkness, and made that part of my undergraduate major. The philosophical and religious question that underlay my vocational search was one that I think many people share though do not acknowledge: "What's the purpose of it all?" I meant, what is the purpose of life, not just of work? And "How can one little life matter in the midst of the countless persons who inhabit the world?" I was looking for meaning in life and I did not know where to find it, or how to find it, or if I would find it at all.

I knew in college that I wanted both a personal and professional life, though I did not think of my personal life as a vocation. I wanted to be married and to have a family, but I also wanted a professional career. At that point, vocation was focused on career for me. But, I also wondered how to find one that would provide meaning and purpose to me and to others. During college, I began to conceive of teaching in higher education as a vocation that I wanted to pursue. I had virtually no role models or mentors. I knew of only two women on the faculty, and I had both of them for classes.

Like Harkness, I made top grades, was a Phi Beta Kappa, received the Outstanding Senior Woman Award upon graduation, and was active in campus activities. Few people ever suggested a profession to me, though one person told me that he thought I would be a very good teacher of small children. I wanted children of my own, and I thought that elementary school teaching was a worthy occupation. However, I had no interest in it personally. I never told anyone about my vocational dream of teaching in higher education. I shared it only with God.

It stuns me now to realize that the female professors whom I had in college did not take an advocacy role with women students. Maybe they were simply overwhelmed with all that they had to do. When I needed a female role model, they were not to be had. However, the presence of two women on the faculty was a witness to the possibility of my becoming a university professor. It was not until my Ph.D. program in the 1970s that I had role models of two women on the faculty at the University of Illinois in Chicago, Professors Marion Miller and Joan Scott, who encouraged me to pursue women's history.

Like Harkness, I was groping to find a kind of work that was open to me that would bring together calling and career in my life, even though I would not have put it that way at the time. I made almost exactly the same alternative choice, forty years later, that she had made. I decided to take a Master's in Religious Education at Yale Divinity School. My specialty would be in religion and higher education, and I would be the director of a university student center, the closest thing to college teaching I could conceive that was open to a woman.

Transformed by Vocation

Georgia Harkness did not become a director of Christian education in a local church, and I did not become a director of a university Christian student center. During mid-life, we journeyed in ways that we did not plan to go, and our lives were broadened, even transformed, by our vocational journeys. Though my life differed from hers, Harkness's vocational experiences gave me a lens for interpreting my own.

First, she experienced the reality that countless women who work outside the home know today: their lives are juggling acts. Gaining a balance between responsibilities within the home and in the public workplace is difficult for women to achieve, whether they live alone, are a single parent, or are part of a dual-career marriage.

For many of her mid-life years, Harkness lived alone, responsible personally to no other adults or children. The juggling that her life demanded, and the heavy toll that it took upon her, came as a result of the fast track of her career advancement. Harkness became *the* spokesperson for women and to women at church events throughout the country and the world. Invitations to lecture and preach at women's groups, church meetings, and worship services came at a heavier rate than she anticipated. She was a delegate to countless national and international conferences, including both the Oxford and Madras meetings of the World Council of Churches in the 1930s. Requests continually came to her to write articles for a wide variety of church publications, at the same time that she was writing one or two books a year.

Brightmann wrote her a letter, in which he expressed his pleasure that she had been invited to speak in the Duke University Chapel, noting that she "must represent all the women of the church." His words conveyed the distinction and the burden placed upon her one set of shoulders. Another time, she made a five-minute speech at the Oxford Meeting of the World Council of Churches on the role of women in the churches in which she described the churches as "the most impregnable stronghold of male dominance." The speech was transmitted back to the United States and she received so many invitations to speak at women's gatherings that she said, "I ran myself ragged."

During these mid-life years, Harkness's experience of vocation not only expanded but was transformed. She became an evangelical liberal, balancing a strong personal commitment to Christ with a socially prophetic witness to the church. After observing first-hand the destruction of Europe and of innocent lives after World War I, "I became a pacifist forever," Harkness pronounced. She spent over twenty years mounting a finally successful campaign for the ordination of women, while simultaneously championing more equitable treatment for lay women. Harkness would not support the merger of the Methodist with the Evangelical United Brethren Church until agreement was reached that the all-black conference of the denomination of the Methodist Church would be abolished and black and white ministers would be ordained in the same geographical conferences. She cried openly at the General Conference of 1974 when the delegates voted that "homosexuality is incompatible with Christian teaching."

Harkness's pioneer contributions challenged the church to truly be the church. However, her vocation became entirely equated with work, and she knew no limits to work in these mid-life years. Other physical, emotional, and spiritual problems entered in, also, including the death of her beloved father. The result of this intense accumulation of strain was a deep

90

depression that began when she came to Garrett Biblical Institute in 1940 and continued for several years. In coming out of this extended depression, she wrote one of her finest books, *The Dark Night of the Soul.* Sharing her experience helped countless people acknowledge and deal with the same realities in their lives.

Vocation transformed Georgia Harkness's life as she came to grips with the reality that work was the sum and substance of her vocation. She was consumed by the good work and the good works that she accomplished. Harkness had to take concrete steps to change her way of life. For one thing, she bought a simple cottage on Lake Champlain, which she named "Hate to Quit It." The cottage, with its name printed over the door, still stands today. A steady stream of family and friends visited her there during summers and she did much of her writing in this quiet and peaceful setting.

Even more importantly, Ernest Fremont Tittle, her close confidante and the pastor of the First Methodist Church in Evanston, Illinois, also bears responsibility for enabling Harkness to find a full and healthy new life and for opening a new meaning and experience of vocation to her. He suggested that she get acquainted with Verna Miller, a woman close in age to Harkness, who had recently moved to Evanston and come to the church. "It is possible that living with her would be very helpful to you," he counseled. Georgia and Verna met, were immediately attracted to each other, and spent the last thirty years of their lives sharing a home together. Harkness now had a committed personal relationship, a person close to her with whom she could share her life.

My understanding and experience of vocation changed radically during my mid-life years, too. It began for me with a personal relationship, my marriage to Bob Keller immediately after our graduations from Yale Divinity School in 1958. He became ordained in the Methodist Church and we moved to Chicago, where we lived for over thirty years. Our two children, Jennifer and John, were born there and are now young adults with vocations of their own. At the time, I had no conception of marriage and family life being a part of my vocation. I would have described my family as at the center of my life, but as a part of my avocation, outside of my vocation of work. In retrospect, however, I realize that if one understands vocation as the way in which one lives the whole of life as a response to God, then raising a family is a vocation.

Like Harkness, I began to expand my understanding of the church's ministry to be both a call to transform individuals' lives and to transform the life of society. I had not embraced ministries of social justice as a part of my commitment to Christian responsibility until we moved into the inner city of Chicago, where my husband received an appointment to a church in a neighborhood going through rapid racial change from white to African-American in the 1960s. We spent the 1960s in this church and neighborhood that were made up primarily of African-Americans, and the following two and a half decades in areas that were mixed among Anglo-Americans, African-Americans, Hispanic-Americans, Korean-Americans, and Japanese-Americans. Almost all of my husband's pastoral appointments were in Chicago, and almost all had interracial and ethnically diverse congregations. Living in multicultural neighborhoods and advocating for inclusiveness became a natural way of life for me. It led me to Garrett-Evangelical United Methodist Seminary and Union Theological Seminary in New York City, schools that place a high priority on the advocacy of diversity as essential to the vocational commitment of the church.

Though I would not have called my personal and church commitments part of my vocation at this time, I now realize that I was developing an understanding of vocation that was much larger than work. However, I did not give up my dream of teaching in higher education. Whether I acknowledged it or not, I know that all this time I wanted both to be married and have a family and also to "do my own thing," as my piano teacher had put it long ago. With my husband's support, and as our children came to school age themselves, I gained the courage to return to graduate school and to gain a Ph.D. at the University of Illinois-Chicago in American and women's history. I was naturally drawn to the study of women in American history, a field that was beginning to be discovered at the time when I was working on a Ph.D. in the 1970s, and I took the first minor field in this subject in the History Department there. Though I didn't realize it at the time, I was also drawn to biography, which together with the history of American women and religion, has become my academic vocational concentration. Writing my dissertation on Abigail Adams and working with Professor Robert V. Remini, the distinguished biographer of Andrew Jackson, as my advisor, formed that area of specialization for me.

My mid-life expression of vocation was one of much juggling, between my academic administrative appointments as a professor of American Church History and an academic dean at Garrett-Evangelical and Union, on one side, and my family commitments on the other. I believe that I have come of age as a woman in a period that has seen the greatest social changes in all of history. For women, of course, much of that change has come in the form of opportunities to enter the professions. However, the deeper I experience my commitment to my vocation, the more I realize how elusive the progress has been and how far we still have to go.

Conceiving New Life

Georgia Harkness was a delegate to six general conferences of the Methodist and United Methodist Church; the last one she attended was in 1972 when she was 81 years old. Meeting on April 21, 1972, the delegates celebrated her birthday by asking her to stand in the plenary session so that they could recognize her as having "long been a champion for the liberation of all men and women." She responded to the Conference, "This is the greatest." Then she used garden imagery, appropriate to the caring of flowers and shrubbery that occupied her in retirement, to describe her state of life in maturity: "It might be said I'm a hardy perennial."

The statement that Harkness made in front of her last United Methodist General Conference in 1972 was one of the shortest speeches she ever made before that assembly, but she said a lot in a few words. More than describing herself as "a hardy perennial," she expressed her joy that the Conference that morning had voted to establish the General Commission on the Status and Role of Women (COSROW), to be an advocate, monitor, and catalyst for full participation and equality of women in the church. Harkness's last words to the General Conference were these: "With the action taken this morning in regard to the place of women in the church, I can say that I believe *the Kingdom is nearer than we believed*" (italics mine).

Though a strong advocate for inclusiveness of women in church and society, Harkness never went so far as to use and advocate inclusive language. However, the Reign of God was nearer for her personally than she might have believed. She died two and a half years later, unexpectedly, on August 21, 1974. Her description of herself as "a hardy perennial" sums up her later years vocationally, just as it did the entirety of her life. She continued to sprout up anew and to conceive new life vocationally. She did not wither away; her roots were identifiable from year to year, and she lived fruitfully during her years of older adulthood.

In the last twenty years of her life, from her early sixties until her death at 83, Harkness increasingly experienced vocation as embracing both her work and her personal life. She came to Pacific School of Religion when she was 60, taking a half-time position in Practical Theology. The arrangement enabled the seminary to bring Charles McCoy onto the faculty and allowed her to have the continued vitality of teaching and writing, while at the same time mercifully scaling back her work. Even so, she maintained her active involvement in social concerns, illustrated by her celebration of the inauguration of COSROW and her determination to attend the nightly late sessions to draft legislation for peace in Vietnam at the 1974 General Conference.

During her last spring in 1974, Harkness preached at Garrett Theological Seminary and at the Northern Indiana Conference of the United Methodist Church. Even in early August, she made two trips to Alaska to speak. Her book, *Understanding the Kingdom of God,* was published in 1974, and the manuscript of her last one, *Biblical Backgrounds of the Middle East Conflict,* close to completion when she died, was finished later by Charles Kraft.

Discerning vocation as the way we live the whole of our lives as a response to God, we see the depth of vocation in Georgia's personal life, in her relationship with Verna Miller, as a balance to her commitment to good work. Friends in their later life point to the complementarity of the two. Georgia was known for her seriousness, and Verna for her sense of humor. Verna effectively brought levity to Georgia's personality, and Georgia enjoyed Verna's "craziness."

A letter written to "Dear Friends Far and Near" at Thanksgiving, 1972, gives an idea of their fruitfulness and contentment in older adulthood. "The story of our year will not require many words. We have taken three trips of some duration away from Claremont, and the rest of the time our lives have moved along quite uneventfully with the usual activities to keep us happily busy," they wrote. "We both remain in excellent health, troubled only by a few cricks in the bones such as one expects on growing older. For this, and for much else, we give God grateful thanks."

As I grow older, Georgia Harkness's vocational image of the "hardy perennial" is increasingly appealing to me. I want to continue to sprout up anew and to blossom afresh vocationally. I have been fortunate in opening doors and having keys turned for me to enable me to experience vocation in new and creative ways. I continue to experience God's call in my life and to find, both personally and professionally, that when I believe I am "set-

94

tled down," vocationally new and unexpected paths appear. I hope that will continue to be a part of my story as it was for Harkness.

*   *   *

There is one more story to tell. I opened this essay sharing my experience of the beginning of my kinship with Georgia Harkness when I started writing her biography. I end this writing with a very personal story. In the very moments that I was writing the final pages of that book and drawing Harkness's life to a close, my own mother, Mary Morley Skinner, died on March 5, 1992. The phone call from Vera Watts, the pastoral counselor in the intensive care unit at the hospital and a dear friend of mine, came just as I completed this sentence on the second to last page of the book: "The kingdom was nearer for Georgia, personally, than she believed, for in the midst of her regular round of devotional and active living, she died unexpectedly on August 21, 1974." As soon as I heard the phone ring, I knew that my friend was bringing me this news.

My mother was ninety-three years old. She had been in the hospital in a coma for a week. Every day I had gone to her bedside, sung hymns and prayed with her, and told her that I was nearing completion of the biography. The night before she died, I spoke to her in her coma and told her I would be back to see her the following afternoon as soon as the final few pages were completed. I told her that I realized how tired she was and that it was all right for her to go on if she needed to do so. I am confident that she heard me.

She was happy about my venture and was trying to help me through to its completion. She stayed until she knew that I was through. She helped me.

Who can explain the mystery of kinship? It is a part of all of our lives in faith. Both my own mother and Georgia Harkness contributed much to my vocational journey. I thank them for that.

THEOLOGICAL TEACHERS
IN THEIR CLASSROOMS

Teaching as Conversation

SUSAN M. SIMONAITIS

"In this [teaching] fantasy, I am absolutely fabulous. With my students, I break open the word of God, showing them its awesome complexity, inviting them to fall in love with the texts as I have, teaching them what it means to read as if your life depended on it, and being taught by them to read again as if it were the first time."

Marsaura Shukla, in the graduate
program at Fordham University

"At this point, I sometimes find myself wondering where my thirst for learning has gone. As my freshman year draws to a close, I often feel that my ears are jaded and my brain lethargic. What can be done about this? What awakening does my intellectual soul need?"

Katrina Domingo, in her freshman
year at Fordham University

"Is it not important for the teacher to give his or her soul to the students in order to mold a moral, compassionate, intellectual, and infinitely original future? It is not enough for teachers to be brilliant scholars. Nor is it enough for teachers to be entertaining circus side shows. Teachers must be brilliant, passionate, intense, insistent, compelling, and relentless."

Mark Savicki, in his freshman
year at Fordham University

I SPENT THE LAST THREE YEARS talking with students, asking them to think about their learning experiences, their teaching fantasies. A number of students, at my invitation, wrote short reflections on their understanding of what can and should happen in the classroom. Both in conversation and in writing, students proved to be insightful about the current problems of our teaching/learning paradigms. Moreover, students shared fantasies of teaching/learning experiences that conveyed energy, excitement, curiosity, and risk. To my surprise, many students seek a type of religious experience in the classroom. They believe, as Katrina Domingo tells us, that their souls are at stake, and they hope, as Mark Savicki describes, that professors will give their own souls to students in a process that produces "a moral, compassionate, intellectual, and infinitely original future."

Because these students correlate effective teaching with inspiration, passion, and transformation, I have begun to examine closely the role of teaching in my work. How does what I do in the classroom relate to what I do and think as a theologian? At a faculty colloquium in which my department discussed teaching styles, we considered the general question: "What is going on when you feel successful as a teacher with your students?" The answers were various: "I think I feel successful when I open new horizons." "At my best, I model for my students what it is to learn." "I think my class — when it works — works because I impress my students." "If I can show the students that intellectual reflection on religion is worth it, then I'm doing my job."

Not content with my own answer (my classroom works when the students are unself-consciously engaged in the process of learning), I asked my students what they thought I did. Natalia Imperatori, a senior at that time, offered a succinct response. "Your teaching can be summed up in four words: problematic, commitment, conversation, and text." In

Natalia's view, but expressed here in my words, my teaching practices emerge from a conviction that religious worlds and theological systems are constructions. They are human responses to rich, complex experiences of the sacred and/or God. At the same time that these religious worlds and theological systems are powerful and persuasive, they are also "problematic."

The problematic elements in and of religious systems and practices, though perhaps experienced as threatening by believing adherents, are tightly woven into the fabric of these comprehensive worldviews. If we look closely at problematic elements, we often see that they are the unacknowledged or excluded or "other" of what is strong and beautiful — of what is, for believers, unsurpassable and of God. My teaching style emphasizes that we can (and should) interrogate the complex interpretations of the sacred offered to us by believers. Moreover, whether or not we consciously affiliate ourselves with a particular religious tradition, we can (and already do) make choices that aggregate into life commitments. These commitments express — perhaps even invoke — "the God we practice."[1]

Sometimes we articulate and intellectually defend our commitments. More often, I believe, our commitments are revealed in unreflective choices (habits of living, ways of relating, etc.). Genuine conversation, "a game" we are told by scholars, with hard rules,[2] is one approach that helps me glimpse the commitments that shape my life, that I practice in and as my life. Students soon recognize that my teaching style requires participation in the difficult discipline of genuine conversation. We work to develop

---

1. "The God we practice" is a paraphrase of Mary McClintock Fulkerson's suggestion that "The crucial inquiry of a liberation theological epistemology, as Sharon Welch says, is not, Does God exist?, but What kind of God is to be practiced?" See Chapter 1 of *Changing the Subject: Women's Discourses and Feminist Theologies,* by Mary McClintock Fulkerson (Minneapolis: Fortress Press, 1994), and *Communities of Resistance and Solidarity: A Feminist Theology of Liberation,* by Sharon Welch (Maryknoll, N.Y.: Orbis Books, 1985).

2. See David Tracy's discussion of conversation in Chapter 1 of *Plurality and Ambiguity: Hermeneutics, Religion, and Hope* (New York: Harper & Row, 1987). Tracy views his discussion of the game of conversation "to be in basic harmony with the position on the implicit validity claims in all communication defended by Karl-Otto Apel and Jürgen Habermas." The "hard rules" of genuine conversation require us "to say only what you mean; say it as accurately as you can; listen to and respect what the other says, however different or other; be willing to correct or defend your opinions if challenged by the conversation partner; be willing to argue if necessary, to confront if demanded, to endure necessary conflict, to change your mind if the evidence suggests it" (*Plurality and Ambiguity,* p. 19).

habits of thought and practice that allow us to enter worlds of discourse, both our own and those of others. When we enter worlds of discourse, we do so with respect. These places are beautiful, complex, comprehensive, and subtle. Certainly they are beyond the mastery of any and all descriptions, no matter how broad and deep those descriptions are. We can never "sum up" a world of discourse. However, in the classroom, profound respect for religious worldviews also finds expression in the "reflective skepticism" that is critical thinking.[3] Introduced to a world of discourse, we ask questions, we challenge assumptions, and we grapple with the plurality that exists both within particular religious traditions and between different religious worlds.

If we take our task seriously, I tell my students, we get caught up in something beyond the intellectual exploration of religious worlds and theological constructions. If we work hard, accepting both the responsibilities and the risks of genuine conversation, we might, in the end, discover (. . . or unearth . . . or construct . . .) commitments that shape us even as they point toward an inadequate but awesome portrait of God.

*   *   *

Mark Savicki asks me what I "give" when I teach. Do I offer my soul? I flip through student reflections on teaching and learning, and pause on freshman Tim Hart's comments. "The most primal and basic reality which I as a student face when walking into a classroom," he writes, "is the fact that I do not have home turf advantage." In Tim's view, the power of a teacher can distort into "a detrimental dictatorship" (in which case, Tim advises students to learn "to artificially adapt," to "grow an outer skin" to survive). Even if a teacher does not abuse power, there exists a dilemma for students nonetheless. Students must learn to flourish ("prosper" is the word Tim uses) without "sacrificing one's true self." Students must learn to adapt, but not artificially.

Tim's concern about adaptation raises questions about the power granted to teachers. As teachers, we possess power. What do we do with

---

3. See Stephen D. Brookfield's depiction of reflective skepticism as the culmination of (1) identifying and challenging assumptions, (2) developing contextual awareness, and (3) imagining and exploring alternatives in "What It Means to Think Critically," chapter 1 of *Developing Critical Thinkers* (San Francisco: Jossey-Bass Publishers, 1987).

it? Can I give my power to students, and is this an adequate response to Mark Savicki, who says he wants my soul? While thinking about these questions, I select yet another set from my stack of student reflections. The focus in this reflection is on teaching, not learning. It is written by a doctoral student.

Julia Brumbaugh says she wants "to be a teacher in, with, and for the [Roman Catholic] church." She writes:

> I believe that the vision, the way of life, the meaning of life proposed by Christianity is the good life (not that this excludes the possibility of other paths offering "the good life"). I also think that in our culture, we often don't employ tools for discriminating between competing claims to truth and goodness.

In her view, good teaching is "very pastoral." She writes:

> I want to suggest to young people, in the very time that they are deeply engaged in assessing the meaning and purpose of their lives, that it would behoove them to consider the place of God in their lives. . . . In addition, I'm interested in giving them (or encouraging the use of) the tools of critical thinking which enable persons to handle and discern among competing claims for truth, value, and meaning.

To many, this doctoral student's understanding of teaching is familiar and inviting. Located within a church community, Julia wants the power of teaching to be used in the service of guiding students to "the good life" proposed by Christianity.

Yet, can this familiar, pastoral fantasy allow for the unexpected, for what theologian David Tracy identifies as the "different *as* possible"? Within a pedagogical paradigm of conversation, important questions emerge. What is going on in the classroom if the power in and of teaching is deployed for the purpose of guiding students toward the good life proposed by a particular form of religiousness? Does authentic conversation take place if one participant has the power (and uses her power) to determine not only the subject matter, but also the outcome of a particular conversation?

Even if I believe the goal is good (even if the outcome is authentic Christian living), I find I cannot use my power in the classroom to predetermine the outcome of our conversations.[4] Even in conversations that I have introduced to students, that I work to facilitate in my classroom, I anticipate unknown, unexpected outcomes. To anticipate anything else is to repress what is genuine (not to mention exciting) about conversation as a teaching style. Even further, if I claim control over the outcome of a genuine conversation, I contradict my commitments, my life as it invokes "the God I practice." This contradiction is a problem *for me;* it is not necessarily a problem for my students, who often wish I would tell them what I want them to say, to think, to believe. No, the problem of dominance is my problem, and to the extent that I misuse the power of teaching, I fail, as a theologian, to teach well.

My commitment to the open-ended quality of genuine conversation in the classroom emerges from a theological understanding of what it means to "converse with" texts of religious traditions. In *The Analogical Imagination,* David Tracy argues that we can engage the classic texts of a religious tradition only if we let go, get caught up in, become a participant in rather than a spectator of the reality offered to us in each text.[5] Tracy modifies some elements of *The Analogical Imagination* in a later work titled *Plurality and Ambiguity.* He does so, in part, to emphasize that if the game of conversation is "an exploration of possibilities in the search for the truth," it must include the uncertain outcomes that are introduced by difference and otherness. "To attend to the other as other, the different as different," he writes, "is also to understand the different *as* possible."[6]

It seems that conversation as a paradigm of teaching must foster attention to possibilities, particularly those that are unexpected. In a practi-

---

4. Sometimes teachers talk about the "Socratic method" in order to describe the use of questions to guide students toward an identified (and predetermined) outcome. The question of whether or not such a style of teaching and learning is authentically Socratic invites us to engage again Plato's influential accounts of Socrates at work. But if a teacher employs the "Socratic method" to guide students to a predetermined outcome, he or she is not, I would argue, carefully and critically using conversation as a style of teaching and learning. To use conversation effectively in the classroom is to risk — as *teachers* and students — the vulnerability, the trust, and the not-known-in-advance outcomes of genuine conversation.

5. See chapters 3-5 of *The Analogical Imagination: Christian Theology and the Culture of Pluralism* (New York: Crossroad, 1986).

6. Tracy, *Plurality and Ambiguity,* p. 20. It is important to note that Tracy's understanding of "truth as manifestation" (his emphasis on "disclosure/concealment-recognition") remains constant in both Tracy's earlier and later writings. "Without manifestation," Tracy writes, "thought is too thin. Truth, in its primordial sense, is manifestation" (p. 29).

cal sense, this paradigm asks us to be hospitable to difference — to the other as other, to the different as possible. It asks teachers to deploy power in a "game" in which *all* of us lose our "usual self-consciousness in the movement of the play itself."[7] In the teaching/learning context, when teachers join the movement of play, when we enter the game, the unexpected is more likely to take place. It is difficult for teachers to do this because the game of conversation demands that I, too, risk what comforts me, what is familiar to me, what has to this moment shaped the boundaries — indeed the horizon — of my life. When we join our students in genuine conversation, we risk ourselves. We say, "this is not confrontation; this is not debate; this is not an exam." Rather, "this is questioning itself; it is willingness to follow the question wherever it may go."[8]

When we follow the question wherever it may go, "we find that we are never pure creators of meaning."[9] Yes, as teachers we select texts and put together course outlines on the basis of what we know. Yes, we have influence over and, in large part, construct our classroom conversations. But when conversation takes place, gathers momentum, is in motion, we — as teachers — have a choice to make. We can enter the risk of a conversation, or we can stop the motion, control the outcome. Though a student who does not allow a text to claim her attention does relatively little harm to the overall conversation of the class, a teacher's refusal does great harm. The questions in and of classic texts are domesticated into data. As teachers, we can manipulate that data and devise tests that determine whether it has been memorized (or forgotten) by students. If this happens, teaching becomes an experience of control for the teacher and domination for students.

Perhaps more toxic is the ability teachers have to require students to reflect back to us our own worldviews, our own commitments, our own treasured practices. Students can be trained to mirror us back to ourselves. Certainly this is a repression of otherness. Certainly this is a form of narcissism. But this practice of control in the classroom is also a rejection of the movement of time and the effects of history. As teachers, we de facto participate in the many movements that press the present into an unknown future. In our classrooms, we have the power to pretend (and to ask our students to reassure us) that we exist apart from time, outside of his-

---

7. Tracy, *Plurality and Ambiguity*, p. 17.
8. Tracy, *Plurality and Ambiguity*, p. 18.
9. Tracy, *Plurality and Ambiguity*, p. 19.

tory. The heady experiment of suppressing our own risk in history is difficult to resist. But we must resist what is, in the end, cowardice. Instead of
hiding from history by pretending that we do not belong to history, we
must deploy our power in the classroom by joining our students in history.
We must work with them in a search that does not romanticize, that does
not exoticize, but that does not deny the different as possible or the future
as original. In any given semester of class meetings, we may prepare for the
possible and the original without experiencing it. But once in a while, our
work allows us to glimpse something "other" that may come to be, that
may flourish and grow, beyond the scope of our control.

Kevin O'Neill, who took several of my courses at Fordham University,
presses the issue of control even further. Kevin, like Tim Hart, knows that
teacher-student relationships will "forever be riddled with power issues."
But after Kevin read a draft of this article, he wanted to discuss how conversation as a style of teaching can become problematic if the emphasis is primarily that of submission (even if that submission is the risk of an unknown future, the different as possible, etc.). "As a student of yours," he
writes, "I think you down-play too much the theme of resistance in your
teaching philosophy." Kevin endorses my focus on teaching as conversation,
but he notes that "risk, commitment, and effort" do not encompass fully
enough the struggle embedded in all authentic conversations. Kevin writes:

> what I gained from your teaching is the ability both to submit and to re-
> sist particular paradigms. *That* action (resisting and submitting) pro-
> duces an authenticity that is rarely found in traditional teaching meth-
> ods. . . . Your students definitely learn how to read and to enter
> conversations, but they also learn how to discern between "what I
> should accept and what I should deny to make *my* beliefs, actions, and
> thoughts authentic to me.". . . I think you instruct your students on how
> to find that freedom, that authenticity.

In Kevin's comments, resistance is as important as submission. He refuses
to romanticize the conflicts that pervade genuine conversation. He says
(and I agree with him) that in genuine conversations, resistance is productive, as long as we risk ourselves at the same time.[10]

10. Kevin's comments prompt me to admit that I am not fully conscious of the strategies I use to "instruct" students on how to "resist" in the process of producing a sense of

Let us take an example. We often hear that our students do not consider institutional churches to be vibrant or even relevant. At the same time, we also hear that many students embrace an individualized, personal spirituality. Does my pedagogical paradigm of conversation require teachers to reject institutional religiousness in order to join students in conversation? No. But I do think we must risk ourselves in a conversation that interrogates what we know about — and how we live — institutional religiousness. Likewise, I think students must risk themselves. Kevin makes explicit that each of us must also construct for ourselves an authentic (and not romantic or reactionary or wishful) practice of commitment.

It is not uncommon to hear students say that institutional religiousness is hypocritical and corrupt. In Paul Wadell's essay in this volume he explores in more detail the perspective of "Generation X," a generation of students who are profoundly suspicious of traditional communities and cynical about the authorities that transmit institutional religiousness from one generation to another. In Wadell's account, student suspicion and cynicism prompt theologians (who have been shaped intellectually and personally by confessional affiliation) to recognize that they themselves are the decidedly "other" to Generation X. Moreover, Wadell sees loneliness and sadness beneath student cynicism, and he suggests that students might benefit from the companionship of authentic religious community, of "church" in the best sense. The classroom can be an authentic community, a place where the seeds of church can be planted, fostered, and allowed to flourish.

---

their own authenticity. In almost every syllabus, I write a variation of the following (enthusiastic) remarks:

> The professor is trained as a theologian who uses, and who takes seriously, a variety of methods and approaches to the study of religion (including philosophy, psychology, sociology, anthropology, cultural theory, critical theory, etc.). She will not agree with all the texts/approaches that we explore, nor will she expect students to agree with everything submitted for examination. However, she will insist that students "submit" themselves to the discipline of learning through perspectives that may or may not be ultimately embraced, and she will encourage students, in the process of this submission, to persistently and courageously discover and develop their own perspectives, their own voices, their own (informed) views, their own projects.

Maybe this statement, which is also repeated in class, is enough to invite students to struggle toward authenticity. I don't know. Kevin's comments on teaching and learning prompt me to think more deeply about the role of resistance in my pedagogical paradigm of teaching as conversation.

107

When I listen to the reasons students have for leaving (or, really, never joining) institutional religiousness, I wonder what form of community students seek to find. My fascination with the unknown future emerges as I hear students casually point out that they no longer look to "the church" for answers. I wonder what forms of religious community may develop (if Fordham senior Natalia Imperatori is right), as the people who "turn away from the locations of traditional religion, . . . seek 'religious' experiences in other places, one of which is the classroom."

Given the loneliness of a present that appears to have lost the rich and valued communities of the past, it is understandable that some graduate students and many theologians want the classroom to be an experience of confessional formation. Julia Brumbaugh speaks for many in her desire "to be a teacher in, with, and for the [Roman Catholic] church." But this practice, which is perhaps instinctive in those who experience a vibrant sense of church themselves, stands over and against the questions asked by our students. To join our students, to ask *their* questions, is to notice that students experience something unique in our current situation. They are not "at an earlier stage" of formation that we can identify as essential — but transient — in *our* religious lives and affiliations. What happens if we take David Tracy's advice and willingly "follow the question wherever it may go"? Our students seem to think that *right now*, in *this* moment of history (forty years after the Second Vatican Council of the Roman Catholic Church, thirty-some years after the flush of civil rights activism, in the midst of both religious indifference and religious fundamentalism) new and different ways of encountering God and engaging community are emerging.

When I listen to my students, one of the things I hear is that they experience each other (. . . and their professors . . . and God) to be irreducibly "other." The culture of individualism that can produce a positive and powerful sense of individual identity also has the power to strip us of an assumption that we are easily and authentically connected to others, either in intimate relationships or in larger communities.[11] David Tracy, in *On Naming the Present*, describes himself "as a white, male, middle-class,

11. It is outside the scope of this argument to discuss the flip side of student isolation, loneliness, and self-reliance. Lack of personal boundaries and intense, pathological attachments also emerge in relationships shaped by individualistic constructions of the self. In many ways, my suggestion that we need to explore ways of relating to the other *as* other emerges also as a response to the inability to allow others to be others.

American, Catholic professor and priest" who lives and works within a "troubled, quarreling center of privilege and power."[12] From his perspective, "our deepest need, as philosophy and theology in our period show, is . . . to face otherness and difference."[13] He observes that

> a fact seldom admitted by the moderns, the antimoderns, and the postmoderns alike . . . is that there is no longer *a* center with margins. There are many centers. . . . The others must become genuine others for us — not projection of our fears and desires. The others are not marginal to our centers but centers of their own.[14]

I think that many of our students already experience others *as* others, and that they are working through (or rather, living towards) forms of community not yet imagined by scholars and theologians. And their starting point may be different from those in the quarreling center of privilege and power. In *On Naming the Present*, Tracy reveals an interest in the formerly repressed and/or presently threatening other.[15] In contrast, it seems to me that our students are not particularly interested in *that* other. They embody a different concern with otherness, and they ask us to enter (or at least to explore as possible, in the context of our classrooms) new ways of relating and new constructions of community.

Who is the other that so preoccupies our students? My students have described feelings of loneliness and isolation. They expect themselves to be stoic, self-reliant, self-contained. For many of them, daily life is characterized by encounters with others who are not "repressed others" or "threatening others." These others are simply inscrutable, unreachable. These others are neighbors who cannot be approached, classmates who want what I want and thus threaten my access to what appears to be a scarcity of

---

12. David Tracy, *On Naming the Present: God, Hermeneutics, Church* (Maryknoll, N.Y.: Orbis Books, 1994), p. 4.

13. Tracy, *On Naming the Present*, p. 4.

14. Tracy, *On Naming the Present*, p. 4.

15. Tracy writes: "Those others must include all the subjugated others within Western European and North American culture, the others outside that culture, especially the poor and the oppressed now speaking clearly and forcefully, the terrifying otherness lurking in our own psyches and cultures, the other great religions and civilizations, the differences disseminating in all the words and structures of our own Indo-European languages" (*On Naming the Present*, p. 4).

goods and relationships that might, if I acquired them, constitute a stronger, more confident, more self-reliant self. These others are potential or actual lovers who seem distant, unreachable even in intimate moments of disclosure or romance. Faced with such others, students become skilled at identifying and analyzing the lack in relationships, the distance between themselves and others who are very near, who are not repressed, who are not threatening but also not accessible. As teachers, we might hear their concerns and yet find a way to answer that the past offers answers for both individual and communal relationships. If we do this, we ignore what Tracy calls "the unsettling reality of our polycentric present." We fail ourselves and our students, for we deny the plurality and ambiguity of living in *this* present, in *this* situation where many centers press toward multiple futures. The polycentric present lived by our students prompts us to think differently, to live practices that might transform our intimate and communal lives.

This polycentric present — lived by our students — challenges the modern assumption that relationships and communities are strongest if they emerge from (or are headed toward) common experience. Sharon Welch suggests that the desire for communities based on common experience is unrealistic and potentially oppressive. It is, she writes, "hope for a utopian world in which there is complete uniformity."[16] Such a desire for complete uniformity undermines the possibility of genuine community. Why? Because it "leads to impatience and intolerance with conflict of any sort." When success in community is characterized by the absence of tension, implicit and explicit forms of oppression often can be detected.[17] As an alternative to such oppression, Welch asks us to adopt different practices of community. She asks us to boldly experiment with communities that emerge in and through difference. Such communities are not abstract. They are not ideas. They are real people risking their lives in actual experiments.

Tim Hart, who in his freshman year observed the dynamics of power in the classroom, would agree with Welch that an experiment of practice (and not merely of philosophy) is necessary. His fantasy of excellent learning emphasizes practices (from "the teacher listens" to the physical arrangement of student desks). Tim writes:

16. Sharon Welch, *Feminist Ethic of Risk* (Minneapolis: Augsburg Fortress, 1990), p. 34.

17. Welch, *Feminist Ethic of Risk*, p. 35.

110

Okay, my fantasy: a classroom environment where the teacher listens, we sit in a semicircle, and the teacher leads the discussions but we, as students, are active participants. . . . The physical setup of the classroom I feel is also a key factor for a class to succeed. Keeping desks in straight rows is too formal, and a circle, or a table, is too informal as well as too uncomfortable. . . . When a class sits in a semicircle, it creates an openness which will further conversation and comfort.

Tim is talking about desks. But I would argue that he is also talking about the construction of authority and the possibility of community in the classroom. Tim doesn't want to be a subordinate in "the teacher's kingdom," but he also doesn't want the classroom to be an uncomfortable, artificial, closed community. He notes that sitting in a closed circle forces students "to find a comfortable place" for their eyes to rest. This comfortable place is, in Tim's experience, always outside the circle.[18] Forcing intimacy on our students (at least in Tim's view, at least in the relationships dramatized by the arrangement of desks) is not going to work. A different practice — or set of practices — must be tried.

Current educational theorists readily discuss the role of power and the formation of community in the classroom. Nicholas Burbules, Stephen Brookfield, and many others suggest that the teaching task is not to deny power, but rather to deploy power fairly, critically, and with consciousness of the fact that "no action you take will produce universally felicitous consequences."[19] In Burbules's view, the need to make choices as a teacher reflects the fact that those in power always make choices that "normalize" or standardize what counts for knowledge. Though current views of education (and, I would add, approaches to the study of religion) stress diversity and tolerance, Burbules writes,

18. Tim's argument against the circle format is really interesting. He believes that a circle breaks down communication "because when you sit in a circle, you are forced to find a comfortable place for your eyes, which usually ends up being a nice paint chip on the wall or a stain on a rug, thus distracting from the flow of learning." Having students sit in a semicircle "creates an openness that will further conversation and comfort." The semicircle appears to be Tim's way of concretizing "a happy medium where maturity is expected and respected, where all views are taken seriously," where students and teachers alike have room to "maneuver."

19. Stephen D. Brookfield, *The Skillful Teacher: On Technique, Trust, and Responsiveness in the Classroom* (San Francisco: Jossey-Bass Publishers, 1990), p. 199.

111

any educational practice, however fluid and multifaceted, has the inevitable effect of making people more alike, at least in some respects. One can label this phenomenon favorably as the "melting pot," or one can label it critically as Foucauldian "normalization." Either way, diversity is lessened to the extent that a common syllabus, a common set of evaluation criteria, a common classroom culture, have an effect.[20]

Such a perspective, which Burbules identifies as "tragic," can be used to foster a strong sense of hope in education, if that hope is tempered by "an awareness of the contradictory character of what we might count as 'success,' an understanding that gains can always be seen also as losses, and an appreciation that certain educational goals and purposes can be obtained only at the cost of others."[21]

From a different point of view, Stephen Brookfield asks us to recognize the cost of remaining unconscious of the play of power in the classroom. If we repress a critical recognition of our power as teachers, then we remain unconscious of but nonetheless participate in values, norms, and practices defined for us by others. Brookfield writes:

> forces present in the wider society always intrude into the classroom. Classrooms are not limpid, tranquil ponds, cut off from the river of social, cultural, and political life. They are contested spaces — whirlpools containing the contradictory crosscurrents of struggles for material superiority and ideological legitimacy that exist in the world outside.[22]

For Brookfield, there are no neutral teaching practices. Even Brookfield's selected goal — to work democratically and cooperatively with students and faculty — is reached through practices that themselves work ambiguously.[23] Because classrooms "mirror the structures and inequities of the wider society," Brookfield argues, the practice of teaching is an "intensely

20. "The Tragic Sense of Education," by Nicholas C. Burbules, in *Teaching and Its Predicaments*, ed. Nicholas C. Burbules and David T. Hansen (Boulder, Colo.: Westview Press, 1997), p. 69.

21. Burbules, "The Tragic Sense of Education," p. 65.

22. Stephen D. Brookfield, *Becoming a Critically Reflective Teacher* (San Francisco: Jossey-Bass Publishers, 1995), p. 9.

23. See chapter 1 in *Becoming a Critically Reflective Teacher* for an analysis of power in different, "progressive" classroom practices.

political occupation."[24] Because teaching engages life, it journeys into uncertainty.

Sharon Welch also discusses the dangerous and potentially liberating play of power in the classroom. Her observation that classrooms are *not* "safe spaces" initially seems to stand against her overall desire to work toward democracy, accountability, and change. In the end, however, safety is *not* authentic community. For Welch, the trusting relationships in and of genuine democracies grow and flourish only if we are willing to risk conflict, disappointment, and change. Welch writes:

> it is crucial to know that . . . this class is not a safe space. We are discussing volatile issues and there will be areas of profound disagreement. We enter this discussion as individuals and as groups with radically different histories and experiences. There are power differentials between us. . . . In trying to learn from each other, to learn how to work together, it is essential that we acknowledge that this is painful, difficult, and possibly exhilarating work. We do not know if we can trust each other. . . . [W]e are *likely* to offend, disappoint, and surprise each other, and we will probably be hurt and challenged. We are not, therefore, in a safe space. However, we are in a space for learning, a space in which we may learn how to work with conflict and how to learn from each other.[25]

In Welch's view, it is "dangerous to assume that we can balance all needs, that we can insure there will be no harm, or at least no undue harm."[26] It is dangerous because the desire to be all things to all people slips easily into a fear of conflict, an avoidance of honest criticism, and a pretense that caring is never manipulative. For Welch, we need "an ethic of conflict" as much as, perhaps more than, we need the "ethic of care."

What might an ethic of conflict look like in a classroom dedicated to genuine conversation? From one perspective, it looks similar to the "hard rules" of conversation identified by David Tracy and others. We dedicate ourselves

---

24. Brookfield, *Becoming a Critically Reflective Teacher*, pp. 266-67, and *The Skillful Teacher*, p. 191.

25. Sharon D. Welch, *Sweet Dreams in America: Making Ethics and Spirituality Work* (New York: Routledge, 1999), p. 107.

26. Welch, *Sweet Dreams*, p. 130.

to say only what you mean; say it as accurately as you can; listen to and respect what the other says, however different or other; be willing to correct or defend your opinions if challenged by the conversation partner; be willing to argue if necessary, to confront if demanded, to endure necessary conflict, to change your mind if the evidence suggests it.[27]

From another perspective, I think, an ethic of conflict in the classroom requires us to learn to pay attention, to hear others *as* other, the different *as* possible.

The different as possible, the other as other: learning to listen, to pay attention, is fostered in my classroom through the discipline of reading texts. I rarely use the lives of my students as the "texts" of the class. I use *texts* as texts. Books. Odd books that my students would not read if they were not assigned. Students readily engage in the meaning and conflicts of their own lives, but can they work to engage the world — and their relation to the world — of an "other"? The sheer difficulty of reading texts, particularly for students whose lives are profoundly ordered by the visual and audio media of contemporary culture, propels students headlong into the complexity, the richness, the strangeness, and the puzzle of the other.

Students tell me that my expectations are intimidating. Students say they are afraid they will disappoint me, that they don't know how to please me. Liz Tamborra, as a freshman undergraduate, described her feelings in the following way:

> Okay, so this is how it goes: I read the material. I think I've got it figured out (I do pretty well in most of my classes), and then you come into class and ask a question or make us read a passage that is totally confusing. I can't predict what will happen. It's clear that you emphasize critical thinking and class participation, but the way you do it is *very* intimidating.

William Kiernan (a classmate of Liz Tamborra) also acknowledges the confusion of teaching as conversation. He, however, makes a distinction between the "average" student and the student who is willing to take intellectual and personal risks in the classroom. Most students, he says, are average students. They "memorize, execute, and forget." William does not

---

27. Tracy, *Plurality and Ambiguity*, p. 19.

want to be an average student. He wants "to comprehend, apply, and retain." But William, like Liz, becomes anxious when we read *texts* in order to "follow the question wherever it may go."

I have developed teaching strategies that seem to help students engage texts in conversation. The first two strategies ("generative lectures" and "structured improvisation") allow me to converse with students even though I possess more knowledge and more power than they do. The third strategy helps students learn to converse with texts. Before texts can be an active part of genuine conversation, they must be carefully, critically read.

Within an undergraduate classroom, formal lectures often promote passivity in students. The professor, well-prepared, demonstrates to her students the relevant knowledge, the relevant questions, and, in the end, the correct answers to previously identified relevant questions. A generative lecture, in contrast, takes place within and for a conversation. Though it does interrupt the flow of conversation to present information in an organized, often schematic way, it is meant to support the questioning that is conversation. At times, generative lectures begin a conversation, and they present — in the vocabulary of a particular time period or text — the topics, conflicts, or puzzles that accumulate into the questions in and of the text. Most often, generative lectures emerge when classroom conversations reach a puzzling impasse. In order to keep the conversation going, I provide "the occasional interruption of argument, theory, explanation, and method."[28]

Structured improvisation is a variation of the generative lecture. Whereas generative lectures are an interruption of the flow of conversation, structured improvisation is an orchestration of critical reflection, a means of keeping a conversation in motion. In this strategy, I ask the students to direct our conversation by selecting an important or intriguing quotation from the text. At the same time, my own preparation for and participation in this conversation emerges from an informed interpretation of what sections of the text (and what questions related to or generated by it) are most important to most interpreters. Before actual classroom conversations take place, I know which quotations have a good chance of prompting careful, critical conversation. But when the class meets, I have not decided when I will interject my selected quotations or specific questions. It may be the case that students will offer questions and

---

28. Tracy, *Plurality and Ambiguity*, p. 41.

text citations that are better, more pressing, more revealing than the ones I have prepared. Taken together, generative lectures and structured improvisations allow me to share with my students the power I possess as "an expert" in theology and religion.

Finally, my third strategy is related to the fact that I ask students to read what they would normally not read (and what they have little practice reading). If students cannot read a text, it remains inert and irrelevant to the conversation at hand. On the surface, one might say that an inert text has been reduced to (or domesticated into) data, discrete pieces of information to be memorized. On a deeper level, an inert text is dead. We converse with this thing that is so boring, so cumbersome, so profoundly dead.

Several years ago, I began to address the potential deadness of texts by reading selections of assigned readings aloud, during class time. A sore throat prompted me to ask students to volunteer to read for me. Finally, I developed the strategy of dedicating an entire class (early in the semester, without advance warning) to reading aloud an assigned text for the class. Taking turns, we read word by word, sentence by sentence, paragraph by paragraph, stopping when we need to, figuring out what is unimportant to the class, what is important but unfamiliar, etc. We look up unknown words in the dictionary (at least one student in every class carries around a battered little Webster's dictionary). We might repeat — by reading aloud again — sentences (even paragraphs) after we have deciphered the meaning of unfamiliar words, concepts, etc.[29] There is a subtle shift during the first half hour of this exercise. If timed well (and if a good text is used), students begin to read with curiosity and openness.

I cannot teach every class in this way. In most cases, I conduct conversations in class with the presumption that, prior to class, students have read the assigned material with a dictionary at hand (and perhaps one or two fellow students within calling distance). This reasonable presumption, however, produces yet another need. Students must learn to read *outside* of class. To meet this second need, I invite students to meet in small groups

29. For example, in an upper-level undergraduate class (which is scheduled to meet for 75 minutes), it took an hour to read the introduction and first 14 pages of Rita Nakashima Brock's *Journeys by Heart: A Christology of Erotic Power* (New York: Crossroad, 1988). We stopped at that point and used the last fifteen minutes of class to review what we had read. Students identified the content, issues, and structure of the text while I recorded (and organized) our thoughts on the chalkboard.

with me outside of class. The reading groups, held at definitively non-class hours (8 at night, 7:30 in the morning, Sunday afternoon) draw between 4 to 12 students. Most often, different students attend each reading, and no more than three reading groups are scheduled over the course of a semester. According to student accounts, these reading groups make a significant difference in student confidence regarding both the world of a particular text and the ability to read for the class in general.

I've noticed a difference between the close readings that take place in class and what happens in the voluntary reading groups. The reading groups outside of class are significantly more successful. Why? Partly, I think, because I bring food, we make mistakes, we follow a few tangents. Unlike the close reading demonstrated in class, the reading groups are small, interruptions are frequent, and no time limit is imposed. By the end of about two hours, however, everyone in the group is tired, punchy, and ready to quit. We rarely finish an entire text (or even chapter, or even article). But students unambiguously express that they have learned *how* I want them to read.[30]

The observation of my students that they can learn how I want them to read prompts me to revisit the question of power in my teaching practices. Because I take to heart Michel Foucault's argument that what counts as knowledge is a matter of power, and that truth is a product of power relations,[31] I am well aware that controlling the data of a text is perhaps less damaging (or at least less dangerous) than disciplining students to read "a certain way." Obviously, training students to imitate "my" way of reading is an insidious, even pervasive exercise of the power I have over students. I want to "control" *more* than what items of knowledge they possess. I want to control the very way that they encounter and construct worlds of discourse.[32] I want students to engage texts in a certain way, a way that gener-

30. When a colleague of mine heard about the success of my reading groups, he decided to incorporate them into his teaching. Soon, however, he (and his students) began to refer to the meetings as "study groups," and the emphasis shifted from reading to reviewing important definitions, topics, and themes of the class. Students also began to correlate the study group with preparation for quizzes and exams. Meeting outside of class for review of material in class is very different from meeting outside of class to *read* a text.

31. See Michel Foucault, *Power/Knowledge: Selected Interviews and Other Writings 1972-1977*, ed. Colin Gordon (New York: Pantheon Books, 1980).

32. This control remains even in my attempts to allow students, in Tim Hart's words, "room to maneuver." Yes, I tell my students that they can "pass" on the invitation to enter a

ates a specific kind of conversation (a "genuine" one, according to my standards). Can this conspicuous (and potentially addictive) power *over* learners become "power *with* learners" in my classroom?[33]

The pedagogical issues raised by this conflict (my desire for control over and for power with students) have been addressed earlier in this essay, when I amiably agree with educational theorists who argue that effective teaching is the just and fair deployment of power. But if we turn briefly to the religious issues and theological commitments raised by the fact that I can (and do) "discipline" my students, I am led to ask if the formative practices of my teaching strategies are any different from those practiced by Julia Brumbaugh, who admits candidly that she wants to use her power as teacher to form faithful members of the Roman Catholic Church.

Julia's contemporary, progressive, and yet doctrinal Catholic theology shapes her teaching strategies. What theology is revealed in (or betrayed by) my teaching strategies?[34] I must ask myself the same question I pose to my students: What God do I practice as a theologian who teaches,

---

conversation, that they should work toward becoming conscious of their own projects, their own commitments. I even tell them that our class is not meant to be a threat to their present religiousness. I say: I am not here to destroy your faith. But I also say that everything we learn, in the end, can have unexpected (sometimes welcome and sometimes unwelcome) influence on our choices, our lives, our practices, our struggle to be authentic.

33. Brookfield, *Becoming a Critically Reflective Teacher*, p. 9.

34. It seems to me that all teaching theologians should periodically evaluate (a) the theological/religious convictions that they want to express in their work as theologians, (b) the ways that syllabi and bibliographies and course outlines correlate (both positively and negatively) with these theological/religious convictions, and (c) the potential blindspots and sites of conflict between teaching strategies and theological commitments.

As an undergraduate, I double-majored in Religious Studies and Psychology. At the time, I was amused by the tendency of theology professors to emphasize "final judgment" (for they reserved a large percentage of the course grade for final exams or term papers). Psychology professors, it seemed, endlessly evaluated us "in process": every month or so we were asked to show what we were learning. The final course grade in a psychology class often reflected many tests and papers, with even the final exam having only a modest impact on the overall grade for the course. Psychologists, I thought at the time, had a better appreciation for the learning process (and our brain's capacity to retain information over time).

On the surface, any two strategies of evaluation can be assessed by their outcome. To what extent does a method of evaluation help students learn, recall, and integrate knowledge, and demonstrate critical thinking? Beneath the surface, however, every strategy employed in a classroom reveals deeply held, though perhaps unconscious, convictions of the teacher. This observation, when applied to teaching theologians, asks us to identify the religious/theological convictions embedded in the structures, books, evaluations, etc., we se-who has power and influence in a classroom, who is granted the authority to shape the religiousness of (subordinate) others?

I can answer my question with a list of desires: I seek to practice a God in and through hospitality to the other, the strange, the alien, the unexpected. I believe that everything sacred begins in and endures through unmanageable abundance. I hope that genuine conversation, like authentic religious experience, is itself an unmanageable but powerful and giving abundance. When conversation slips out of an economic mode of "knowledge" and wanders into the abundance that funds theological discourse and bankrupts certainties about "God," something uniquely religious happens. Contact is risked: the strange, the demanding, the complex, the other is invited *as it is* into our lives. If we are not to colonize the other, we must learn to genuinely converse with the other. And genuine conversation "is not confrontation . . . is not debate . . . is not an exam." Rather, genuine conversation "is willingness to follow the question wherever it may go."[35]

As preparation for teaching, I select texts. I establish boundaries. I decide that we read this text and not another. In the classroom, I help my students engage texts so that the other, the different, and the strange are welcome. In the space of the classroom, new space is opened for the other as other, the other as possible. This new space is not merely the arrangement of old space. It is often the sacrifice of filled space. In this new space, my students and I might become questions that have no predetermined answers. Though we remain a well-ordered circle that labors to read texts and listen to others, though we struggle to be authentic and yet do not know the scope of our freedom, once in a while the circle of learning becomes the site of a bonfire. Now and then, fleeting manifestations of the sacred blaze up, and the God who speaks consumes us.

---

lect. For good or for ill, sustained interrogation of teaching strategies reveals powerful and often unarticulated religious commitments. We must think about our tendency for final judgments. Is it really an "innocent" teaching practice?

35. Tracy, *Plurality and Ambiguity*, p. 18.

Teaching as a Ministry of Hope

PAUL J. WADELL

NOT LONG AGO I CROSSED the Great Divide. After thirteen years of teaching graduate students at a school of theology in Chicago, I packed my bags and headed for the strange new world of undergraduate teaching. I knew the change would be more than geographical. But never did I think it would leave my tidy universe in pieces.

The first day I walked into a classroom of thirty-five undergraduates to embark on our fifteen-week journey through the Introduction to Theology, I knew I had left my old world behind. My boast that nothing is more interesting than God was shipwrecked by looks of practiced boredom and determined dismay. My promise that nothing is more relevant than theology sank deep into a sea of blank, empty stares and not-so-subtle checks of watches. By the end of the first week I was haunted by the question of how to connect with students who seemed to inhabit a universe so different from my own. Though only a few inches separated us in the classroom, I felt as if some immeasurable chasm stood between us. Am I speaking some strange foreign tongue? Is my passion for theology bizarre?

If today's teachers feel that students are like orphans left on their doorstep from some alien world, we must explore that world and know how to address it if what is truly a graced vocation is not to disintegrate in defeat. We won't salvage hope by blaming students for all that is demoralizing in undergraduate teaching today. Truth is partner to hope and the truth is, these students are creatures of our own making. Thus, if teaching is to remain a ministry of hope, even of joy, we must probe the world of our students to wrestle with what makes so many of them strangers to us and we, most certainly, to them.

In this chapter I want to explore four things: (1) to identify and analyze the effects of three characteristics of our dominant culture of consumerism and mass communication on the attitudes, perceptions, values, beliefs, and behavior of students; (2) to diagnose the more enduring effects of this culture on the souls and spirits of our students; (3) to consider how teachers of theology can challenge students to reimagine their lives in a more hopeful way; and (4) to explore what virtues and practices teachers of theology need to cultivate if teaching is to remain a vocation and ministry of hope.

The World of Our Students: How We Have Misled Them

Everybody follows some gospel and today's college students have been baptized into the gospel of consumerism; it is the cultural mood they bring with them into the classroom like the backpacks on their backs. For many of my students, television is their meditation chapel, shopping malls their temples, and food courts their place for eucharist. Evangelized through the catechesis of consumerism, they have learned it is not seeking and loving and glorifying God that makes us human, but marketing, producing, buying, purchasing, and consuming. Like any gospel, consumerism has provided them with answers to the most pressing questions of life: What does it mean to be human? What should I do with the life I have been given? Where will I find happiness and hope? Answers are shouted back every time they flick on the television, open a magazine, or stroll through a mall: Who you are is what you own and the more you own the more you are.[1]

In a society where capitalism is not only an economic system but an entire way of life, to be human is to be a consumer[2] and everything, including ourselves, is a commodity whose value depends on its marketabil-

---

1. For an excellent treatment of this point see John Kavanaugh, *Still Following Christ in a Consumer Society* (Maryknoll, N.Y.: Orbis Books, 1992).

2. On this point see Larry L. Rasmussen, *Moral Fragments and Moral Community: A Proposal for Church in Society* (Minneapolis: Fortress Press, 1993), especially pp. 34-60.

ity. One no longer goes to college for intellectual and moral development — such notions sound quaint to most students today — but to learn what one needs to market oneself successfully in order to get the best job at the highest salary as quickly as possible. If there was a time when a college education meant crafting the soul as well as the mind, for many students today college has the strictly utilitarian value of equipping them with the facts, skills, and connections they will need to be financially successful. As William H. Willimon and Thomas H. Naylor report, when students in a prominent School of Business were asked what they wanted of their faculty, their response was neither wisdom nor inspiration, but "Teach me how to be a moneymaking machine."[3]

No one is going to learn "how to be a moneymaking machine" in a theology class. For students who have been formed far more by consumerism than by Christianity, the problem with studying theology is that God has so little cash value. What relevance can God have for people whose minds and hearts have been assaulted with the message that human beings are economic creatures whose vocation is to produce, purchase, and consume, not religious beings called to love, worship, and praise God?

This is where our universes collide. As a Christian I believe human beings are inherently religious beings because we live in, from, and for God. The defining feature of our humanity is not our ability to purchase or consume, but the gracious invitation to live in communion with the Triune God who befriends us in grace, Christ, and the sacraments. I believe we should study theology not principally because it is intellectually gripping or personally compelling, but because our lives depend on knowing and loving God. But the very thing that brings joy and hope to my world is what makes me strange in theirs.

A second characteristic of contemporary American society that has shaped the perceptions, beliefs, and behavior of many students is an intellectual and moral relativism that undermines any claims to truth and objectivity. But this is no surprise. They have been raised in a world of spin doctors and talk shows where slick manipulation matters more than truth; a world of constantly changing images designed to exploit the senses, not transform them; and a world where appearances matter most because ap-

3. William H. Willimon and Thomas H. Naylor, *The Abandoned Generation: Rethinking Higher Education* (Grand Rapids: William B. Eerdmans Publishing Co., 1995), p. 38.

pearance is all there is: Beneath the surface, behind the smile, lies not the soul, but nothingness. No wonder they have learned not the cult of the saints, but the cult of celebrity.

And so the skepticism of college students today is far deeper than that of previous generations. The uncertainty many young people have about truth stems not primarily from the difficulty of knowing it, but from the more radical conviction that there is no truth to be known. Bluntly put, they are disillusioned with the very idea of truth; consequently, the Christian claim that there is some ultimate meaning to life we need to discover and to live if we are to be successfully human seldom rings true for them. Like pilgrims who drift without a destination, they have wandered beyond the conventional skepticism of late adolescence and early adulthood into the barrenness of intellectual and moral agnosticism. In that desert where the sands shift constantly, there are no standards of excellence and no sure ways to distinguish truth from falsity.

An example may illustrate this point. In my Introduction to Theology class I have the students read, and write an essay on, Robert Bolt's *A Man for All Seasons,* the story of Thomas More. Recently, a student asked why he had not received a higher mark for his essay. I told him that, among other reasons, there simply was no truth to his claim that Thomas More lacked a strong identity and a clear sense of self; in fact, that he professed this made me doubt he had read the play. But instead of being embarrassed or contrite, the student was defiant, arguing that my assessment of Thomas More was "only my opinion," and since interpreting literature involves nothing more than offering one's opinion, his point that Thomas More lacked a substantive identity had as much merit as my claim that More could go to the guillotine only because his identity before God was so strong. The story illustrates that in a culture where there are no truths, only opinions, teachers and students are equals and differences are resolved not by reasoned arguments, but by subtle intimidations.

A third characteristic of the culture of mass communication and consumerism that is especially prevalent among college students is the expectation to be amused and entertained. Sometimes when I am teaching I think students picture the classroom to be a rather uncomfortable lounge in which they, unwilling spectators, must sit several times each week. I imagine they envision the front of the classroom as a giant video screen and see me as some not very entertaining media creature they are forced to watch because on this unfortunate television there is only one station. Things are better if they can bring their snacks and drinks to the show, but without a cascade of channels to distract them it isn't long before they tune me out. As Peter Sacks remarked in *Generation X Goes to College,* these students "have grown to expect amusement in virtually every aspect of their lives."[4] Or as a student told Sacks, "We want you guys to dance. We expect so much more from everything now because of the media. You guys can't compete."[5]

The very skills and practices necessary for education, such as critical thinking, reflection, patience, inquisitiveness, humility, silence, and solitude are precisely what our entertainment culture devalues. Students have been taught that nothing is worthy of their attention for an extended period of time but, as Simone Weil made clear, learning is a matter of patiently fixing one's attention on a subject long enough to be drawn into it, absorbed by it, and even changed by it; in this respect, genuine learning is an act of love.[6]

Take, for example, the study of theology. To study theology is to grow captivated with God; however, this is possible only when students first make themselves available to God. This availability is what Christianity, particularly Roman Catholicism, has traditionally called contemplation, the practice of fixing one's attention on God long enough truly to gain wisdom of God. Contemplation entails openness and receptivity, it demands waiting quietly and patiently, and it requires the kind of single-hearted vulnerability to something greater than ourselves that ultimately leads to the transformation of ourselves.

At its best, the study of theology ought to be transformative, but that cannot happen unless students first cultivate attentiveness, patience, humility, and solitude, all elements of contemplation. This will not be easy because they have been taught the best life is the distracted life, the life that is continually attentive to nothing because it must be potentially available to everything. In classical Christian spirituality, not to fix one's attention on God shriveled the soul. Sadly, students today have been formed to be-

---

4. Peter Sacks, *Generation X Goes to College* (LaSalle, Ill.: Open Court Publishing, 1996), p. 143.

5. Sacks, *Generation X Goes to College,* p. 144. In an informal survey Sacks conducted with his students, nearly half cited entertainment as the quality they valued most in their teachers. Close behind was the expectation that a teacher be friendly and warm. See *Generation X Goes to College,* p. 55.

6. Simone Weil, "Reflections on the Right Use of School Studies with a View to the Love of God," in *Waiting for God* (New York: Harper & Row, 1973), pp. 105-16.

lieve that sustained attentiveness to God is a sign of boredom, not peace. What quiets the restless heart is not union with God, but novelty. Thus, not surprisingly, the highest praise a teacher can receive is not that a class changed a student's life, but that it was fun.[7]

A Diagnosis: How Souls Have Been Malformed

What has a culture of consumerism and individualism made of students today? How has it shaped their sense of life? Their understanding of self? Their hopes about the future? There are many ways to answer these questions, but three things seem most important.

First, there is a quality of "lostness" to many students. True, this has always been characteristic of adolescence, but today there is a difference. If in previous generations young people drifted before settling down, at least they believed there was some journey they were meant to take, some destination in life they should reach if their lives were to be judged a success. I do not sense this with my students today. It is not so much that they get lost along the way and simply need to be nudged back to the right path; rather, they believe there is no right path to take or destination to reach if their lives *as human* are not to be judged a failure. Language about goals to reach, a *telos* to achieve, or a transformation to partake in if one is to flourish as a human being strikes many of them not only as quaint, but as nearly incomprehensible because it suggests happiness and fulfillment are not a matter of unimpeded choices, but of being initiated and formed into a definitive way of life.

In a culture where choice is the highest good, suggesting that happiness demands being apprenticed into a particular way of life makes little sense. Similarly, it is hard for students to understand how anyone can fail at being human when what it means to be human is something everyone must decide for themselves. This is what makes my Christian faith so strange to them. Christianity argues that fullness of life is found in knowing and loving God, and that we learn best what it means to be human in faithful discipleship with Christ and joyful imitation of the saints. It is in living this story that we discover who we truly are and are transformed in a way that makes genuine happiness possible.

7. Sacks, *Generation X Goes to College,* p. 93.

125

If Christianity does anything, it locates one's life within a story; it tells us *who we are* by telling us *where we stand.* But citizens of consumerism do not stand, they float, moving from one possibility, one amusement, one distraction to the next. One reason many students have little idea of what they think is good is that they do not picture themselves standing within a story that helps them make sense of their place in the world.

A second way the pathologies of the culture have misshaped the young is seen in their conviction that there is no such thing as an enduring, stable identity because the self is little more than the backdrop for constantly changing choices. We see this, for example, in the way many young adults approach sexual relationships. One reason, I believe, they enter into sexual relationships so casually is that they do not believe they have a self or identity deep and lasting enough to be damaged. Relationships can constantly change because the self constantly changes; thus, who I am today has no necessary connection to who I was yesterday or who I shall be tomorrow. If everything constantly changes, so does the self, and if novelty is prized by technology and consumerism, should it not also be the hallmark of true individuality?

Many students exemplify what Charles Taylor calls the "neutral self." He means by this a self that is not identified by any set of constitutive concerns; a self that is so thoroughly *disengaged* from any overarching narrative framework that it is, as Taylor puts it, perpetually "at sea."[8] Previously, of course, such a predicament would be so ontologically and existentially disorienting that it would precipitate an identity crisis; you cannot know who you are unless you know where you stand, and the "neutral" self stands nowhere.[9]

Now, however, what once would have been judged an unbearable predicament is extolled as an ideal. The appeal in having a life with no fixed reference points is that it allows the self to be continually remade. If selfhood reaches no deeper than our constantly changing desires, then personal identity is not a measure of integrity, but of fancy. Who we are is whatever or whoever has our interest, but since those interests continually change so does our self. I am not suggesting that the self should be immune to change or impermeable to its world; nor am I advocating a rigid

---

8. Charles Taylor, *Sources of the Self: The Making of the Modern Identity* (Cambridge: Harvard University Press, 1989), pp. 26-31, 49.

9. Taylor, *Sources of the Self,* p. 27.

and static self that would not be formed by all the relationships of its world. But I do believe we must be rooted and centered in some relatively stable commitments and concerns in order to have a self at all, and it is this conviction I find missing in many undergraduates. They have been taught that novelty, not fidelity, is the key to identity and that permanency is more a sign of sterility than integrity.

Of course there has been a cost to this philosophy of the self. There is a deep loneliness to many of my students today, a loneliness that has been part of their lives for so long they cannot imagine themselves without it. But this should come as no surprise. If our identity is little more than what momentarily has our interest, how can anyone ever come to know us? If who we are today has little connection with who we shall be tomorrow, is friendship truly possible? One reason many student relationships that bear the name of friendship are actually fairly trivial is that an increasing number of them lack the kind of moral identity necessary to make rich and rewarding friendships possible. The best friendships extend over time, but a friendship can last no longer and be no deeper than the self we bring to it. Thus, what first appears to many students to be freedom for the self is actually a state of permanent and paralyzing estrangement.

A third effect of the culture glimpsed in probing the souls of my students is depression. Young people today may be entertained, but that does not mean they are happy. Lost in many of them is any confidence that life is graced and promising, or that the future holds hope. Never has a generation been given so many options and possibilities; seldom has a generation been so demoralized. They have been told they have every reason to be happy, but they sense something is missing. We have tutored them to believe freedom of choice is the secret of happiness; however, their anxiety tells them if all that holds our lives together is "the slender thread of choice,"[10] despair is bound to follow.

Many of my students — and many of their teachers as well — show all the symptoms of acedia, a dangerous form of depression and an aptly named deadly sin.[11] Acedia describes a pervasive sadness and discontent that descends upon the person who no longer believes great things are possible in life. It is a deep listlessness of spirit — a life-robbing sadness —

10. I am indebted to Scott Bader-Saye for this expression.
11. For an excellent treatment of acedia, see Henry Fairlie, *The Seven Deadly Sins Today* (Notre Dame, Ind.: University of Notre Dame Press, 1979), pp. 113-30.

that characterizes the person who moves through life engaged by nothing. Henry Fairlie described acedia as "a morbid inertia" that immobilizes one's spirit.[12] Acedia is dejection in its most toxic form. What makes it especially dangerous today is that many students are barely aware of the malaise that cripples their lives because they are numb to their own despair. This is the darkness we must shatter.

Reimagining Life in a Hopeful and Promising Way

How then can we help students envision their lives graciously? How can we encourage them to see their life in the world as blessed? There is a scene in Walker Percy's novel *The Second Coming* in which Allison Vaught, who has just escaped from a psychiatric hospital, encounters a woman who hands her a pamphlet. The first three sentences read: *"Are you lonely? Do you want to make a new start? Have you ever had a personal encounter with our Lord and Savior?"*[13] These would be good questions to ask our students because they touch the disenchantment and disillusionment many of them feel. Like Allison Vaught, many have been depressed for a long time and are not sure why. Percy suggests one way "to make a new start" is to probe the depression, to investigate the discontent.

A first step in helping students imagine better possibilities for their lives may well lie in exploring their disenchantment. Sometimes the most momentous changes are born from disenchantment because it is only when we are thoroughly disillusioned with one kind of life that we find the energy and courage necessary to search for a better life. Disenchantment is a powerful source for moral and spiritual change because it provides the energy necessary to break free from conventional but deadening practices and mesmerizing but empty ideologies in order to search for something more. Realizing we are not satisfied with the life our society says should content us, and finding the courage to imagine new possibilities and more hopeful expectations, can be the start of a life-saving transformation.

Perhaps the greatest sign of hope in many young people today is

---

12. Fairlie, *The Seven Deadly Sins Today,* p. 113. See also Paul J. Wadell, *The Primacy of Love: An Introduction to the Ethics of Thomas Aquinas* (New York: Paulist Press, 1992), pp. 103-5.

13. Walker Percy, *The Second Coming* (New York: Pocket Books, 1980), p. 37.

their suspicion. Despite the daily bombardments of consumerism, they are skeptical enough to wonder if what is presented to them as the good life is not life at all, but only death disguised. Such suspicion, though initially disconcerting, is a saving grace. Teachers need to seize this suspicion and stoke it. We need to pay attention to the intimations of discontent because only then will students feel free to question the way of life they are constantly encouraged to accept.

But probing disenchantment is not enough to restore hope. We must give them something to replace their disillusionment and if, like Peter and John, we have neither silver nor gold to offer, we do have the gospel. But we should not think it is a message they are instantly ready to hear, because it is precisely the cultural mood they have embodied that makes the Christian gospel seem so strange. We have to teach them to hear. We have to help them struggle with a message that initially will seem so odd and disconcerting it can hardly be good news. Many students have been nursed on a vision of life so bereft of promise it makes the very notion of grace strange. This is why reimagining their lives more hopefully must begin with unlearning — and breaking free from — the lies of the culture. Such rehabilitation of the soul will not be easy precisely because many are addicted to the social and cultural ideologies even when they know they are pathological.

Christianity is bound to seem crazy in the consumerist world of our students and, if we are honest, teachers of theology crazed. But that's all right, even a little exciting. Let us seem crazy if it is enough to catch a student's attention, and let the gospel be far-fetched if it will make them curious. The craziness of the gospel to many students is exactly the radical alternative it offers. Against the frantic emptiness and ultimate sterility of consumerism and individualism, it envisions a world embraced by the befriending goodness of God. In other words, what makes Christianity shocking to many students is that it is full of hope.

Grasping that hope requires being initiated into a community whose traditions and practices should help us recognize the darkness in order to shatter it. That community should be the church, but unfortunately too often the churches have conformed to the seductions of the culture instead of resisting them. What makes the gospel believable to students is not teaching it but living it. They need to see in the church (and in us) people who embody the hope, joy, challenge, and truth of the gospel. They need to see disciples bold and courageous enough to live lives of resistance not in order to be different, but because in Christ they have found a life that sets them free. And, perhaps most of all, they need to see in the church a community that welcomes them and cares enough about them to invest itself in helping them learn the challenging but liberating language of God. Will we teach them to speak?

Teaching as a Ministry of Hope

A few years ago I was talking about teaching with Charles Pinches, a colleague and good friend. Charlie commented that teaching theology to undergraduates is "an enterprise full of self-doubt." I laughed not because I thought Charlie was exaggerating, but because I knew his insight was distressingly true. Teaching theology can leave us feeling disheartened and defeated; even worse, it can make us cynical. But we should fight those temptations with fury because to settle into cynicism or defeat would betray the grace entrusted to us. If we embrace theological education as a vocation it means we envision what we do not as a job or career, but as being faithful to a grace. What we do with the gifts and talents entrusted to us is determined not primarily by our interests and inclinations, but by our conviction that teaching is what God calls us to do; it is a commission more than a choice, a ministry as much as a profession. As Greg Jones observes in his essay in this volume, we should seek a vocation that will make *more of us,* not a job in which we make more for ourselves. How then do we sustain our appreciation of teaching as a vocation? Despite the challenges and setbacks, how can it remain a ministry of hope? It depends on cultivating certain practices and virtues, and I want to suggest five.

First, we must cultivate the virtue of reverent and truthful vision. As Ignatius of Loyola reminded us, Christians are challenged to "find God in all things," a feat not easily achieved every time you walk into the classroom. God is not what comes to mind when you look out on faces marked by indifference, defiance, or just plain boredom. But if God really is present wherever we are, then God lives in those students. The question is not whether God can be found in our students, but are we willing to look beyond the surface, are we willing to see beyond the obstacles they put in our way? Such vision is not a natural aptitude, but a precious moral skill that is the result of patience, determination, and hope. There is promise and goodness in every student we teach because the God who fashioned them lives in them, but we must train ourselves to see. To use Enda McDonagh's metaphor, the challenge is to see those before us as gift rather than threat.[14]

But it is not our temptation to allow the threat to triumph over the gift? Do we not sometimes let the vacant stares of students shrivel our vision so that we see them as adversaries, not as images of God? Seeing is everything, but seeing involves more than just opening our eyes because we can open our eyes and miss the beckoning presence of God before us. And sometimes our vision simply becomes twisted. Fatigue, disappointment, and a sense of our own limitations prompt us to see our students ungraciously. But if we look upon our students through eyes of mistrust, fear, anger, or resentment — if we see them as enemies instead of gifts — we have declared that God's grace may be present in the world, but it is not present in them. Thus, as Bonnie Miller-McLemore writes in her essay in this volume, "Far better to ask, how can we enhance our capacity to meet God in and through others who are dependent upon our charity and wisdom for their well-being?"

Second, if teaching theology is to be a ministry of hope, we must become experts in the virtue of hospitality. In *Hospitality to the Stranger,* Thomas W. Ogletree argued that we need others, especially those who are different from us and who may not experience, know, or see the world as we do, to open, expand, challenge, and renew our world. For Ogletree, the stranger cracks open our world, sometimes turning it upside down. But however disconcerting, the stranger is truly a gift because the stranger brings something graced and surprising into our world, and in doing so rescues us from the false security of arrogance.[15]

Is any group more "stranger" to us than our students? If the stranger is the person whose experiences, perceptions, attitudes, tastes, inclinations, and interests are dramatically different from our own, who fulfills this salutary role better than our students? And if Ogletree is right that our deliverance comes through the strangers who enter our world and show us what we fail to see and teach us what we did not know before, then we should give thanks for our students, not fear them. Precisely in their differences they de-center us enough to make us teachable.

14. Enda McDonagh, *Gift and Call: Towards a Christian Theology of Morality* (St. Meinrad, Ind.: Abbey Press, 1975), pp. 34-39.

15. Thomas W. Ogletree, *Hospitality to the Stranger* (Philadelphia: Fortress Press, 1985), p. 2.

But they cannot work their magic unless we risk letting them into our lives, and this can only happen if we are willing to listen to them. We always fear what we do not know and perhaps the reason we most fear our students is that we never take time to know them. Parker Palmer says "good teaching is an act of hospitality toward the young,"[16] and hospitality begins with attentive listening. We want students to listen to us because we want to share our truth with them; but students have their truth to share too, and perhaps the greatest respect we can extend to them is to take their truth seriously. Hospitality in teaching is a harbinger of hope because the more we attend to the insights, experiences, fears, joys, and humor of our students, the more we not only see their goodness *precisely in their otherness,* but also realize how they can bless and enrich our lives.

Third, teaching remains a ministry of hope when it is embraced as an act of stewardship. Here it may be helpful to draw a parallel between the stewardship entailed in teaching and the stewardship of human beings towards the earth. As James A. Nash makes clear, stewardship towards the earth describes the distinctive moral responsibility human beings have to respect and care for God's creation.[17] Because we are creatures blessed with intelligence, moral awareness, and free will, God entrusts the goodness of creation to us with the expectation that we will not destroy the handiwork of God but nurture it. Stewardship means the creation that comes to us from God as a beautiful gift should be presented back to God as a beautiful gift; in short, the earth should not be the worse for having known us.

Neither should our students. If teaching is a form of stewardship, we should see our students as gifts God entrusts to us. They are not ours to possess, manipulate, or control; rather, they are God's and God gives them to us with the expectation that we will continue God's good work in them by caring for them, respecting them, and, above all, nurturing the image of God in them. This makes teaching a sacred trust and a solemn responsibility; it makes teaching a noble vocation. As Nash observes, "Christians are called to honor and nurture what God honors and nurtures,"[18] and if this is true with the good things of the earth, it certainly is true with our stu-

16. Parker J. Palmer, *The Courage to Teach: Exploring the Inner Landscape of a Teacher's Life* (San Francisco: Jossey-Bass Publishers, 1998), p. 50.

17. James A. Nash, *Loving Nature: Ecological Integrity and Christian Responsibility* (Nashville: Abingdon Press, 1991), pp. 102-8.

18. Nash, *Loving Nature,* p. 100.

dents. If teaching is a Christian vocation, indeed a ministry in the church, then to teach is to receive our students as beautiful gifts in order to offer them to God as beautiful gifts. This is not limp piety, it is what the person of humility and gratitude simply knows.

Fourth, no one can persevere in the vocation of teaching theology without courage. Courage helps us deal with fears and difficulties, with the inevitable discouragements and hardships of life, and with all the things that make us lose hope. It is the virtue that teaches us how to endure in hope despite whatever difficulties and disappointments might face us. Aquinas said courage equips us to deal with the "oppressing difficulties" of life, and in teaching they can be manifold: our own limitations and short-comings, fatigue and loss of zeal, frustration at lack of results, lack of insti-tutional support and cooperation, apathy and resistance in students, social and cultural dynamics.[19] In teaching theology, "oppressing difficulties" abound, and if we do not learn to confront them courageously and pa-tiently, our teaching will degenerate to little more than grim determina-tion, a joyless endurance contest rather than a ministry of hope.

It is important to understand, however, that courage is not a matter of denying or minimizing the obstacles and challenges we face, especially if we envision teaching as a *vocation and ministry;* rather, the power of cour-age rests precisely in its realism and its hope. Aquinas, for instance, noted that courage comes into play when we are tempted to "retreat from a diffi-cult situation" or flee a "formidable evil" on account of fear.[20] He did not flinch from acknowledging that any good person in any good life will eventually have to wrestle with adversity, even evil, but she need not be overcome.

Nor should she simply suffer silently. If the first part of courage is pa-tient endurance, the second part of courage is daring. Daring is not reck-lessness, it is the energy, imagination, insight, and determination we need to overcome the "oppressing difficulties" whenever we can; otherwise, courage too easily looks like stoic surrender. Our first response to the inev-itable hardships, setbacks, and even desolation in teaching should not be to surrender but to attack. If our students seem lethargic and disengaged, we should challenge that, not endure it. If we find ourselves growing disen-

19. Thomas Aquinas, *Summa Theologiae* (New York: McGraw-Hill, 1966), II-II, 123,1.

20. Aquinas, *ST,* II-II, 123,3.

chanted and cynical, we must work to exorcise those demons, not honor them. Classically, the primary setting for courage has been the battlefield. There are days the classroom can seem a battlefield and teaching a war we are losing. But like any good soldier, our first response should not be surrender, but to do what is necessary to complete the mission entrusted to us. This is why Aquinas insisted that daring is as integral to courage as patient endurance.[21]

Finally, there is friendship. We are less likely to get lost on a journey if a friend accompanies us along the way, and this is certainly true with the journey of teaching. Teaching theology is an exciting adventure, but it can also be a perilous one. There is no way any of us can survive the journey, much less delight and flourish in it, without the support, encouragement, and companionship of friends, including friendship with the God who called us to the journey in the first place. If teaching is to be a ministry of hope and of joy, it requires the companionship of friends who care about what we care about and care about us caring for it. We need others to remind us of the value and importance of our vocations. We need people who are committed to the causes and projects we have made our own.[22] It is in company with them that we remember why teaching theology is a vocation born from love.[23]

And so I do not regret crossing the Great Divide and entering the world of undergraduates. It has been an adventure full of challenges, surprises, and occasional perils, but it has also been full of grace. True, sometimes my students can exhaust me and sometimes they can exasperate me, but they have also stretched me, challenged me, and enriched me. Most importantly, they have shown me that to be called to teach is to be given a noble vocation I should cherish, not lament. If I can remember all the reasons I have to be indebted to them, my teaching will remain a ministry of hope.

21. Aquinas, *ST,* II-II, 123,3.

22. See Paul J. Wadell, *Friendship and the Moral Life* (Notre Dame, Ind.: University of Notre Dame Press, 1989), pp. 59-61.

23. I am grateful to Rebecca Welch, Jennifer Johnson, and Emelie Broullire, students of St. Norbert College whose insights, reflections, and comments were immensely helpful for me in preparing this paper.

Teaching as Cultivating Wisdom
for a Complex World

LOIS MALCOLM

...be infants in evil, but in thinking be adults.

1 Corinthians 14:20, NRSV[1]

ONE OF THE FIRST THINGS I discovered when I started teaching was that I could not rely on my intuitions. My students were very different from me. And the difference between us was not simply due to the fact that I as a theology professor was more theoretical and my students, who were preparing to become pastors, were more practical. The difference had to do with what some of our fundamental theological questions were and why we were studying theology in the first place. This is not to say that I didn't enjoy my students and find teaching to be a tremendous delight. I did. It is simply that I discovered when I began teaching that we were, for the most part, different. And I could only be an effective teacher if I truly

1. I am grateful for the helpful comments of the members of the consultation on the vocation of the theological teacher on earlier drafts of what was a very different paper. I am also grateful for many conversations with students at Luther Seminary, both in and outside of the classroom, especially those with my teaching assistants, Paige Evers, Laurie Johnson, and David Lyle (who also commented on an earlier draft of a very different paper). Your input helped me radically rethink what I was about in this paper.

135

understood what they, as people very different from me, needed and not simply what I would have wanted if I had been sitting in their place.

Like many sons and daughters — and in my case also a granddaughter — of pastors and missionaries, I had studied theology at least initially to understand more fully, and to some extent to distance myself from, an intensely religious background. I needed to figure out what it meant to be human and a contemporary person before I could reappropriate or make my own the Christianity I had inherited. As a graduate student, I identified with many modern theologians' quest to rethink the Christian faith they had inherited — from Schleiermacher's desire to become a "Moravian of a higher order" to James Gustafson's attempt to rethink his father's Swedish pietism. I read with interest books like David Tracy's *Blessed Rage for Order* and Langdon Gilkey's *Naming the Whirlwind,* carefully tracing their arguments for why Christianity was still viable after the Enlightenment critique of traditional religious belief.[2] I fully resonated with Paul Tillich's observation that true theology — what he called "theonomy" — completed and did not efface the human capacity to think, reason, and ask questions.[3]

By contrast, many of my students had self-consciously decided to become Christians as teenagers and adults, coming out of either nominally Christian or secular backgrounds. Christian faith was not necessarily something they had inherited but something they had quite intentionally sought out. Even those who had been raised in Christian backgrounds were clearly making an intentional choice to go into ordained or lay ministry — a choice that often countered other cultural expectations. And far from needing to distance themselves from a faith they had inherited, they sought solace in Jesus Christ — a solace from more concrete vicissitudes like job lay-offs, depression, drug or alcohol addictions, violating sexual experiences, their own or their parents' divorces, and so on. Of course, not

2. See David Tracy, *Blessed Rage for Order: The New Pluralism in Theology* (New York: Seabury, 1975), and Langdon Gilkey, *Naming the Whirlwind: The Renewal of God-Language* (New York: Bobbs-Merrill, 1969). Note, of course, that both theologians have developed theologically in a range of different directions since these early books. Note, e.g., the direction Tracy's work has taken since writing the *Analogical Imagination: Christian Theology and the Culture of Pluralism* (New York: Crossroad, 1987). See his most recent work on God as exemplified in "The Hidden and Incomprehensible God: The 1999 Palmer Lecture," *Reflections: Center of Theological Inquiry,* vol. 3 (Autumn 2000): 62-88.

3. See, e.g., Paul Tillich's autobiographical reflections in *The Boundaries of Our Being: A Collection of His Sermons* (London: Collins, 1963), pp. 285-350.

all my students had dramatic conversion experiences. But most were very eager to receive *catechesis,* a basic introduction to Christian faith. Indeed, they preferred more concrete explications of what to believe than surveys of what a range of theologians might think about a particular topic. My teaching evaluations were highest when I spoke with an apodictic confidence that what I was teaching was God's truth, a truth they needed to hear existentially there and then. Of course, there was great diversity among my students. Not all could or wanted to fit into the same mold. Factors like age, gender, ethnicity, race — even personality style — greatly influenced why students were studying theology and what their needs and interests were. Nonetheless, it was possible to generalize about a certain trend that was evident especially in students born after the 1960s.[4]

In addition to wanting *catechesis,* my students were aware that both the church and the world around them were changing. They could no longer expect that Lutheran churches could go on as they had serving primarily Scandinavian or German immigrant communities. They were familiar with the statistics demonstrating that only those churches capable of reaching out to new people could flourish in the twenty-first century. They also knew the statistics about mainline Protestant churches in general — that for the most part they were on the decline, and that the role these churches had played as part of the cultural establishment in the United States was now shifting.[5]

But the very forces — both global and local — that were contributing to the decline of this former establishment were also contributing to the emergence of new but largely diverse religious movements. Indeed, the number who identify themselves as Christians and who worship regularly in the United States has actually risen, but this group tends to be evangelical Protestant or Roman Catholic. If a sociologist of religion like Peter Berger

---

4. It is interesting also to note that theologians who consider themselves to be "revisionist" were often raised in Christian backgrounds with very clear Christian identities (e.g., John Cobb and Gordon Kaufman), whereas those who are converts to the faith tend to argue for and presuppose Christian beliefs in their more traditional forms (e.g., Wolfhart Pannenberg and Eberhard Jüngel).

5. The most influential text on this is Loren B. Mead, *The Once and Future Church: Reinventing the Congregation for a New Mission Frontier* (Washington, D. C.: The Alban Institute, 1991). See also Stanley Hauerwas, *Resident Aliens: Life in the Christian Colony: A Provocative Christian Assessment of Culture and Ministry for Those Who Know That Something Is Wrong* (Nashville: Abingdon, 1989), and Douglas John Hall, *The End of Christendom and the Future of Christianity* (Valley Forge, Pa.: Trinity Press International, 1997).

or a theologian like Harvey Cox had predicted that we would be entering an era of secularization at the turn of the century, then their most recent work has argued for something very different.[6] The very issues that Tracy and Gilkey sought to address in books like *Blessed Rage* and *Naming the Whirlwind,* issues having to do with the post-Enlightenment critique of traditional religious belief, no longer seem to be issues for large segments of the population. Cox, who wrote *The Secular City* in the 1960s, best describes the new religious situation in a recent book on Pentecostalism:

> Even before I started my journey through the world of Pentecostalism it had become obvious that instead of the "death of God" some theologians pronounced not many years ago, or the waning of religion that sociologists had extrapolated, something quite different has taken place. . . . The prognosticators had written that the technological pace and urban bustle of the twentieth century would increasingly shove religion to the margin where, deprived of roots, it would shrivel. They allowed that faith might well survive as a valued heirloom, perhaps in ethnic enclaves or family customs but insisted that religion's days as a shaper of culture and history were over.
>
> This did not happen. Instead before the academic forecasters could even begin to draw their pensions, a religious renaissance of sorts is under way all over the globe. Religions that some theologians thought had been stunted by western materialism or suffocated by totalitarian repression have regained a whole new vigor. Buddhism and Hinduism, Christianity and Judaism, Islam and Shinto, and many smaller sects are once again alive and well. For many people, however, it is not always good news that religions that were once thought to be safely moribund or at most peripheral have again become controversial players on the world stage. We may or may not be entering a new "age of the Spirit" as some more sanguine observers hope. But we are definitely in a period of renewed religious vitality, another "great awakening" if you will, with all the promise and peril religious revivals always bring with them, but this time on a world scale.[7]

6. See Peter Berger, *The Desecularization of the World: Resurgent Religion and World Politics* (Grand Rapids: Eerdmans, 1999).

7. Harvey Cox, *Fire from Heaven: The Rise of Pentecostal Spirituality and the Reshaping of Religion in the Twenty-First Century* (Reading, Mass.: Addison-Wesley Publishing Company, 1995).

Ironically, the very factors linked with the decline of the influence of mainline denominations — factors like a global economy, a mass media of universal scale, and the pluralistic culture these engender — also seemed to correlate with the resurgence of traditional forms of religious belief and practice. Such belief and practice is often a direct response to the uncertainties of being part of a global capitalized economy where a mass media and potential for social mobility threaten the structure and moral fabric of families and the hold of traditional local cultures.[8]

In other words, one of the chief and most pervasive features of the world our students will be entering is that it is "globalized"; it is highly interconnected by a global economy and mass media. But at the same time, as many commentators have noted, such a world is also highly differentiated. It is characterized by high levels of reflexivity. Its different domains — such as the economic, the political, and the mass media — act upon and are, in turn, affected by one another.[9] As we have noted, even the spiritual and the religious — which, of course, includes what Christian communities do and who they are — are deeply enmeshed in this world, whether in their critique of it, or even in their participation in it.

Ironically, the very move toward globalization makes us only more aware of how *different* local cultures and traditions are. Indeed, as sociologists of religion have noted, globalization itself spurs on a desire to preserve those traditions in the face of uncertainty and change. The very decline of mainline Protestantism and the rise of other forms of Christian faith — and even other forms of religious and spiritual expression — cannot be divorced from other factors going on in the culture.

My students — especially the younger ones — were aware of something their elders were only vaguely becoming aware of. Many in the cul-

---

8. See, e.g., Martin Riesebrodt, *The Emergence of Fundamentalism in the United States and Iran* (Berkeley: University of California Press, 1993) and *Die Rückkeher Religionen: Fundamentalismus und der 'Kampf der Kulturen'* (Tübingin: C. H. Beck, 2000).

9. William Schweiker makes this point in an unpublished essay, "Beyond the Captivity of Theology: Toward a New Theology of Culture," presented at the Theology and Continental Philosophy Group, American Academy of Religion, November, 2000. Note the growing literature on globalization. See, e.g., Saskia Sassen, *Globalization and Its Discontents* (New York: New Press, 1998), and Roland Robertson, *Globalization: Social Theory and Global Culture* (London: Sage, 1992). For a theological discussion, see *God and Globalization*, vol. 1, *Religion and the Powers of the Common Life*, ed. Max L. Stackhouse with Peter J. Paris (Valley Forge, Pa.: Trinity Press International, 2000).

ture were ripe for what they had to offer as pastors and spiritual leaders, but the ways they would have to go about the task of Christian ministry would have to be very different from that of their predecessors who had studied at our seminary. What they wanted from seminary education was not only a set of skills or techniques for manipulating trends but insight into how God was present and active in this new and increasingly complex world. How could we best prepare them for the world they would be entering? How could we best educate them to be leaders of Christian communities who were, in the words of our seminary's missionary statement, "called and sent by the Holy Spirit, to witness to salvation through Jesus Christ and serve in God's world"? If their burning issues were not the "crisis of cognitive claims" that theologians like Tracy and Gilkey had responded to several decades ago — if, indeed, the spiritual potency of Christian belief already seemed to make sense to them — then how could we best prepare them to perceive and respond to God's presence and activity in the world, a world in which they were reflexively participating in forces both within and beyond their control?

An Institutional Context: From Abbey and Academy to Apostolate

I was not asking these questions in a vacuum. David Tiede, our seminary's president, was leading our institution in a shift from having been an "abbey" and "academy" to now becoming an "apostolate."[10] The predecessor institutions of our seminary had been established to train pastors who would minister to the primarily Scandinavian immigrant communities that had immigrated to the upper Midwest.[11] Initially these seminaries had functioned as "abbeys" in which seminarians lived, worshiped, and attended classes for several years before they went out into congregations to serve as pastors. In the 1950s and 1960s, as some of the brightest of these seminarians went off to graduate school in Germany or the major divinity

10. See David Tiede's address on the Lutheran and Episcopal agreement (*Call to Common Mission*) entitled "Paths as Yet Untrodden," given in St. Louis, Missouri, November 3, 2000.

11. For a discussion of the early immigrant communities that were the first constituencies of our seminary's predecessor institutions, see Todd Nichol, *All These Lutherans: Three Paths Toward a New Lutheran Church* (Minneapolis: Augsburg, 1986).

schools in the U.S., these "abbeys" were transformed into "academies." The historical-critical method, neo-orthodoxy, and process thought, among other emphases, were introduced into the seminary curriculum. The older inner-Lutheran debates between confessionalists and pietists in the seminary were now redefined in relation to conversations that were taking place in the larger theological academy. A new paradigm of seminary education emerged, with the "academy" providing the standard for what was to occur in the classroom. Lutherans were entering the American Protestant mainstream.

But just as they were entering that mainstream in the years after World War II, that mainstream was in decline. And as mentioned above, the very forces leading to the decline of mainline Protestantism were enabling the ascendancy of other forms of Christianity, and other forms of religious expression as well (such as New Age spiritualities). When Tiede became president in 1987 he was beginning to receive a new message from alumni and others in the church at large. To put it in the words of one blunt pastor, that message was: "Quit preparing your graduates for a church that no longer exists."[12] The seminary became aware of its need to address a new day and a new set of issues. A new paradigm was emerging, one oriented toward mission. Under the leadership of key faculty members like Patrick Keifert and Rollie Martinson, a curriculum reform took place that made mission the center of the seminary's education. In recent years, this reform has culminated in a series of initiatives both within the institution and among its "stakeholders" in the Lutheran church — members of congregations, donors, alumni, board members, the denomination's leadership, and so on — oriented toward rethinking the institution's structure and educational design so that it could prepare pastors for this new era.[13]

What surprised me was my ambivalence about these developments. I had grown up in the Philippines, the daughter of missionaries; my grandparents had been missionaries in China. My father had been part of a team of Filipino church leaders who trained lay leaders to start and nurture congregations. Theological education occurred in workshops and conferences

12. Quoted in Tiede's address, "Paths As Yet Untrodden," p. 3.
13. For work by faculty members that represents some of the thinking informing these shifts, see Partrick Keifert, *Welcoming the Stranger: A Public Theology of Worship and Evangelism* (Minneapolis: Fortress, 1992), and Craig Van Gelder, *Confident Witness — Changing World: Rediscovering the Gospel in North America* (Grand Rapids: Eerdmans, 1999).

held in congregations for short periods of time. We lived on the island of Mindanao in the southern Philippines, a frontier open to new ideas and new ways of thinking. Our island was not only a scene for interreligious conflict between Muslims and Christians. It was also a place where new religious, educational, and political ideas could flourish, not in intellectual ivory towers but at a grassroots level — from the many forms of consciousness-raising groups that emerged in post–Vatican II Catholicism to the range of charismatic revivals and Pentecostal movements that also flourished. As a young adult, I found a niche in similar environments, but in different parts of the world — Minneapolis, Toronto, and a refugee camp in Luzon in the northern part of the Philippines. Among other things, I taught English as a second language to Southeast Asian refugees preparing for resettlement in the United States and a "barefoot approach" to language learning to missionaries preparing for assignments where there would be no language school. I was deeply committed to ways of thinking and learning that empowered people to think and learn independently and in new and creative ways.

I intuitively associated participating in the reign of God that Jesus preached about and the ongoing activity of the Spirit in the church and world with this kind of learning and teaching.[14] When I began teaching at Luther Seminary after graduate school, I used the story of Cornelius and Peter in Acts 10 as a paradigm for thinking about theological education.[15] Recall that in this story Cornelius, the learner, is as actively involved in the learning process as Peter is. His vision, in which an angel tells him to invite Peter to his house, is the culmination of a life of prayer and giving alms to the poor. In turn, he is not the only one who undergoes a conversion in the story. Peter, who gives a speech about Jesus of Nazareth in Cornelius's household, a speech that leads to their conversion, also undergoes a conversion. He too receives a vision, in which a voice tells him to eat food that for him as a Jew is ritually unclean. Finally, throughout the story, both Peter and Cornelius are responding to a power and presence beyond them, the Holy Spirit that is guiding and leading them.

If, indeed, this had been my experience and those were my commit-

---

14. For a helpful discussion of the Holy Spirit and the reign of God, see Michael Welker, *God the Spirit*, trans. John F. Hoffmeyer (Minneapolis: Fortress, 1994).

15. I offer a theological exegesis of Acts 10 in *The Lectionary Commentary: Theological Exegesis for Sunday's Texts*, ed. Roger Van Harn (Grand Rapids: Eerdmans, 2001).

ments, why did I have such ambivalence about my seminary's shift from being an "academy" to being an "apostolate"? Why did I fear a loss of the "academic" thrust, especially when that thrust was no longer in touch with not only the expressions of Christianity that were taking hold in the United States, but even with the range of spiritual and religious movements outside of Christianity? Why in faculty meetings did I find myself sounding like a reactionary wanting to cling to an older phase in the seminary's life with its predictable debates between liberals and neo-orthodox confessionalists? What was I trying to preserve?

As I examined my reactions, I realized that I wanted to preserve a place for the kind of distance — the kind of reflection — I myself had sought in studying theology. What I wanted to preserve was a place for "leisure," to use a term Patrick Keifert introduced into our faculty deliberations. I wanted to preserve a place for "theory" understood in both senses as a kind of contemplative knowledge *(sapientia)*, on the one hand, and a technical specialization knowledge *(scientia)*, on the other. What I wanted to preserve was precisely the time and space in the Peter and Cornelius story for not only having visions but also for figuring out what they are about.

I had very specific fears about what would happen if the time and space for such theoretical reflection were lost. And here I was deeply informed about what I had intuited as a child and young adult growing up around charismatics and Marxists, missionaries and rebels. The leading of the Holy Spirit and the work of God's reign in the world is always more complex and nuanced than initially meets the eye. If a secularity and an overly intellectual Christianity had lost its potency — as the decline of mainline denominations was suggesting — then there were other dangers to avoid as well. One was a smug confessionalism, which could easily veer into a fideism that failed to be self-conscious of its own humanity and potential for perversity (or in theological terms, its own creatureliness and sinfulness), on the one hand, or the ways God was at work in the world outside of its preconceived categories, on the other. I had known too many evangelists or advocates for political change who, like Peter's first reaction to his vision, refused to acknowledge where the Spirit might be active elsewhere outside their own particular movements or positions, their own notions of orthodoxy or orthopraxy. Another danger was a pragmatism, or even an eclecticism, that simply worked with what succeeded, what enabled one to achieve one's objectives or meet one's needs, without relating the different dimensions of one's life to an overarching vision of how God was working either in one's own life or the worlds one found oneself in.[16]

I need to make clear that these were my *fears* and not the reality of what was being articulated in the various proposals for rethinking our seminary's curriculum. I wholly agreed with the overarching direction Tiede and other faculty members were leading the seminary. I simply wanted to ensure that the best from the "abbey" and "academy" phases of our institution's life were integrated into its new movement toward becoming an "apostolate." Thus the question: How could the range of theoretical inquiries (from, say, the social sciences and humanities) needed to help our students understand the complex, interconnected "globalized" world they were entering be integrated with a theological understanding of God's activity and presence in the world? How could we best learn and teach the apostolic tradition handed down through Christian history so that we and our students might best be prepared for the new transformations in thinking that would be required of us in a new era of mission in the world? How might our Lutheran confessional tradition be interpreted so that the full fecundity of its key concepts could be tapped for their generative power — concepts like "finite is capable of bearing the infinite" (*finitum capax infiniti*), giving witness to what bears Christ *(was Christum treibet)*, the justification of the ungodly and the priesthood of believers? How might the story of Cornelius and Peter be paradigmatic for how teaching and learning might occur in an era of mission? How might we as learners and teachers best prepare ourselves — whether we find ourselves in seminaries or even in congregations — for being open to the new gestalts, the new visions of ourselves and the world, that the Holy Spirit might be leading us into as we delved more deeply into the story of Jesus of Nazareth and interpreted its full implications for our highly complex and interconnected world?

---

16. It is interesting to note that in the recent encyclical *Fides et Ratio*, the current pope identifies these difficulties in the contemporary theological and intellectual context in a critique of "fideism" and "biblicism," on the one hand, and "pragmatism" and "eclecticism" which lead finally to "nihilism," on the other. For an interesting comparison, see Paul Tillich's discussion of "reason" in *Systematic Theology.* vol. 1 (Chicago: University of Chicago Press, 1952), where he questions "absolutist" reasoning (whether of a traditionalist or revolutionary kind) and also forms of pragmatism and cynicism.

Discerning God's Presence In, With, and Under
the Complexity of Our Lives

The kind of world we have described — this highly globalized world, with its interconnections and rapid change — is one that is going to need special kinds of leadership, special kinds of insight and maturity. In the words of psychologist Ellen Langer, what will be needed is not merely intelligence but "mindfulness," which she identifies with a range of capacities such as being able to perceive novelty and new distinctions as they emerge, being self-conscious of how context influences how one perceives and responds to the world, and being able to see things from multiple perspectives.[17] This is why "spirituality" has become so popular nowadays — especially in management and leadership literature — because it helps individuals and organizations get in touch with their core commitments and values and thus cope better with a rapidly changing environment. As we have noted, a global economy of unprecedented competitiveness is a continual challenge to human ingenuity and belief in ourselves. There is an increasing demand on individuals at every level of every institution, and not just at the top but throughout the system, for self-management, personal responsibility, self-direction, a high level of consciousness, and innovation.[18]

Within such a context, how the individual self thinks and feels becomes extremely important. Many contemporary people have been turning to spiritual exercises of all kinds because they have recognized that it is only when one surrenders to life that one can truly enact one's intentions. But at issue is not simply a means to better achieve one's goal or in the words of a best-selling self-help title, *How to Get What You Want and Want What You Have.*[19] At issue for Christians is discerning and responding to God's justice and mercy — which may not always lead to success, at least not success as many would define it. Luke's Jesus warns the rich, the full,

17. Ellen Langer, *Mindfulness* (New York: Perseus, 1990).

18. See Nathaniel Branden's description of the major developments in the past few decades in the national and global economy that have led to "making the need for self-esteem more urgent for all those who participate in the process of production, from the leader of an enterprise to entry-level personnel" in *The Six Pillars of Self-Esteem: The Definitive Work on Self-Esteem by the Leading Pioneer in the Field* (New York: Bantam, 1994), pp. 228-29.

19. John Gray, *How to Get What You Want and Want What You Have* (New York: HarperCollins, 1999).

the laughing and those whom all speak well of, and instead blesses the poor, the hungry, those who weep, and are hated, excluded, and reviled (see Luke 6:20-26). Of course, to feel "blessed" when one is being excluded one must have a fairly good sense of self-definition. Indeed, the culminating event of Jesus' career was the crucifixion, and though the stories of his life end with the resurrection and his sending of the "Holy Spirit with power" to his followers, they also make clear that this was not the end those followers had expected.

So how do we teach? And for those of us who teach, how do we ourselves learn how to perceive where God is acting, where the Holy Spirit is leading, in a fashion similar to the way Cornelius and Peter perceived it? How do we learn to interpret events so that it is God's justice and mercy we enact and not merely our own individual ends or those of groups that promote our interests — or the interests of our class, gender, race, ethnicity, theological or political persuasion, and so on?

The Lutheran theological tradition has some highly fruitful conceptual resources for understanding how to go about this task, which Tiede, our seminary's president, has appropriated for understanding our school's theological task in an age of mission.[20] One such concept is encapsulated in the phrase, *finitum capax infiniti* or "the finite is capable of bearing the infinite." It is rooted in the affirmation that God's promise and presence are at work *in, with, and under* the physical elements (bread and wine). Emerging out of the debates in the sixteenth century over the sacraments, the phrase expresses St. Paul's point in 2 Corinthians 4: "We have this treasure in clay jars so that it may be clear that this extraordinary power belongs to God and does not come from us." If we take the incarnation seriously — that the Word, indeed, became flesh and dwelt among us, and that God's glory is truly found there — and if we interpret this to have universal implications for what God is doing through Christ throughout the world, then certain implications follow. A central one is that all cultures can give witness to God's glory, and not merely in an arbitrary sense, but in a truly sacramental sense of being in and of themselves, in their very concreteness, the place where God's presence and activity is fully known and experienced. This means that any people's vernacular language, even religious practices of those formerly outside the faith, can bear Christ. It also

---

20. I have adapted these four concepts from Tiede's address, "Paths as Yet Untrodden."

means that no one particular human tradition can be sacralized because that would oppose the radicality of Christ's incarnation and its universal significance for all people (all human "flesh").

Of course, this makes the task of discernment highly essential. This is not a pantheistic affirmation that God *is* the world. It is still *God's* presence that is discerned in the finite. The criterion for Christians for discerning this presence is "what bears Christ" *(was Christum treibet)* — and Christ as Christ is depicted in the full complexity of the early church's interpretation of his life, death, and resurrection. All texts, practices, and traditions, even the Bible itself, are interpreted and judged by this norm. And this norm is quite remarkable. "Whatever does not teach Christ," Luther contends, "is not apostolic even if Peter or Paul teaches it." On the other hand, "whatever preaches that [Christ] is apostolic, even if it is done by someone like Judas, Ananias, Pilate, or Herod." What is at stake here is not simply some inner-Christian point for distinguishing among different Christian witnesses. What is at stake is the freedom to discern what, say, the disciples and James discerned in Acts: that the Holy Spirit was already at work among the Gentiles, preparing them for a similar encounter with the Holy Spirit.

The criterion of "what brings Christ" is accompanied by a corollary theme: that God justifies the ungodly. It is because of God's grace that we are made whole and complete, that our sins are forgiven and our wounds healed, not because of what we have achieved or possess. This, for Lutherans, is the confession by which the church stands or falls. What we are discerning is a power and love that we cannot control, a power and love that truly does transcend us. What this means is that any doctrine we formulate, any practice we enact, any decision we make — if it is to give witness to this power and love — can only be made in an act of repentance and gratitude. The Christian cannot boast of what he believes or what she has accomplished — politically, ethically, emotionally. She can only cling in faith to God's gift of grace in Jesus Christ and realize that her life has value precisely because it is gift — a gift she has received both as a creature and a forgiven sinner.

This means that she is able to shift the focus off of securing herself, by way of achievements, what she possesses. She need not control others, nor seek their approval. She knows who she is in God's eyes and that is enough. This gives her the freedom to attend to what others need. In classical Lutheran language, she is now free to "seek the good of the neighbor."

She or he is free to see things clearly — whether as a father or mother, a pastor, or a teacher; whether in business, education, or politics. And she or he can do this in the very messy complexity of life — in the very complex global world we find ourselves in, where different systems act upon each other, and choices, especially spiritual and ethical ones, are indeed complex and at times deeply ambiguous. She or he is free to do what can best enact God's justice and mercy, whether in the complex nuances of interpersonal relationships, in roles she or he plays, or simply through being a consumer and a political agent in a democracy.[21]

But to develop that sensitivity — that capacity for insight and transformation — she needs to be trained. Habits, ways of thinking, need to be cultivated over time. Cornelius was only able to perceive that something new was happening with the Christian movement because he had lived a life of prayer and gave alms to the poor. Peter was only able to break the rules because he knew what the rules were in the first place. He had been a good Jew and had struggled quite intensely with what it meant to be a faithful disciple of Jesus.

Thus, my students' desire for *catechesis* is right on target. They need to know what the Christian Scriptures teach along with key texts in the history of theological reflection on the life of faith. They need to know something of the history of interpretive strategies for approaching these texts, from the patristic and medieval allegorical methods (with their focus on a range of interpretive levels within a text — the literal, the moral, the anagogical, and the allegorical) to the Reformation focus on law and gospel to the modern and contemporary use of not only the historical-critical method but also the range of literary and sociopolitical forms of critique and analysis. As the global character of Christianity becomes more apparent, the multiplicity of approaches for reading the biblical and traditional texts will become even more apparent as previously ignored texts and aspects of those texts come to the fore. Increasingly, for example, we will be reading Christian texts in light of Muslim, Buddhist, Hindu, and especially in the United States, New Age questions about Christian faith.[22]

Throughout, the purpose is not simply to repristinate ancient texts

---

21. See David Tracy, *Plurality and Ambiguity: Hermeneutics, Religion, and Hope* (New York: Harper and Row, 1986).

22. See, e.g., Gavin D'Costa's argument in "The End of Systematic Theology," *Theology* 95 (Sept./Oct., 1992): 324-34.

(as though each new interpretation of them does not enact new meanings) nor to find some singular "essence" that they are really intending (as though the meaning of the texts were *actually* found, say, in some historical or existential world that lies beyond the text).[23] Rather, the purpose is to read them in their full complexity (as texts and the actual genres they represent). That task will involve rethinking many of our highly abstract common sense notions of how God is active in the world in light of the rich and complex relationships among the "multifarious witnesses of Scripture."[24] Following John Polkinghorne's observation in the Gifford Lectures of 1993/94 that "many theologians are instinctively top-down thinkers," Welker suggests a "bottom-up" reading of Scripture, one that takes seriously the complex ways God's presence and activity are depicted in creation, in Jesus' life, death, and resurrection, and in his Spirit's ongoing presence.[25] The result, he contends, will be an even richer understanding of "the vitality and *doxa* of God" and "the creative freedom of creatures." It will also entail destabilizing "old, long-transparent forms of dominion and self-preservation" in our thinking about God and God's relation to the world in order to appreciate — and experience — more fully "real joy in God's vitality, genuine fear of God, and the vitality of human experiences of God."[26] Such an inductive reading entails reading these texts not only in their original settings in life but in the range of ways they have been interpreted over time (their "efficacious history," to use Hans-Georg Gadamer's phrase), on the one hand, and in the range of ways they are interpreted and appropriated by Christians and Christian communities in the contemporary context, on the other.

Further, the point of mastering these texts is not simply to master some arcane body of knowledge or enclose oneself in a ghetto — either conceptual or communal. The purpose is precisely to be able to see ourselves and the world more clearly, that is, the very interpersonal and

23. See Paul Ricoeur, *Figuring the Sacred: Religion, Narrative and Imagination* (Minneapolis: Fortress, 1995).

24. See Michael Welker, "Christian Theology: What Direction at the End of the Second Millennium," in *The Future of Theology: Essays in Honor of Jürgen Moltmann,* ed. Miroslav Volf, Carmen Krieg, and Thomas Kucharz (Grand Rapids: Eerdmans, 1996), pp. 73-88.

25. See Welker's reference to John Polkinghorne, *The Faith of a Physicist: Reflections of a Bottom-up Thinker* (Princeton: Princeton University Press, 1994), p. 4 in his essay "Christian Theology," p. 78.

26. Welker, "Christian Theology," p. 75.

global worlds we find ourselves in. As pointed out earlier, the very complexity of a "globalized" world entails reflexivity. Different domains act upon each other and affect each other reflexively (e.g., the mass media, the economy, and even what is identified as the "spiritual" are in a very real way profoundly linked). As human agents we cannot divorce ourselves from this reflexivity, although we may find ourselves thinking, feeling, and acting amid circumstances we do not feel we as individuals have much control over. This is why so much leadership and management literature stresses the importance of "self-mastery" and "self-organization"; one has to be highly self-conscious about how one is responding to human-made systems that themselves act upon and influence each other.[27] If the spiritual intelligence we have been talking about has anything to do with how one actually lives in this world, it cannot be divorced from this reflexivity.

But for Christians the purpose of this spiritual intelligence cannot simply be about self-mastery or achieving one's purposes in the midst of a rapidly changing and sometimes chaotic world. The purpose is to discern how best to participate in God's justice and mercy in this world. A classic Christian understanding of what it means to die and rise in Christ is especially appropriate here. We have been baptized in Christ's death — and thus have "died to sin" — so that we too, like Christ, might be "raised from the dead by the glory of the Father, so that we might walk in newness of life" (Romans 6:4). At issue here is not only a death to being self-centered or "curved in on ourselves" *(incurvatus in se)* in an individualistic sense, to use a classical Lutheran phrase, desiring only our own ends as individuals and not the broader sweep of things (although it is also that). At issue as well is how we participate in systems — economic, political, and cultural — that seek particular interests, many of which are incompatible with God's reign of truth and justice (see, e.g., Romans 8:38-39 and its list of things we might fear would separate us from God's love).[28] Indeed, Jesus' death resulted from his confrontation with political and religious authorities.

But, further, it is not only critique and death that we are about but primarily life. The purpose of testing our biases and distortions — or more fundamentally our sin — is so that we can perceive the rich density

---

27. See, e.g., Peter Senge, *The Fifth Discipline: The Art and Practice of the Learning Organization* (New York: Doubleday, 1990).

28. Welker makes this point in "Christian Theology," pp. 84-86.

of God's goodness in the world, both in the natural world and in the very webs of interconnectedness we find ourselves in, whether on an interpersonal or institutional level.[29] For example, classical Protestants from Luther and Calvin to John Wesley and Jonathan Edwards presupposed conceptions of "vocation" that received "concrete institutional embodiment" in a range of spheres, such as the family, the government, and the church. In a different but nonetheless analogous vein, Roman Catholic ethics presupposed a differentiated, hierarchical conception of human goods or ends, in which human beings have a natural right to self-preservation even as they participate in a common, social good. Both sets of theological resources presuppose God's presence and activity. In the former, the norms and purposes of life are rooted in conventional patterns of interaction ultimately founded in God's fidelity to creation. In the latter, natural ends — human flourishing of individuals and communities — serve supernatural ends. These legacies offer complex symbolic and conceptual resources for thinking not only about how we might order our family lives in the contemporary world, but for how we might even think of ourselves and the Christian communities we are a part of as "ecumenical, worldly forces that can and may and must counterbalance [even] transnational, global agents."[30]

Thus the spiritual cannot be divorced from the cognitive. *Sapientia* (spiritual or theological wisdom) must embrace *scientia* (the other disciplines theology is reliant on, like the humanities, the social sciences, and now, even the natural sciences). Cognitive claims — that is, the rationality and intelligibility of beliefs — cannot be wholly abandoned. We only need to understand them in their full complexity. The very entanglements of our lives — whom we commit ourselves to love, what we buy, how we vote, how we spend our time, the basic attitudes, beliefs, and values we allow to influence our perception of the world — these are all the grist for

29. Bernard Lonergan's very helpful discussion of biases and distortions in theological reflection should not be overlooked. See *Method in Theology* (New York: Crossroad, 1979), especially chapter 10 on "Dialectic" and chapter 11 on "Foundations." Iris Murdoch is also helpful on this. See, e.g., *Metaphysics as a Guide to Morals* (London: Penguin, 1992).

30. William Schweiker, "Responsibility in the World of Mammon," in *God and Globalization*, vol. 1, *Religion and the Powers of the Common Life*, pp. 105-39. See also Mary Stewart Van Leeuwen's very insightful essay on the family in the same volume, "Faith, Feminism, and the Family in Age of Globalization," pp. 184-230.

the mill of theological reflection. These are precisely the places we experience the beauty and goodness of God's creation, the reality of sin and tragedy, and the healing and forgiving power of Jesus' resurrection and the new creation it entails. As Christians we live out of the hope of this new creation — in theological terms, we live eschatologically. As theologians like Paul, Luther, Pascal, and Kierkegaard have pointed out, such an eschatological perspective offers a radical critique of the limits of human rationality. But such hope is neither an otherworldly one that has no connection with our lives nor simply something enforced or juxtaposed upon facts that present a very different reality. If it is the true reality out of which we live our lives, then it has to be in touch with the reality of our lives, as that reality is understood from a range of perspectives. And that means the messy, often complicated, situations we find ourselves in — whether as individuals, families, institutions, or participants in a global economy.

The specific form such insight takes will vary. The complexity of the biblical texts themselves, and their rich diversity of genres, is testimony to that variety — from the "wisdom" that accounts for the best in nature and human intelligence (Proverbs 8) to the "folly" of the cross that confounds the wise and the debaters of the age (1 Corinthians 1:20-25). But the point of such insight is to perceive where God is at work healing and forgiving, even as the whole creation awaits its full redemption (Romans 8). The intelligence needed for such insight is, to quote a modern Jesuit mystic, François Roustang, "the power of the attention to the real, a respect for the facts that impose themselves upon us, an absence of obstinacy and a keen desire to penetrate the heart of things, beings or events."[31] Such intelligence is humble. It rejects ready-made theories, never thinks it knows enough, and doubts whether it has understood. It is open to new truths, continually capable of being surprised, and has a youthfulness of mind that consents to receive life from what actually is.[32]

So what is actually to take place in the classroom? The activities of teaching and learning will vary greatly depending on the learners and teachers — their personalities, needs, the situations they find themselves in, their age, social class, race, ethnicity, gender, and so on. Seminaries in this century will find that their shape and form will vary greatly — from

---

31. François Roustang, *Growth in the Spirit* (New York: Sheed and Ward, 1966), p. 201.
32. Roustang, *Growth in the Spirit*, pp. 201ff.

more traditional classroom settings to offering courses online with mid-semester retreats to workshops and sessions in local congregations. I would argue that there remains a place for the seminary as "abbey" — a place for retreat from the rest of life's complexity for concentrated study and prayer in community. And there remains a place for the kind of intellectual rigor the "academic" phase of seminary has required. But the way these dimensions of seminary education will be woven into the overall pattern of "educating leaders for Christian communities" will vary greatly in this century. What is not up for grabs is the task — that of discerning how God is at work *in, with, and under* the reality of our lives, discerning when it is Christ who is preached (whether by a friend or a foe, or by an insider or an outsider to the Christian community), discerning when and how God's goodness is being replaced by some blasphemous effort to be God (whether by the power of an individual or the systems that individual is participating in), discerning when and how to enact God's justice and mercy in the often messy complexity of life. Perhaps a Jesuit education remains one of the best models for learning and teaching in an apostolate, with its stress on a basic core set of practices and beliefs as outlined in the *Spiritual Exercises,* patterned directly after an understanding of how the Christian might intentionally participate in Christ's life, death, and resurrection. Such highly reflexive practices turn the participant outward toward apostolic engagement with the world, both Christian and otherwise, precisely as they help one develop a sense of interiority before God.

Much more could be said. More could be said about actual methods and modes of teaching. My own style combines Mortimer Adler's reading of classical texts with Paulo Freire's approach to reflecting on the circumstances one finds oneself in,[33] but each teacher must appropriate what works best for him or her and his or her own students. I have only dealt with the experience of a Lutheran seminary. Much more could be said about other Protestant seminaries, both evangelical and mainline, and Catholic and Orthodox seminaries. Much more could be said about what is going on in theological education throughout the world, especially as we become more fully aware of the fact that Christianity is truly a global phenomenon.[34] I have focused primarily on the seminary as an institution,

33. See my essay "Mortimer Adler, Paulo Freire, and Teaching Theology in a Democracy," *Teaching Theology and Religion* (June 1999).
34. I am grateful to Frederick Norris for his stress on this point.

but much more could be said about the new forms seminary education will take — from its use of online education and congregational sites to other patterns that will emerge in the future. More could also be said about the implications of my argument for the ongoing formation of adult Christians, on the one hand, and the design of Ph.D. studies, on the other.

My argument in this paper has simply been this. As my students and the leadership of our seminary have pointed out — along with other theological and sociological prognosticators — seminaries need to attend to the fact that they are educating leaders for a very different world than the one they prepared students for in the past. The model of "apostolate" may be a much more fruitful way of thinking about the design of the seminary than that of "academy." At issue in this new context may not be the task of defending Christianity's cognitive claims as much as learning how to use spiritual power appropriately. But that entails discerning God's justice and mercy in the full complexity of life, and to do that we cannot escape the difficult task of integrating the multiple dimensions of our lives. The difficult task of thinking remains, a thinking that requires not only self-consciousness about what we are doing as individuals, but self-consciousness about how we are part of much broader systems — interpersonal, economic, even natural — that act upon each other. Only that kind of hard thinking and teaching and learning can do justice to the truth and mercy of being "called and sent by the Holy Spirit, to witness to salvation through Jesus Christ and serve in God's world."

Teaching and Learning
as Ceaseless Prayer

MICHAEL BATTLE

But we appeal to you, brothers and sisters, to respect those who labor among you, and have charge of you in the Lord and admonish you; esteem them very highly in love because of their work. Be at peace among yourselves. And we urge you, beloved, to admonish the idlers, encourage the faint hearted, help the weak, be patient with all of them. See that none of you repays evil for evil, but always seek to do good to one another and to all. Rejoice always, pray without ceasing, give thanks in all circumstances; for this is the will of God in Christ Jesus for you. Do not quench the Spirit. Do not despise the words of the prophets, but test everything; hold fast to what is good; abstain from every form of evil.

1 Thessalonians 5:12-22 NRSV

I AM A PRIEST. I am also a professor. I am a theologian whose vocation is visible through the covenants of teaching and prayer. Through my vows as a priest and my work as a professor, I have come to understand my teaching vocation in a divinity school classroom as the kind of ceaseless prayer that the apostle Paul calls all Christians to in his first letter to the Thessalonians. If we understand the classroom as a collection of individual strivers, this may make no sense. But if we can imagine our classrooms as discerning communities working together toward a common goal, Paul's words might have much to say to us.

Paul teaches the church in the above passage of Scripture that to pray without ceasing assumes that we have entered into a covenant in which we pledge to seek the other's good, never repaying evil for evil, rejoicing always, always being thankful, being at peace and helping the weak. It is my belief that Western Christian spirituality has so focused on the individual's relationship with God that it has lost sight of the role such covenants must play in the life of prayer. Without covenants, ceaseless prayer is unintelligible, its practice impossible. Paul teaches us that prayer need not be understood solely in an individualistic sense. Such an expanded understanding of prayer without ceasing has had an enormous impact on my classroom teaching.

I wish to argue that ceaseless prayer, practiced within a community undergirded by covenants, ought to be recovered as part of the sensibility of the theological teacher. I will begin by reflecting on my own experience as a professor and priest. I will then offer a definition of prayer as the ceaseless activity of practicing God's presence. I will propose apophatic prayer as a form of ceaseless prayer that is crucial for our healthy relationship with God as opposed to our worship of an idol: to worship ourselves, to be trapped in individualistic spirituality apart from community, dries up prayer and causes it to cease. I will then discuss my understanding of covenant as a form of ceaseless prayer that is practiced through the maintenance of authentic community. Finally, I will offer a portrait of what such community looks like in a classroom.

My Vocation of Prayer

Not long ago, listening to a friend of mine preach in a maximum-security prison unit, I heard an inmate interrupt the sermon to rebuke some inconsiderate inmates talking in the corner. "Shut up!" he growled, staring at them with wild eyes. The others laughed as he gritted his teeth. Earlier, I had seen this same inmate beating the top of his head with both hands to the beat of "Blessed Assurance." A black man, ill clad, wearing white and faded blue, he lived in a different world than the rest of us and he wanted to get on with "church." But his interruption did not seem to stop the others.

With peculiar gyrations he repeated his command to "Shut up." In the middle of my friend's sermon he screamed at these black men, "Are you in church or where you at?" A peculiar question, I thought. How could he really expect others to believe this was a real church service in the middle of a maximum-security prison unit? Sure, they had sung hymns, and there were ministers in the room, and there was a lectern posing as a pulpit, and there were musical instruments for praising God, and the chairs were lined up in the room for an assembly of people, and they even prayed to God as if God were truly there. But how could he really expect to be "at" church? The rational explanation is that he had never learned to perceive reality accurately. His command to "Shut up" and his question, "Are you in church or where you at?" provoked me to analyze the nature of my vocation in a divinity school classroom, a setting that claims to be an environment where people are corporately attentive to the reality of God. Although the analogy between a divinity school classroom and a maximum-security unit may seem incongruous, I contend that the prisoner's question could also be asked by a divinity school professor. How does one introduce spirituality to a group of people who no longer communally practice the presence of God?

In order for a sense of vocation to be intelligible for professors in seminary or divinity school settings there need to be practices of God's presence discernible by both teacher and student. No longer can divinity school professors be ashamed of spiritual disciplines that clearly exhibit their vocation. But such a vocation requires work and patience.

> Then [Jesus] said [to the disciples], "Suppose one of you has a friend, and he goes to him at midnight and says, 'Friend, lend me three loaves of bread, because a friend of mine on a journey has come to me, and I have nothing to set before him.' Then the one inside answers, 'Don't bother me. The door is already locked, and my children are with me in bed. I can't get up and give you anything.' I tell you, though he will not get up and give him the bread because he is his friend, yet because of the man's boldness he will get up and give him as much as he needs. So I say to you: Ask and it will be given to you; seek and you will find; knock and the door will be opened to you. For everyone who asks receives; he who seeks finds; and to him who knocks, the door will be opened. Which of you fathers, if your son asks for a fish, will give him a snake instead? Or if he asks for an egg, will give him a scorpion? If you then, though you are

157

evil, know how to give good gifts to your children, how much more will your Father in heaven give the Holy Spirit to those who ask him!" (Luke 11:5-13 NIV)

Jesus teaches us that prayer is an ongoing pursuit, an activity that never ceases. The verbs to ask, to seek, and to knock in the above pericope are all expressed in Greek in imperfect tenses. Grammatically, this passage teaches that prayer must become our way of life, our way of seeking God's best intentions for our life. The emphasis is not simply on asking and receiving, as some popular evangelists are wont to say, but on the way of life of Jesus' disciples, who have learned to practice God's presence continually. This means that prayer is better understood as our disposition toward God, rather than our words of petition.

On our best days in the classroom, theological teachers are like the inmate, beating our heads, looking for God in unexpected places. Our vocation as teacher is intelligible only through ongoing spiritual practices that continue to make sense of God's presence in our midst. Once such presence is assumed, then our speculation discovers proper agency. Understanding prayer as a way of life that continually practices the presence of God facilitates our needed growth of all that we are — body, spirit, and intellect. The practice of integrated growth toward God, as a grapevine grows toward sunlight, is what I define as ceaseless prayer.

Teachers in divinity school, whose work is to articulate God's presence on behalf of the Christian community, are essential to such growth in others. The church has set aside space and time for divinity school teachers to train in our vocations so that we may help equip pastors and teachers for ministry. As the vocation of a divinity school professor becomes clear through a long education process and often an ordination process, the Spirit through inner promptings prays for us to lead the world out of individualism and academic competition. Like John the Baptist, the teacher warns people who are headed away from the kingdom of God to "shut up" and know God. The vocation of a divinity school professor is not only to articulate how to know God in our midst, it is also to know when to "shut up" in the midst of God's presence. The teacher's vocation is to know how and how not to know God through text and experience.

As a black Anglican priest (ordained in South Africa) and professor of spirituality and black church studies at Duke University, how I make sense of my dual identity is through the practice of teaching others to love

God on a continual basis. This means that my students learn to love God with their minds as well as through their love of neighbor. Teaching my students to love God on a continual basis is what I understand ceaseless prayer to be. I understand prayer to be more than words and thoughts, but a manner of life predisposed to loving God. I avoid prayer as a mere concept because it then becomes either an abstraction that lacks reality or a monologue of an individual's musings. Conceptual prayer has become the normative understanding for the Western world, which places the locus of knowledge with the individual. I name this Western emphasis individualism, which can appropriate prayer only through individualistic practices.

When I was a seminarian, I attended a church in which the pastor proceeded to take out his clipboard during the intercessions. The pastor asked the congregation for "the prayer requests from the Body." He then began to jot down notes and record the antiphonal responses from the congregation. I noticed that most of the prayer requests did not reveal intimate knowledge about the particular person who spoke. The prayer requests were usually to "pray for the mail man who needed Jesus" or to "pray for my great grandmother who was entering the hospital." No one ever requested prayers for deliverance from sexual temptation or selfishness. Once these superficial requests came from "the Body" the pastor proceeded to "lift them up in prayer." He proceeded to pray as if he were informing God about things God did not know about. It was as if the pastor needed to wake God up from some kind of slumber. "Dear God, we just want to ask you right now to be with us, to help the mail man who is struggling with his faith, to visit Jenny's great grandmother who just entered the hospital."

As a result of such a redundant understanding of God's presence, I now teach my students, who lead their congregations in prayer, that if prayer is to be intelligible, prayer must be understood as continuous and communal. My mantra in teaching is that understanding prayer as "my personal relationship with God" is the bane of Western spirituality. In order to counter such individualistic assumptions, I have learned through my experience to define prayer apophatically. To define what prayer is does not help my students, formed in an individualistic culture, to understand their complicity in superficial practices of God's presence. Of course, the best practices of prayer are both conceptual (cataphatic) and critical (apophatic), but I privilege apophatic prayer in the teaching context because it helps my Western students see that the apostle Paul's understanding of ceaseless prayer makes sense through the practices of recognizing God's presence. Apophatic prayer is the process of stripping cultural and anthropomorphic images of God so as to remind the community that what we think of as God is not the living God. God is always much more than we can think or imagine. Since we will always be cultural and communal beings, apophatic prayer must be a continuous and ceaseless process of reminding Christian disciples that God is not our creation.

Praying Apophatically

Apophatic prayer is prayer without ceasing, a spiritual discipline that requires us to be constantly removing stagnant images and concepts that often replace the presence of the living God. Simone Weil helps me explain, through her concept of attention, how apophatic prayer is ceaseless prayer. Weil believes that our love for God is cultivated as we learn to bring our whole attention to God. For Weil, love does not seek to produce anything greater than ourselves. Love only produces mutuality. Any effort of love stretched toward God does not reach God without God's grace. For Weil, it is only after a long and fruitless effort that ends in despair, when we can no longer expect anything, that, from outside ourselves, the gift of God's presence comes as a marvelous surprise. This stripping process is needed because it provides a history in which we can recognize the false sense of fullness and finally recognize God's presence. In other words, we cannot know God without a history of mutuality. This is also Augustine's understanding that "to know God is to love God."

Weil's concept of attention helps me see that the call of Christ is to love God and others even through despair. Our love for God, which produces our knowledge of God, makes us long to increase our attention to God's presence. This need to seek God in all things facilitates a coherent understanding of my vocation as priest and professor in which I no longer polarize academy and church. In other words, I no longer see my vocation in either the church or the academy. I can no longer accept the church's conviction that by an onrush of emotion the skepticism of the academy can be permanently dissolved, or the academy's that skepticism is as virtuous as critical thinking.

In order to bridge the gap between church and academy, I propose that prayer contains elements of both hope and despair, faith and skepticism. Our restlessness for God contains within it the tensions that often represent both the church and the academy. In prayer, I learn as a priest and professor that I must constantly be attentive to God in our midst without convincing myself that I understand God. In other words, I learn to practice God's presence apophatically, which ironically offers me a contentment I have not had before. I learn that I need not simply play the role of a professor or the role of a priest. Practicing the living presence of God through apophatic prayer allows me also to understand my vocation as teaching others to love God so that they may know God. Apophatic prayer, however, requires both a history and a community in order for it to be understood.

Apophatic prayer requires a history in the sense that I learn to recognize God retrospectively. A history has to occur in which I can see how I have responded to God and my neighbors as priest and professor. And from such a history my experience has been that people identify either with my priestly vocation or my professorial vocation. Perhaps I just don't know what it would mean or look like for someone to relate to me as both priest and professor. To be granted such cohesion to my vocation, however, to be both priest and professor, is a matter of grace, because the academy and the church are usually vying for sole vocational allegiance, for a choice between prayer and scholarship. In other words, neither the academy nor the church seems able to receive one's full, complicated history.

Prayer requires a community because I cannot just rely on my own experience of God to come to know God; I must rely on others' experience with God to make God known to me. Through such mutuality I gain a better understanding of my integral vocation as priest and professor, in which I am able to answer why I teach certain courses and read and write certain books. And, as I will discuss shortly, what I understand as authentic community is largely understood through my particular narrative as a priest and professor who understands unity in diversity, especially as such unity relates to the broad spectrum of instructional techniques in a classroom. As diversity becomes a more significant concern in the academy, the teacher's attention toward God, three persons in one nature, ought to influence how he or she can facilitate the learning of diverse students in one classroom.

Prayer and Covenant

Jesus teaches the disciples that prayer occurs where two or three gather; in other words, prayer is not the monologue of an individual making requests to the deity. Instead, prayer is more like a form of covenant among a community. More particularly, ceaseless prayer is understood and practiced through covenants because we learn the authenticity of our prayers through our covenants with each other. In other words, to know if our prayers make sense, we need to test them out in a community. In this sense, the pastor with his clipboard may have rendered a good service to his congregation by helping them test their prayers. But that pastor could improve his congregation's prayer life by facilitating a history of common prayer in which the congregation learns to discern an authentic presence of God.

As a community recognizes their history of prayer together, they will see retrospectively where their prayers were authentic or where they were simply entertained by their own monologues and shopping lists. From a history of common prayer my experience has been that people's prayers are flavored with either hope or despair. Prayers are hopeful as the pray-er looks back, with the help of community, and discovers personal symmetry with God's will. More and more I am convinced that prayer is understood retrospectively. It can only be recalled through communal covenant. Jesus teaches the disciples that his presence is discovered through covenant: "Again, truly I tell you, if two of you agree on earth about anything you ask, it will be done for you by my Father in heaven. For where two or three are gathered in my name, I am there among them" (Matthew 18:19, 20). At the very least, a historical covenant has to occur in which I can see what I in fact needed and how I in fact survived the situation in which I was praying.

Prayer requires mutual covenant because no one can know God alone. To know God is to love three persons in one nature, an image of God that disallows individualistic spirituality. Loving God with all of who we are and loving our neighbor as ourselves makes sense of ceaseless prayer. As I discuss below regarding a diverse classroom, the greatest difficulty is practicing this covenant in which we must pray with and for those who are much different than ourselves. The constant struggle to love those we would rather not love becomes a ceaseless prayer. Therefore, the call to love God and neighbor is indistinguishable from our call to prayer. Walter Wangerin states,

You discover *what* the covenant is in the painful, passionate business of living it out. And, if the covenant is real, if the commitment is real — even not knowing the future, even though we have no idea what the covenant is going to be — then a third being comes to exist between us (the parties who make the covenant).

Prayer derived from covenant has a life of its own, and it will grow given the opportunity. But, when an individualistic society lacks communal sensibility, covenants cannot flourish. Community is important to a definition of covenant because community acts as buffer against the inevitable suffering that will come under the covenant and with the covenant, but it is not a wasted suffering. Often, it is a generative suffering, a creative suffering, though it is nonetheless suffering. Wangerin says also:

> . . . but if [suffering] arises out of covenant, then those who have made the covenant can grow wise and strong. They can grow into something different from what either one of them was, because the suffering forced them into new territory. Then the covenant becomes the blessing.

This is why the community is crucial to an understanding of prayer without ceasing. Not only must an individual make a covenant between the self and God, the individual must enter community in order to solidify the covenants we have with God and our neighbor. Through community we determine through grace and gritted teeth to what extent our covenant with God and each other is real. Indeed, we discover such reality or illusion in the confines of the church. Our covenant with God is a blessing from the beginning even though at times it feels like imprisonment. Our journey is difficult because we find it hard to believe that there is such a thing as covenant anymore. It blesses individuals into community because it holds a communal attention together while individuals discover what the covenant is and what the communal relationship is going to be. The covenant describes a new and different world in which to discover and work out what may seem like disparate relationships. Hence, covenants take time, in fact, require time. There must be trust that the other person is not going to cut and run. When students are too eager to retreat into individualistic modes of education, covenants cannot flourish.

The vocation of teaching is integral to the communal process of discerning the flourishing life of God, because what is learned is learned in the midst of covenant. People do not select their deepest relationships beforehand; they are discovered in life's journey. So, too, persons discover God's continual presence through the communal process in which one may look back and reflect that there was in fact an abiding presence of God. "I'm so glad I decided to teach Isaac the Syrian," a professor may pray as the discovery is made that her former student has just completed a dissertation on a spirituality of tears. Or a Hebrew Bible professor may despair as she listens to her former student preach an anti-Semitic sermon. In both cases, the act of remembering allows the professor to see the vocation of prayer more clearly. Those who pray hopefully describe their careers and jobs as vocations in which God calls them to new and exciting responsibilities. Those who pray with despair often do not understand their groans and sighs as prayer, only as complaints and self-mutter. Those who despair often think that their fragmented response could never be a language of prayer. But all of this, all of this, is the ceaseless prayer of the teacher.

Prayer in School

So far in this essay, I have sought to show how prayer is more accurately understood as ceaseless prayer, namely, that one cannot know God without the desire of the whole being to love God and neighbor on a continuous basis. For the remainder of this essay, I address the connections between this understanding of prayer and my vocation in the classroom. A classroom should be an environment of prayer akin to the miracle of God's presence at Pentecost, in which God's Spirit helped people in a multicultural context discover a common language by which to describe reality.

> When the day of Pentecost had come, they were all together in one place. And suddenly from heaven there came a sound like the rush of a violent wind, and it filled the entire house where they were sitting. Divided tongues, as of fire, appeared among them, and a tongue rested on each of them. All of them were filled with the Holy Spirit and began to speak in other languages, as the Spirit gave them ability.
>
> Now there were devout Jews from every nation under heaven living in Jerusalem. And at this sound the crowd gathered and was bewildered,

because each one heard them speaking in the native language of each. Amazed and astonished, they asked, "Are not all these who are speaking Galileans? And how is it that we hear, each of us, in our own native language?" (Acts 2:1-8 NRSV)

These questions of amazement present the problematic in what I propose: What does it mean to pray in the classroom? "I don't pray in my classes," one of my colleagues told me, "because I don't want my students to confuse the difference between thinking and feeling." The rationale against prayer in the classroom usually follows this logic: Teaching, after all, requires objective criteria by which scholars dispense information to their students in such a way that a critical facility is needed; therefore, prayer in the classroom prevents any serious intellectual growth by students as they need to learn how to think clearly about the subject matter.

I cannot see the logic in such dichotomizing. Further still, I am against the above logic because of my own classroom experience. The following narrative proves my point.

My class, in which about twelve Master's students grappled with theological texts on forgiveness and reconciliation, met on Tuesday afternoons. For each class my students are required to read and write on a regular basis; for each of them this means short papers each week. This discipline has a twofold purpose: first, to prevent the survival mode of merely cramming for courses, and second, to create stimulating and pithy discussions by having each student come better prepared for class. It was the second purpose that created the critical incident.

One particular student made me see myself as more than an objective teacher. In fact, this student made me see teaching as my vocation of prayer. For the purposes of this essay I will call her Nancy. It was a typical class period. I lectured the first half of the class — the subject for the day was the concept of theodicy and the irony of forgiving God. The reading assignment was from David Blumenthal's *Facing the Abusing God*. When our class took its usual break, Nancy passed out her written work, as required, to the entire class. Each student was required to present his/her weekly writing to the entire class; the class would listen to the student's presentation and then proceed into class discussion and make written comments on the paper. At the end of the class everyone would return their copies to Nancy.

We were ready to begin. As Nancy began reading her paper she stopped suddenly in tears. She slowly resumed her reading pace as she described her survival of an attempted rape. Although I seek the kind of classroom that Parker Palmer describes as a space to "invite the voice of the individual and the voice of the group," we were nevertheless shocked by Nancy's honesty and vulnerability. Literal silence prevailed for an extended time on that Tuesday afternoon. My confusion in the silence had me wrestling with which identity to assume: teacher, police officer, counselor, priest, etc. One male student was visibly angry and told Nancy she should prosecute the "son of a bitch" who attempted the rape. Another female student rose from her chair and put her arms around Nancy.

In many ways this class session is what I have in theory longed for, i.e., an encounter in the classroom in which students and teacher abandon the pretense of objectivity and commence with the difficult work of being conscious of who each other is in relationship to the text. When I experienced this critical incident in my teaching, however, through Nancy's powerful engagement with my class and her own life, I discovered that I was leading my class in what I have articulated as ceaseless prayer. They had developed a history in a mutual covenant that allowed them to risk intimate knowledge of the other. In other words, they were seeking God not only in the text but through each other's lives in relationship to the text. I call this mutual seeking ceaseless prayer, but such prayer did not lessen the stripping process of how a classroom came to know God in their midst.

If I understood my vocation in some static sense, I would have aborted the life of prayer in our classroom. When Nancy took our classroom beyond the normal boundaries of self-disclosure, we discovered ourselves similar to those in Acts who gathered at Pentecost. We all should have been confused by Nancy's different language of conviction, but surprisingly we were not. I should have been confused as to what my identity as teacher should be in this critical incident with Nancy, but I was not. To our surprise, we understood each other's language. Even though I work to give my students such openness to the unexpected, I learned with Nancy that such work in a classroom also involves transformation of individuals into a community.

Because I am a self-conscious, academic person my attention was on the proper etiquette of academic discussion. I wanted to avoid an onrush of emotion that might turn my classroom into a therapy session. But Nancy evoked from me my true vocation as a teacher. I was in need of the other to know myself.

A new image came to mind: teacher as mediator of transformation. Such transformation in the classroom is a movement from pretense to authenticity. It is from this incident in the classroom that I formulate the vocation of theological teaching through the transformative movement of prayer. Teaching is a communal process that relies on the desire to move from ignorance to understanding. These are the movements of prayer in the Christian mystical tradition, in which the movement of prayer contains three levels of ascending order: purgation, illumination, and union. In this regard, Paul in his Epistle to the Romans illustrates my meaning of ceaseless prayer through the following pneumatology: "Likewise the Spirit helps us in our weakness [ignorance]; for we do not know how to pray as we ought, but that very Spirit intercedes with sighs too deep for words. And God, who searches the heart, knows what is the mind of the Spirit, because the Spirit intercedes for the saints according to the will of God" (Rom. 8:26, 27 NRSV). It is my conviction that such a vision of ceaseless prayer becomes vital to sustaining the vocation of the theological teacher.

An understanding of how prayer is integral to the meaning of community guards against what I understand as a prayerless classroom, an environment void of transformative movement. Here, I do not take the so-called fundamentalist position of classroom prayer in which you pray in the same tone as you pledge allegiance to the flag. For my colleagues who overcompensate to avoid such a fundamentalist label, I offer them the irony that teaching as ceaseless prayer increases diversity in the classroom. Nor do I assume a Western individualism in which prayer is an individual's manner of informing God of what God does not know. What I have in fact proposed in this essay is an unconventional understanding of the vocation of a divinity school professor, in which the one who prays may function as a teacher who may increase the skill of discernment among students. I attempt now to display what such unconventional prayer looks like in a multicultural classroom.

Prayer and Diverse Community

In the Acts of the Apostles we learn that God's Spirit at Pentecost teaches a diverse community to live in mutuality. Because of the Spirit, the community's prayers have a life of their own, and given the opportunity such prayers will grow into a single chorus. God's Spirit blesses our diverse dis-

167

course in a way that we can be intelligible to each other, allowing us to learn how to pray more continually, without ceasing, through community. Such prayer occurs as the Spirit prays in us while holding us together through our covenants. In unceasing prayer, diverse persons discover what their covenant is and what the relationship is going to be. Herein is the vocation of the theological teacher, namely, to describe among one's students a new and different reality of God that is continuously practiced through each other's relationships. More particularly, the vocation of a theological teacher tends to be marked by the following characteristics:

(1) covenantal (gets class to agree to covenant in the beginning);
(2) discerning (adjudicates students' progress in a wholistic manner);
(3) adaptive (responds spontaneously to the needs of the class);
(4) innovative (allows for the creative potential of students);
(5) interpersonal (facilitates communal identity of a classroom).

Few instructors can be expected to exhibit all of these characteristics, but student success seems to correlate with the presence of these characteristics in the classroom. It is up to individual departments, deans, and provosts to provide the types of incentives that foster the enhancement of these teaching competencies in the classroom. One must be careful, however, not to seek immediate results.

By understanding prayer without ceasing in relationship to the classroom, I have learned that I will seldom see the results of my vocation as a priest and professor. As a professor trying to get my students to make a true confrontation with evil in our lives, by what criteria would I measure the difference I've made in their lives anyway — letter grades? The rewards of the vocations of priest and professor are not easily discernible. In the story of the judgment in Matthew 25, Jesus teaches that we cannot know what is best for us without reference to our neighbor.

Observance of the difference a theological vocation makes in how we teach, write, and read involves *attente*, attention to God's love, an operation that cannot be hurried. Herein is the arduous nature of our vocation to both love God and teach about God — namely, we are required to have humility, perhaps the ordering virtue for my hybrid identity as priest and professor. Humility is the subjective counterpart of the operation of grace itself. As Simone Weil states, "Humility is endless, and *attente* is humility in action."

168

Proper attention to God's will, namely, prayer, tests the intentions of the person praying; i.e., true attention to God's will disallows the treatment of others as means for ends. So it will always be difficult for me to see what difference I make in people's lives, because prayer will continually train me not to seek rewards. True prayer trains persons beyond the contradictions of survival and grace.

In all of this I find an affinity with the Eastern Church, which places emphasis not on the typical Western dualisms of rationality and faith, of freedom and will, but on our relation to what God has already revealed in the world: most importantly, the salvation of the world in Christ. But such a revelation does not require control or domination on our part; neither does it claim a banal observation of a "new heaven and new earth" already complete on earth. Instead, because this approach aligns with my own particular history as a priest and professor, it better enables me to see that God created us to be responsible for others, in fact to know our identity through them. God desires that our movement toward the divine life be a movement of participation, a life that implies freedom.

Bibliography

Anderson, J. "Cognitive Styles and Multicultural Populations." *Journal of Teacher Educators* 39, no. 1 (1988): 2-9.

Carter, R. T. "Cultural Value Differences Between African Americans and White Americans." *Journal of College Student Development* 31, no. 1 (1990): 71-79.

Cooper, G. "Black Language and Holistic Cognitive Style." *Western Journal of Black Studies* 5 (1981): 201-7.

Friere, P. *Pedagogy of the Oppressed*. New York: Seabury Press, 1970.

Gilligan, Carol. "Remapping the Moral Domain: New Images of Self and Relationship." In Carol Gilligan, J. V. Ward, and J. M. Taylor, eds., *Mapping the Moral Domain: A Contribution of Women's Thinking to Psychological Theory and Education*. Center for the Study of Gender, Education and Human Development, no. 2. Cambridge, Mass.: Harvard University Press, 1988.

Gollnick, D. M., and P. C. Chinn. *Multicultural Education in a Pluralistic Society*. New York: Merrill, 1990.

Green, M. F., ed. *Minorities on Campus: A Handbook for Enhancing Diversity*. Washington, D.C.: American Council on Education, 1989.

Hale-Benson, J. E. *Black Children: Their Roots, Culture, and Styles* (rev. ed.). Baltimore: Johns Hopkins University Press, 1986.

Jackson, B. W. "Black Identity Development." In L. Golubschick and B. Persky, eds., *Urban Social and Educational Issues.* Dubuque, Iowa: Kendall/ Hunt, 1976.

Kochman, T. *Black and White Styles in Conflict.* Chicago: University of Chicago Press, 1981.

Kolb, D. A. "Learning Styles and Disciplinary Differences." In A. W. Chikering and Associates, eds., *The Modern American College Responding to the New Realities of Diverse Students and a Changing Society.* San Francisco: Jossey-Bass, 1981.

—————. *Experiential Learning: Experience as the Source of Learning and Development.* Englewood Cliffs, N.J.: Prentice Hall, 1984.

Lesser, G. "Cultural Differences in Learning and Thinking Styles." In S. Messick, ed., *Individuality in Learning.* San Francisco: Jossey-Bass, 1976.

MacGregor, J. "Collaborative Learning: Shared Inquiry as a Process of Reform." In M. D. Svinicki, ed., *The Changing Face of College Teaching.* New Directions for Teaching and Learning, no. 42. San Francisco: Jossey-Bass, 1990.

Palmer, Parker. *The Courage to Teach.* San Francisco: Jossey-Bass, 1998.

Ramirz, M., and D. R. Price-Williams. "Cognitive Style of Three Ethnic Groups in the U.S." *Journal of Cross-Cultural Psychology* 5, no. 2 (1974): 209-12.

Tomlin, E. W. F. *Simone Weil.* New Haven: Yale University Press, 1954.

Wangerin, Walter. "The Door Interview." *The Wittenberg Door,* 1989.

—————. *A Miniature Cathedral.* San Francisco: Harper & Row, 1987.

Weil, Simone. *Gravity and Grace.* New York: Putnam Press, 1952.

THEOLOGICAL TEACHERS
IN THEIR SCHOOLS

"Yea, the Work of Our Hands, Establish Thou It": On Stability in the Academic Life

CLAIRE MATHEWS McGINNIS

Introduction

The Rule of St. Benedict is a sixth-century document outlining a way of life for monastic communities that is at once both unflinchingly practical in its details and thoroughly spiritual in its aim. While on the one hand it addresses such mundane issues as the proper amount of food and drink, on the other it speaks of the monastery as "a school for the Lord's service" whose pupils learn to "run on the path of God's commandments," their "hearts overflowing with the inexpressible delight of love."[1] Perhaps it is Benedict's insistence that these two, the mundane and the loftier aspects of our lives, go hand in hand, that is responsible for *The Rule's* enduring influence not only on monastics, but on the lives of lay persons as well. But surely what has been equally fundamental to its perceived applicability to the laity is the fact that, although the pattern of life Benedict sets out is meant for a monastic community, its goal is that shared by all Christians, namely, "responsiveness to . . . the gospel and the Spirit."[2] As Esther de

---

1. See *RB 1980: The Rule of St. Benedict in English* (Collegeville, Minn.: The Liturgical Press, 1981), chs. 39-40 and Prologue, p. 49.
2. Daniel Rees et al., *Consider Your Call: A Theology of Monastic Life Today* (London: SPCK, 1978), p. 49.

Waal observes in her discussion of Benedict's use of Scripture, "The primary concern of the Rule is to confront us as forcefully as possible with the Gospel and all its demands."[3] And it is for this reason, because *The Rule's* goal is "to confront us . . . with the gospel," in such a distilled and practical form, that *The Rule* still has something to say to us, more than fourteen centuries after its composition.

In this essay I will argue that *The Rule* addresses the vocation of the theological teacher in a special way. But, given that Benedict's *Rule* is the expression of wisdom gained from his own trials and experience as a Christian and monastic, it seems fitting first to say a word about how the suggestion that *The Rule* might have a special applicability to the life of the theological teacher arose within the context of my own life. Perhaps it is not too great an exaggeration to say that *The Rule of St. Benedict* saved my life. It happened during my first year of motherhood. I had been an assistant professor for four years, and was granted a research leave. My husband and I spent this leave time at the Institute for Ecumenical and Cultural Research in Collegeville, Minnesota, which happens also to be housed on the campus of St. John's University and Abbey, now the largest Benedictine monastery in the world. During that year we were also graced by the birth of our first child, a daughter, Killian. When we returned to Baltimore, and I to teaching, I found myself torn between conflicting demands in an unprecedented and painful way. The conflict was one that arose both out of the limitations of time, and of the question of identity. I was not happy to keep my daughter in day care for long days to enable me to teach and keep up in my research in the manner to which I had grown accustomed. While I had once been content to live, as it were, in my office, putting in long hours even after dinner, I now found myself having to cram a full day's work between the hours of 10 and 3. When Killian was home with me her needs were all-consuming and unrelenting in a way I had never imagined. And so I was consigned, it seems, to a life of total chaos: of coming to class feeling ill-prepared, of walking away from the office in mid-task, the piles of papers accumulating around me as I tried desperately to shift gears from play dough to Plato and back again. Parenthood is not conducive to the reflective life.

Perhaps it would not have been so bad had I had a simple nine-to-

---

3. Esther de Waal, *Seeking God: The Way of St. Benedict* (Collegeville, Minn.: The Liturgical Press, 1984), p. 32.

five job — an occupation. What I had instead was a vocation — a task that came as a call, and as such, gave both great meaning to life and a strong sense of identity. But my newly acquired vocation to parenthood seemed to reveal fault lines in the old one. How could I consider myself a "real" academic when I seemed to be reading and writing so little, when I was conducting class on a wing and a prayer, when the first thought on my mind when having lunch with departmental colleagues was how they handled certain parenting issues, rather than how they read a particular section of Thomas Aquinas? I loved my job, yet not a day went by when I did not think of quitting it, not only for Killian's sake but for my own.

This is where St. Benedict entered in. I was spending much larger amounts of time in the car than ever before, and I found here an opportunity: not only an opportunity to pray, but to read. I searched and found on our shelves a single book on tape, Esther de Waal's *Seeking God: The Way of St. Benedict;* it would have to do. I found in de Waal's exposition of *The Rule* a way of holding the seemingly fragmented pieces of my life in a coherent whole; of reconciling my vocation as mother and academic as part and parcel of the same. I discovered that the three Benedictine vows of stability, obedience, and *conversatio morum,* as limiting as they might at first seem, help one make peace with the disorienting array of demands that arise from wearing multiple hats. But equally important, or more so for the present discussion, I found that approaching one's vocation as a theological teacher in the light of these vows opens up a way for an academic to find coherence among the varied activities of teaching, research, and service; to develop an institutional relationship that nurtures one's growth as a scholar; to broaden one's view of one's vocational trajectory; and to deepen one's understanding of the vocation itself.

I have already suggested that one primary reason *The Rule* is applicable to monastic and lay persons alike is because its goal is to confront the reader "as forcefully as possible with the Gospel and all its demands."[4] It should also be noted, however, that the Benedictine life is one characterized by a sense of balance among one's activities, and by moderation, for, as Benedict himself writes, "In drawing up [these] regulations, we hope to set down nothing harsh, nothing burdensome."[5] It is these factors that also contribute to *The Rule's* relative accessibility to the laity as opposed, for in-

---

4. de Waal, *Seeking God,* p. 32.

5. *RB 1980,* Prologue, p. 46. See de Waal's discussion of balance in *Seeking God,* ch. 6.

stance, to more extreme forms of the religious life. But what is it about *The Rule,* or about the vocation of the theological teacher, or even about the academic life, that makes such a Benedictine analysis of our profession particularly appropriate? The staples of Benedictine life are *ora et labora* — work and worship. Indeed, the monk's day, as Benedict envisioned it, would have been divided up by periods of prayer, manual labor, and (religious) reading. In this regard, the monastic's day would have borne some resemblance to our own, ideally, although the amounts of time spent at each activity surely differ. This similarity is not a superficial one. For the monk's engagement in reading was akin to the hours spent in the oratory, the aim of both being to have the word of God take root and dwell in one richly. For the modern academic the act of reading has arguably been corrupted: we are pushed by the ever expanding corpus of publications to read faster, to read widely rather than deeply, to know what has been said in our field rather than reading to know the one by whom we are known. But ideally, inasmuch as the aim of the theologian is the knowledge of God, though in a peculiarly intellectual way, then the act of reading ought also be for us an activity that is complementary to, and in fact, a kind of prayer.[6]

With regard to manual labor, Benedict saw its value partly in its warding off idleness. But work also serves as part of an integrated life in which the monk perfects the ability to move from one activity to another in such a way that he or she gives full attention to each and so achieves the "stability of heart" which is the aim of the monastic disciplines.[7] The old stereotype of the academic is of one who cannot be bothered with manual labor. But for many of us, the manual tasks of one's life, or the kind of manual labor one might choose, such as chopping wood, serve as moments of refreshment. One cannot do intellectual work all the time. But even those tasks that don't clear the mind, grading papers for instance, have an analogy in the thankless tasks that all the monks of the monastery, regardless of previous station in life, were asked to share. And so, I will argue, we have much to learn from them about how tasks that don't seem to relate directly to the practice of our vocation might be seen, at least, to have a bearing on it.

6. On the recovery of religious reading see Paul J. Griffiths, *Religious Reading: The Place of Reading in the Practice of Religion* (Oxford: Oxford University Press, 1999), and Michael Casey, *Sacred Reading: The Ancient Art of Lectio Divina* (St. Louis: Liquori/Triumph, 1996).

7. On this see the discussion in de Waal, *Seeking God,* pp. 60-64 and 149-54.

My assumption that *The Rule* speaks to the vocation of the theological teacher in a special way is also based on certain assumptions about the relationship between this vocation, and one's vocation as a Christian.[8] The first assumption is that one's vocation as a Christian is the primary one, and one's vocation as a theological teacher is subordinate to the first. Put another way, the commitment to being Christian governs (or ought to govern) the teaching vocation, shaping one's interests, one's decisions about time allocation, and generally, one's choices about how to fulfill the demands of one's job. It also means that, while one could continue to be a Christian were one no longer teaching, if one were to renounce one's Christianity but continue to function as a faculty member, one would no longer be fulfilling the vocation in quite the same way. A more likely scenario, one short of outright apostasy, is one in which the practice of one's vocation is no longer consonant with one's vocation as a Christian — say, if one wrote and taught primarily to advance one's own interests rather than those of the Kingdom of God, or if one interacted with students in such a way as to demean and diminish them. In such a case one might still be teaching theology, but one could hardly consider this fulfilling one's "vocation." It should be apparent from these comments that in speaking of the vocation to teaching as subordinate to that of being Christian I am by no means suggesting that one's vocation as a teacher is ancillary to one's life as a disciple, but is itself one very central way in which we respond, on a daily basis, to Christ's call to "Come, follow me." For those of us who understand our role as theological teachers to be a vocation, and hence in itself a kind of calling rather than simply an occupation, practicing this vocation, and the way in which we practice it, is an integral part of our Christian practice.

My second assumption concerns motivation. I think it's safe to venture that most of us teaching theology, or teaching theologically, were led into this work because it in some way resonated with our own journey toward God. In other words, we are not in this because of the money, or because it is a good job (although surely it is that), or even fundamentally out of a love for students, but because of the love of God. And here I intend all of the ambiguity of Paul in such a phrase: both our love for God, and the

---

8. There is some debate about whether one need be a Christian to teach Christian theology. While recognizing the existence of this debate, I will not attempt to enter into it directly in this essay, which is addressed to those who view teaching theology, or teaching theologically, as a Christian vocation.

love of God for us, if these can be at all separated. Once ensconced in a particular position in a particular university, in the midst of all of the "lesser" tasks such as committee work and grading papers, we may press on simply because it is our job. But in our best moments we press on to know the Lord. And when we envision our vocation in this way, I believe, the three vows of Benedictine life — stability, obedience, and *conversatio morum* — can instruct us in a pattern of life in which our two vocations, as Christians and as theological teachers, might become more fully integrated and more effectively fulfilled.[9] In this essay I will focus on stability, and how attention to this Benedictine vow might inform our lives as theological teachers.

A Posture of Stability

In chapter 1 of *The Rule*, Benedict distinguishes four kinds of monks: cenobites, anchorites, sarabaites, and gyrovagues. The monastic life *The Rule* envisions is a cenobitic one, wherein monks "belong to a monastery" and "serve under a rule and an abbot."[10] His description of the monks called gyrovagues offers some insight into Benedict's understanding of the role of stability in a monk's formation. The gyrovagues, he writes, "spend their entire lives drifting from region to region, staying as guests for three or four days in different monasteries. Always on the move, they never settle down, and are slaves to their own wills and gross appetites."[11] He draws a connection here between these monks' transiency and their enslavement. Conversely, stability, standing in one place, is meant to lead to a kind of freedom.[12] Stability finds its expression in multiple ways. Benedict envisions it on the one hand as communal and geographic stability — a monk makes a commitment to be part of a particular community of persons in a particular locale. On the other hand, communal and geographic stability are not an end in themselves, but a means to an end, which leads us to the

9. In what follows, my understanding of *The Rule* and its application depends quite heavily on the works of Esther de Waal, *Seeking God: The Way of St. Benedict,* and Daniel Rees et al., *Consider Your Call: A Theology of Monastic Life Today,* beyond the material specifically footnoted.

10. *RB 1980,* 1.1.

11. *RB 1980,* 1.10.

12. See de Waal's discussion of restriction versus freedom in *Seeking God,* p. 55.

deeper meaning of stability. What is sought is "stability of the heart," a continual commitment to conversion, to persevering in one's search for God.[13] Communal and geographic stability are a necessary, but not sufficient, means to attain this.

Seen positively, communal and geographic stability meet a fundamental human need:

> The world is not simply something given to man as an object to be examined and put to use. The world is man's home at the present time. But being at home in the world implies a certain rootedness, "a grafting on to the local scene." This human need to be rooted in a particular locality is behind the monastic exercise of stability with reference both to material objects and to people. A tree often transplanted does not bear fruit. A man usually comes to know himself, and in that knowledge to know God, when he dwells for long periods in a stable relationship to places and persons. The sense of belonging which is generated by familiar surroundings tends to create a focus for man's awareness, so that he is able to ask himself, "Who am I? Where have I come from and where am I going?" This sense of belonging grows even more from stability in relation to persons, from knowledge of the constancy and predictability of persons established over a long period of familiarity, and from mutual trust, love, respect, and appreciation which come about only with time and struggle. There is a close link between the questions, "Who am I?" and "Where am I?" Through his incarnate situation man discovers his identity and his true relation to God.[14]

At the same time, "Stability ensures that [a monk] will not evade the cross. . . ."[15] When confronted by difficult circumstances there is always the temptation, the danger, of running away, of avoiding, not only the situation, but the opportunity that situation affords for facing oneself. Ultimately, it means the failure to participate in the sufferings of Christ.[16] While the requirement of one's physical presence in a community cannot ensure that one engages in the process of conversion, it at least makes the

13. Rees, *Consider Your Call,* pp. 137-40.
14. Rees, *Consider Your Call,* p. 141.
15. Rees, *Consider Your Call,* p. 138.
16. See de Waal's discussion, *Seeking God,* pp. 55-58.

possibility more likely. "Stability involves both bearing from day to day the inevitable trials and disappointments which are part of human life *and profiting from them*."[17] De Waal delineates the relationship between stability of place and of heart most sharply in her assertion that "monastic stability means accepting this particular community, this place and these people, this and no other, as the way to God."[18] Obviously, one would not want to claim that God could be found only in this monastery and not that one, only in this way of life and not another. Her claim seems to be, rather, that if one is to find God, it will be in that which is real and present: "The man or woman who voluntarily limits himself or herself to one building and a few acres of ground for the rest of life is saying that contentment and fulfilment do not consist in constant change, that true happiness cannot necessarily be found anywhere other than in this place and this time."[19]

Communal stability, as distinguished from geographical stability or enclosure, "is a matter of commitment to situations and persons," and thus something that can be expected of all persons, and not just monks.[20] It seems especially applicable to, and instructive for, married persons and those with (or in) families, for a family community, no less than a monastic one, daily confronts an individual with difficult circumstances, as well as sustaining ones. As de Waal observes:

> . . . so many people find themselves in the situation of enclosure, in a marriage or a career, with the fundamental difference that by their refusal to accept it has become a trap from which they long to escape, perhaps by actually running away, perhaps by resorting to the daydreaming which begins with that insidious little phrase, 'if only . . .' Family life which is boring, a marriage which has grown stale, an office job which has become deadening are only too familiar. *Our difficulty lies in the way in which we fail to meet those demands with anything more than the mere grudging minimum which will never allow them to become creative.*[21]

She continues by speaking of the role such limitation plays in creativity. "Artists must submit themselves to the necessities imposed upon them by

17. Rees, *Consider Your Call*, p. 138, emphasis added.
18. de Waal, *Seeking God*, p. 57.
19. de Waal, *Seeking God*, p. 57.
20. de Waal, *Seeking God*, p. 58.
21. de Waal, *Seeking God*, p. 59, emphasis added.

paint and canvas, by words or notes or stones." What is true for the artist is likewise true "in the less obviously rewarding situations of daily life." Indeed, ". . . the way in which such limitation can bring both freedom and fulness is the heartening paradox of the Benedictine understanding of stability." The key, she argues, is that one must "attend to the real" and listen "to the particular demands of whatever this task and this moment in time is asking."[22] "When we have discovered that a necessity is really necessary, that it is unalterable and we can do nothing to avert or change it, then our freedom consists in the acceptance of the inevitable as the medium of our creativity."[23]

Although one must exercise caution in drawing too strict a parallel between the monastic and other forms of life, I would argue that the notion of stability can be instructive also in academic life in the way it models a particular approach for relating both to one's work and one's institution.

When I was offered my first teaching job one of my teachers commented that the institution making the offer might be "a good place to tear your pants." I understood him to be saying that it was not a bad place to start out, to make my mistakes, to get used to teaching, to build a repertoire of courses and establish a publishing history before moving on to some place "better," perhaps some place with a bigger name. This comment was troubling to me. It seemed to trivialize what I perceived to be the particular strengths of that school, and to undermine the enthusiasm and commitment I was prepared to bring to the practice of my vocation in that place. In essence, the comment seemed to be saying, "that would be a good institution to pass through." It represented for me one model of relating to one's work and one's institution, characterized by an overemphasis on what the institution could do for me: How much prestige might being at that institution confer, for instance? What might be the mix of so-called "real" work — writing and research — as opposed to "grunt" work — teaching, grading, serving on committees? As it turns out, I have not only torn my pants there, I have mended them. And there I will probably also wear them out. I am lucky, it is true, to have been hired by an institution that was so well suited to my abilities and interests. But it is also true that teaching in that institution has changed me, has changed the way I think

22. de Waal, *Seeking God*, pp. 59, 60.
23. de Waal, *Seeking God*, p. 60. Here she is quoting, although the particular source is not cited.

and the way I teach, the way I write, and how I understand what it is I am doing there. Had I taken my teacher's counsel too seriously, I would inevitably have always been searching for that better offer. Under such conditions, I suspect, I would have found less satisfaction doing the work at hand, found it difficult to become personally invested in the long-term vitality of the school and its student body, and missed the particular opportunities for growth that being at that institution afforded. Such a tenuous institutional relationship would also inevitably have had an impact on how I continued to identify my peers; I would still be thinking of my primary peer group as the "guild" — my colleagues, say, at the AAR/SBL, rather than at my home institution. I am not arguing that a biblical scholar, for instance, ought not think of other biblical scholars as one's peers. But if one thinks of these as one's only peers, or even as one's primary ones, again, one has missed an opportunity to deepen one's own sense of vocation, and one's practice of it.

How might applying Benedictine notions of stability to one's own life as a theological teacher change one's perception of one's work, and as a result, change the way one goes about it? How might Benedictine notions of stability offer a model for relating to the various people and tasks presented by one's being situated in a particular institution? As we have seen, the vow of stability implies a long-term commitment to persons and situations. And at a deeper level it involves accepting "this particular community, this place and these people, this and no other, as the way to God." Given that one finds oneself at an institution relatively appropriate to one's talents, what would it mean to think of one's institutional colleagues and students in such a way? I am not proposing that the workplace replace church, nor that an academic institution be a church. What I am proposing is that we take seriously the Benedictine conviction that work and prayer go hand in hand — that work supports the life of prayer, and indeed, that one's work can and ought to function as a kind of prayer. The goal for the Benedictine is to be attentive and responsive to God at all times, in all tasks. This is the goal of geographic and communal stability. This is stability of the heart.

In my own experience, viewing one's work in *this* place with *these* people as the way to God alters the practice of one's vocation in wonderfully fruitful ways. But notice already how placing one's work within the framework of stability has helped shift one's understanding of what one's vocation is. It is not to advance the state of our knowledge, to publish, or even to teach well. One's vocation is to find and be found by God, and in our particular cases, to find and be found by God through reading and writing and teaching in our own disciplines, in our own institutions.

Placing our work within the framework of stability allows a deepening of one's sense of what one is doing. It is easier not to be distracted by superficial concerns: my standing in relation to others in my department, or the slower-than-expected progress on my research. For our journeys toward God are always strikingly different, and advancement in this real work is never limited by the pace or outward signs of progress. In essence, placing our work within the framework of stability helps us to "keep our eye on the prize." Assuming a posture of stability also allows an underlying coherence to emerge among tasks that heretofore seemed disparate. For no task, whether meeting with students or attending a department meeting, can really detract from one's "real" work — from that which is really one's real work: knowing God, as individuals and as a community of inquiry. Thus one is more able to see how these various tasks, some more welcome than others, fit together in a larger project and work toward a common goal. In light of the ultimate concern toward which one's work is directed, routine consultations with students or colleagues hold new possibilities. One listens, I would suggest, with greater openness, looking for Christ's face in theirs, and seeking to reflect his face in one's own. This does not shield us from the inevitable trials and disappointments that are part of life in an academic community. But even these may be turned to gain inasmuch as one is more able to meet them as an opportunity to persevere with patience, to participate in the sufferings of Christ. And, just as one offers all of one's tasks up to God, so also, when one views one's vocational life as the way to God, one is more easily able to place it in God's hands.

Perhaps what I am saying here might become more concrete through illustrations from my own life. I am in some ways fortunate to find myself in a department of what I consider to be academic superstars; my colleagues are all delightfully smart, boasting long publishing records, and are well-respected in their sub-disciplines. While I am most appreciative to be among them, their accomplishments have also been occasion for comparison to my own, particularly in my years of anxiety — unfounded, as it turns out — over tenure. While many of them are also parents, all but one of them are male and have wives, most of whom do not work full-time, which mitigates the pressures of parenthood. (Not to mention that none of their children have gestated in, come forth from, and been sustained by their own bodies.) I do not begrudge them this. I simply point it out to note how treacherous collegial comparison can be. In moments of greatest self-doubt, what has sustained me is the grace to perceive my academic vocation in a larger framework. First, I had to remind myself why I was teaching in a theology department in the first place: not for my own glory, or even simply to make a living. I had pursued my doctoral degree because I found in my studies a way of coming to know God, and I had chosen teaching as a profession because of its evangelical role — because I hoped that in studying theology my students might also come to know God. Seen in this light, it didn't really matter whether or not I got tenure, for, I realized, my primary vocation was in being a Christian, and I could do that just about anywhere. But, trusting that I would get tenure, I also began to view my contributions to, and standing in, the department in the long term. What did it matter, really, if my professional trajectory didn't directly parallel that of my colleagues? If, rather than a steady upward arc of publications, my "publication graph" showed an upward arc pre-parenthood, which then slowed for a few years, only to resume its course as my children grew more independent? God had surely called me to parenthood, a most Christ-like project in its demands for *kenosis;* how could I perform my duties as a biblical scholar and theological teacher with any integrity if I were at the same time neglecting the most needy in my midst? It is unfortunate that publishing pressures are the greatest early in one's career, when a scholar ought to be building up intellectual capital and deepening his or her thought. And for women, it is unfortunate that the pre-tenure years almost always coincide with the prime childbearing ones. While I am not advocating the abolishment of tenure, I am acknowledging the ways in which the demands of our profession, as currently structured, may have a distorting effect. Placing our work within the framework of stability helps in countering the more detrimental effects of such forces. It may, for instance, temper external pressures to produce published work prematurely, or simply for the sake of publishing.

As I have attempted to illustrate, viewing our work in a context of stability allows a deepening of one's sense of what one is doing, and enables one to keep one's eye on the prize. But a posture of stability also allows an underlying coherence to emerge among tasks that heretofore seemed disparate. I have already suggested above, for instance, that there is an integral relationship between how we respond to our responsibilities as members of particular communities, such as families, and our integrity as

Christian theologians. But let me say more. For a Benedictine, communal and geographic stability is a means through which one might achieve stability of heart, understood as the ability to be attentive and responsive to God at all times, in all tasks. When one has achieved such an inward stability, being asked to move from one task to another is no longer viewed as an interruption or distraction, for one perceives the unity of purpose amidst disparate demands. So, for instance, a professor who embodies such stability of heart would not find that knock on the door — a student come to talk about a paper — an irritant, as much as an opportunity to meet Christ in the student as much as in the text from which one's attention had been drawn. One could say the same of distractions more tangential to the practice of our specific vocation. Brevard Childs used to tell the divinity students at Yale, "If you want to become a better exegete, become a deeper person." Here was the recognition that how we read, how we think, and what we write are informed by the larger contours of our life. If a biblical scholar has any hope of her readings giving flesh to the word, it will only come through the embodiment of that word in her own life. It has been this reminder, along with that from Benedict that all of our tasks point to the same goal, that has given me confidence that tasks such as classroom preparation, time spent with students and with my children, do, and will, ultimately contribute to the quality if not the quantity of my publications. This confidence is proven well founded when I compare, for instance, my first book, a *bibelwissenschaftliche* study of Isaiah 34–35, with a later essay, an "Ignatian" reading of 1 Samuel.[24] The latter grew directly out of teaching biblical narrative to students in a Jesuit context, and my own experiences in discernment. Had I not been attentive to the needs and questions of my students, that study might never have come forth, and yet it is work I consider of far more value than the earlier one.

In providing illustrations from my own life I don't want to suggest that life at Loyola College is by any means perfect. My colleagues have their quirks, not only those within the department, but especially those outside of it. We are not all rowing in the same direction, or even in the same boat,

---

24. I am referring here to *Defending Zion: Edom's Desolation and Jacob's Restoration (Isaiah 34–35) in Context*. Beihefte zur Zeitschrift für die alttestamentliche Wissenschaft, Vol. 236 (Berlin: Walter de Gruyter, 1995) and "Swimming with the Divine Tide: An Ignatian Reading of 1 Samuel," in *Theological Exegesis: Essays in Conversation with Brevard S. Childs,* ed. Christopher R. Seitz and Kathryn Greene-McCreight (Grand Rapids: Eerdmans, 1999), pp. 240-70.

and this does indeed make life together challenging. I was once witness to a query about the relationships among the monks at St. John's Abbey, to which one wise brother responded, "when you know you're going to live with these people a long, long time, you learn to get along." This monk was expressing in personal terms something that can be stated more generally: that in a monastic community stability entails, in part, facing others' shortcomings with patience and acceptance. Daniel Rees describes the patience with one's fellow monks' shortcomings precisely for what it is: incarnate love. "A monk loves his own community," he writes, "not as unchangeable or static, not as already perfect, *but as the sacrament of the divine mercy in his life.*"[25] The community is a tangible expression and a tangible means of God's mercy. Certainly, trust is much more difficult to achieve in an academic setting than in a monastery, for not every individual there will share the same level of commitment or the same understanding of that to which they are committed. Nonetheless, I have found that if one tries to achieve a similar sense that it is in this work and in this community — in this and no other — that he or she is to find and be found by God, the shortcomings of one's colleagues are kept in perspective, and one is rather naturally able to take the long-range view. This may express itself as patience (long-suffering), a willingness to continue to work with those colleagues on committees and projects that shape the institution. Or, this long-range view may be shown in a willingness to invest one's energy in efforts that may not gain one easy recognition or that might bear fruit only in the long run, tasks such as shaping a department, mentoring others, or participating in any of the thankless tasks necessary for the sustained well-being of that institution.

It may seem that I am suggesting that wherever we are, we ought to stay put. But I am not. It may be that one finds oneself at an institution ill-suited to one's training or talents. Not everyone, for instance, is called to undergraduate teaching. And, just as life in a virtuous community may be formative, so life in a community that is not virtuous, in a community that is highly dysfunctional, can be malformative. There may be other more complicated reasons why an academic cannot stay put, such as the demands of a dual-career marriage. What I am suggesting, however, is that wherever we are, for however long, we ought to approach our life and work there in the posture of stability, with a commitment to those persons and

25. Rees, *Consider Your Call,* p. 140, emphasis added.

that situation as the way to God, to the end of achieving stability of heart. "Stability in the sense of some geographical space is unattainable and irrelevant," writes de Waal. "Stability in terms of some internal space, that we can carry around, is something attainable, though not necessarily without considerable hard work and perseverance."[26] She recounts the reflections of Henri Nouwen during his stay in a monastery:

> He knew that he wanted to be different, to attract attention, to do something special, to make some new contribution. Yet the monastic situation was calling him to be the same, and *more* of the same. Only after we have given up the desire to be different and admit that we deserve no special attention is there space to encounter God, and to discover that although we are unique and that God calls us each by name, that is completely compatible with the unspectacular, possibly the monotony, of life in the place in which we find ourselves.[27]

If the God who found us did so by becoming human, then that God can surely be found by us in our quotidian tasks: perhaps more easily in reading and writing, but also in lecturing, slogging through another tedious exam, correcting grammatical errors, assigning grades, sitting on committees. If we cannot find the God who suffered among us there, how shall we find him anywhere? More than likely finding God there will not mean enjoying those tasks any more. It will mean doing them with the mindfulness that in all things God is to be glorified; doing them with the same intensity required of Simon of Cyrene as he lugged Christ's cross to Golgotha.[28]

But stability is also of evangelical value. Writes Rees, "to live in community is to make the approach to Christ more clearly visible."[29] To the degree that an academic community cannot be church, so it cannot serve as the same kind of witness as a community of monastics. But a little leaven leavens the whole lump. At Loyola College in Maryland I have seen how the devotion of one or two individuals, practitioners of the inward and outward expressions of stability I have attempted to describe, have profoundly shaped the attitudes and practices of their younger colleagues, and

26. de Waal, *Seeking God*, p. 61.
27. de Waal, *Seeking God*, p. 61.
28. Luke 23:26.
29. Rees, *Consider Your Call*, p. 142.

so built a community within a community, at least, that models "faith seeking understanding." When the entire faculty was Jesuit, the presence of that community had as deep an impact on the students as the subject matter in the classroom. In theory at least, a lay faculty bears witness to something as well, say, the value of disciplined inquiry, of openness to truth. One hopes, though, that at a religiously affiliated school such as Loyola the witness of the faculty community might be more clear: that we are engaged in pursuit of the truth because of our longing for the one who is Truth; that we are engaged in the pursuit of truth in a manner worthy of it; that we invite you to participate in that pursuit of the truth, with the same rigor, and with the same love that we have shown you in our interactions with you. If we fail to bear witness in this way, then, I think, we have not fulfilled our vocation.

Conclusion

The author of Psalm 90 expresses beautifully the tensions between the centrality of work to human life and its apparent futility in the light of our mortality. His thought moves from the observation that the days of our life are only "toil and trouble; they are soon gone, and we fly away" to an impassioned plea: "Let the favor of the Lord our God be upon us,/and establish thou the work of our hands upon us — /yea, the work of our hands, establish thou it."[30] In his *Rule* for the monastery St. Benedict expresses the same awareness of the dual possibilities of work as simply toil and trouble, or as something of which we might appeal to God, "establish thou it." "Every time you begin a good work," Benedict counsels, "you must pray to [God] most earnestly to bring it to perfection."[31] It is not simply the perfection of the work itself that Benedict has in mind here, but the perfection of the worker as well. And here Benedict sounds a theme that runs throughout the entire *Rule:* that work is not a good unto itself, but a means by which a monk might respond to God's call.

Of all of the monk's activities, the *opus Dei* is, as it were, the first among equals. I have argued that for us also, whose vocation as theological teachers is embedded in our vocation as Christians, it is the *opus Dei,* the

30. Psalm 90:10 and 17 RSV.
31. Prologue, p. 4.

work of prayer and praise, that governs all of our other work. As theological teachers, research and teaching are likewise central to the practice of our specific vocation. But as I have also argued, simply performing the tasks of research and teaching are not enough. In this essay I have tried to point toward, to model even, a particular way of practicing our vocation that has the potential for gathering up all of the various threads of our lives into a seamless whole, but which, more importantly, is appropriate to the end of all theological inquiry — to find and be found by God. Fundamental to this way of practicing our vocation is stability within a community: a willingness to bear from day to day the inevitable trials and disappointments of living and working in a particular setting, based on an acceptance that for me, at this particular place and time, this place and these people — this and no other — is the way to God. The counterpoise to this stance of stability is captured by another of the Benedictine vows, *conversatio morum,* understood in one sense as an openness to change: to allow living and working in a particular community to change us and to change the shape of our careers.[32] But such an openness to change involves, by definition, practice of the third of the Benedictine vows, obedience, in its most fundamental form, namely, as attentiveness: attentiveness to hearing God's word in our reading and writing, of course, but also attentiveness to those with whom we are engaged in a common project, and attentiveness to the demands that present themselves in our unique situations. In practicing our vocation in the light of the Benedictine vow of stability, I contend, we do so in a way that is true to the gospel demand that we lose our lives in order to gain them. We also thereby participate in the plea of the psalmist and St. Benedict himself — an audacious plea in view of our transiency and seemingly inescapable imperfection: Let the favor of the Lord our God be upon us, /and establish the work of our hands — /yea, the work of our hands, establish thou it.

32. de Waal, *Seeking God,* pp. 59 and 69.

Vocation in the Outback

FREDERICK W. NORRIS

VOCATION ALWAYS HAS A HOME BASE, but not all locations are equally attractive. One difficulty for some who have finished Ph.D. or Th.D. programs in religious or theological studies is that their experiences in a fine graduate school have influenced them to forsake considering teaching positions in the outback. Yet the job market remains clogged with many more applicants than posts.[1] These budding teachers long for the colleagues, the libraries, and the cities that have nurtured them toward their present achievements. Some now flounder while teaching part time in more than one institution within a major city, with little or no hope of tenure, health benefits, or retirement security. They sense that only if they stay around the university, where they can finger the pulse of the job market and be on hand for interviews, will they have any chance of success.

Others take positions in the hinterland and dream incessantly of leaving. They go to the cattle calls at national meetings, read lists of openings, write letters of application, and know that soon they will be on their

---

1. In a rather conservative analysis Russell McCutcheon notes that 50 percent of the newly minted Ph.D.s find work. Even that figure is true only if one-year and other temporary appointments are included. While the number of degrees awarded since 1970 has increased 33 percent, the number of available positions has declined 30 percent in public universities and 12 percent in private institutions ("The Crisis of Academic Labor and the Myth of Autonomy: Dispatch from the Job Wars," *Studies in Religion/Sciences Religieuses* 27 [1998]: 387-405).

way. They see publication as the ticket out, so they rush into print rather ill-considered pieces that fail to enhance their chances.

A third group joins prestigious faculties and scraps for tenure. A number of them falter because they cannot meet the criteria now raised higher than the resident faculty themselves could have met so early in their careers. These young scholars slip away to what they consider "lesser" educational institutions and at times cannot find the grit to create a career resembling what they had thought they were entering.

It has not always been so. As one extended example, the fourth-century Cappadocians provide a different model for fulfilling the vocation of a theological teacher. Each of them wound up serving the Church, often quite seriously in teaching and sometimes in "publication," either by returning to their homeland after education and/or appointments abroad or by never leaving it. Together they created a world-class theology that emerged primarily from the outback.

Cappadocia in the fourth century C.E. was quite Hellenized and thus participated in the Greco-Roman culture centered in the great cities of the empire such as Alexandria, Constantinople, and Rome. In many ways, however, it was still a buffer state for the Roman government, one located near that empire's eastern edges facing out toward Persia. Large grassy plains provided food for horses of extraordinary quality by which the region had been famous as early as the hegemony of Assyria in the eighth century B.C.E. That was Cappadocia's major contribution even in Roman times, rather than the development of any outstanding cultural or educational institutions. Its "feudal" society encouraged neither a deep sense of freedom nor the growth of large cities. A local language still competed with the more widely usable Greek. People of means sent their children elsewhere for the best instruction in philosophy, rhetoric, or law.[2]

Gregory Nazianzen (c. 329–390), a Cappadocian called The Theologian by the Eastern Orthodox,[3] fits the pattern of creating an internation-

2. Ruge, "Kappadokia," *Paulys Realencyclopädie der classischen Altertumswissenschaft* (Stuttgart: Druckenmüller, 1919), vol. 10.2, cols. 1910-18.

3. At the Council of Chalcedon in 451 Gregory was mentioned with that title *(Acta Conciliorum Oecumenicorum* 2, Concilium Universale Chalcedonense, ed. Eduard Schwartz [Berlin: De Gruyter, 1922], pp. 1, 3, 114, 14). Philostorgius, the Neoarian historian, had used it earlier, perhaps ironically because it was so often employed *(Historia Ecclesiastica* 8.11, *Philostorgius Kirchengeschichte,* ed. Joseph Bidez, 2nd ed, in *Friedhelm Winkelmann,* Die

ally renowned theology in the outback. His father watched over his early studies in the hometown of Nazianzus, but soon sent his son to Cappadocian Caesarea for intermediate education. The family's wealth allowed Gregory to travel for schooling at Caesarea in Palestine, then at Alexandria, and to finish at the noted center of learning, Athens. He thus received instruction from some of the very best teachers in three important cities far from his homeland. He probably used Origen's library in Palestinian Caesarea and might have met either Didymus the Blind or Athanasius during his stay at Alexandria. In Athens he came to know Himerius, a rhetorician whose reputation is disputed but who may have had not only literary talents but also logical and philosophical ones. Nazianzen also presumably sat under a Christian, Prohaeresius, who taught in Athens and had some hand in the education of the emperor, Julian the Apostate. Gregory was so outstanding in his philosophical rhetoric studies, based on wide reading in philosophical handbooks and selected philosophers as well as intense study in the theory and techniques of rhetoric, that he apparently was offered one of the few chairs of rhetoric in Athens.

During his "graduate education" he had carefully attended to spiritual meditation. He and his friend, Basil the Great, both listened to the lectures, took part in the practice sessions for rhetoricians, and spent time together in prayer and biblical study. Their original intent was to return to their region and set up a monastery based on practice they had heard about from Syria and Egypt. After they returned to Cappadocia, they did take retreats together in a secluded area at Annesi in Pontus, one owned by Basil's family, but the timing for founding their monastery never seemed right. During one of those periods together they evidently assembled the significant collection of quotations from Origen, the *Philochalia*.

When Gregory had finished his studies in Athens, he had made his way back to Nazianzus. There his father and mother pressed him into ordination and ministry alongside his father in his home church, something he despised and fled. Yet he returned and served, under considerable duress. He creatively used the distress as an occasion for writing, among other orations, *An Apology for His Flight*, a painfully personal look at the vocation of a priest. That piece lies behind both John Chrysostom's and Gregory the

---

griechischen christlichen Schriftsteller der ersten Jahrhunderte [Berlin: Akademie Verlag, 1972], p. 112).

Great's treatises on life as a priest, and thus forms a major understanding of religious vocation in both Eastern Orthodoxy and Western Catholicism.[4]

Later he spent nearly a four-year period of retreat in a convent/monastery dedicated to St. Thecla and located at Seleucia; it was a time devoted to study and contemplation.[5] Perhaps because of relatives who worshiped with the struggling orthodox community meeting in a chapel at Constantinople, the Theologian was invited to lead that small group. In the metropolis he doubtless experienced the high point of his public, episcopal career. Most of his speeches and homilies that we still have were probably given there, particularly his brilliant *Theological Orations.* Although soon established by Emperor Theodosius in the large church formerly occupied by his foes, the Neoarians, Gregory in 381 huffily resigned from leadership there and the presidency of the Council of Constantinople. He returned to a stint as bishop of Nazianzen, but then retired to family estates at Arianzus where he spent about seven years writing poetry and editing all his works.

Sadly, Gregory was often disquieted, sometimes deeply offended at his treatment by others. Both his father and his friend Basil did misjudge his sensitivities and tried to force him into places only full rebellion would have kept him from.[6] He is, however, a sterling example of a significant theologian whose doctrinal contributions concerning the Trinity, the Holy Spirit, Christology, and soteriology are only recently being rediscovered to the full. His major opponents on the inside were Eunomians whose leaders, Aetius and Eunomius, were noted for their logical ability and confessed that the

4. *Or. 2, Patrologia Grecae* 35, ed. J. P. Migne and others (Paris: Garnier Fratres, 1886), pp. 407A-513C; *Grégoire de Nazianze, Discours 1-3,* Sources chrétiennes 247 (Paris: Les Éditions du Cerf, 1978), pp. 84-240; Eng. trans. Charles Gordon Browne and James Edward Swallow, Nicene and Post-Nicene Fathers 7 (New York: The Christian Literature Company, 1894), pp. 204-27. John Chrysostom and Gregory the Great both built on Nazianzen's piece in their works. See John Chrysostom, *De sacerdotio, PG* 48, 623-92; *SC* 272, ed. Anne-Marie Malingrey; Eng. trans. W. R. W. Stephens, *NPNF* 9, 33-83; and Gregory the Great, *Regulae Pastoralis Liber, Patrologia Latina* 77, ed. J. P. Migne and others (Paris: Lutetia Parisiorum, 1849), 12A-126A; *SC* 381, ed. Floribert Rommel; Eng. trans. Henry Davis, Ancient Christian Writers 11 (Westminster, Md.: Newman Press, 1950).

5. We do not know in which Seleucia Nazianzen spent his spiritual retreat, other than that it was not in Cappadocia. Seleucia on the Tigris and Seleucia in Isauria are possible candidates. The Seleucia that was the port city of Antioch of Syria had a shrine to Thecla.

6. Jean Bernardi, *Saint Grégoire de Nazianze: Le Théologien et son temps,* Initiations aux Pères de l'Église (Paris: Les Éditions du Cerf, 1995), pp. 101-243. Rosemary Radford Ruether, *Gregory of Nazianzus: Rhetor and Philosopher* (Oxford: Clarendon Press, 1969), pp. 18-54.

Son was a created nature less than God and more than humans. He also recognized that Apollinaris's Christology was deficient. A less than full humanity would endanger salvation.[7] His opponents outside were those who worshiped the Greco-Roman pantheon through its many manifestations.[8]

Various modern theological interests appear in bits and pieces within Nazianzen's works. He ridicules his Eunomian opponents; next they will say God is male. Surely that fits feminism.[9] His trinitarian cosmology offers remarkable insights into ecological concerns.[10] He anticipates Karl Rahner's theme of anonymous Christians by noting that his father, raised among non-Christian Hypsistarii, was with the Church before he became a Christian. The elder Gregory needed to learn the name that defined his virtues.[11] Furthermore, Nazianzen prefigures some of the ways in which Wittgenstein worked out philosophical problems through grammatical analyses.[12] He has a grasp of logic that looks much like the best missiological insights of our era as well as the disputed but fascinating development of quantum logic in modern physics.[13]

---

7. *SC* 208, ed. Paul Gallay with Maurice Jourjon.

8. Frederick W. Norris, *Faith Gives Fullness to Reasoning: The Five Theological Orations of Gregory Nazianzen,* Supplements to *Vigiliae Christianae* XIII, trans. Lionel Wickham and Frederick Williams (Leiden: E. J. Brill, 1991), provides a commentary that deals with the historical context and makes some of those claims clear.

9. *Or.* 31.7, *PG* 36, 140C; *SC* 250, ed. Paul Gallay, 286-88.

10. Sigurd Bergmann, *Geist der Natur befreit: Die trinitarische Kosmologie Gregors von Nazianz im Horizont einer ökologischen Theologie der Befreiung* (Mainz: Matthias-Grünewald, 1995).

11. *Or.* 18.6, *PG* 35, 991B-993A.

12. See my "Theology as Grammar: Nazianzen and Wittgenstein," in *Arianism After Arius: Essays on the Development of the Fourth Century Trinitarian Conflicts,* ed. Michel Barnes and Daniel Williams (Edinburgh: T. & T. Clark, 1993), pp. 237-49.

13. *Or.* 29.9, *PG* 36, 84D-85C; *SC* 250, ed. Paul Gallay, 192-94. Gregory insists that the assertion of contradictories — either the Son existed or did not exist when he was begotten — must be considered in more than one way. The liar's paradox demands that its statement is both true and false. Apparent contradictories may be either true or false, both true, or both false. Competent missiologists for some time have suspected that a universal human logic similar to the system spelled out in Aristotle's Western *Organon* does not function everywhere. Duns Scotus (1266–1308) and William of Ockham (c. 1295–1349) worked on the problems associated with contradictories and anticipated a three-value logic of true, false, and undetermined. The fullest enhancement of a position like Gregory's, however, has appeared in this century in the debate about the relationship between Einstein's and Bohr's work. A minority of physicists with deep interests in logic, while working on the ways in

He studied abroad but polished his theology in the outback. Constantinople was the city where he made public so many of the insights he had developed during his church service in Nazianzus and his monastic retreat at Seleucia, apparently rather far from the cultural and educational advantages of any metropolis. His rich poetry and the final editions of his orations and letters were completed in Cappadocia. And yet the theology he created, along with his friends, has proved to be one of the most interesting and substantial to be produced anywhere at any time.

The rest of those people most often seen as the creators of Cappadocian theology come from a single family. Basil the Great and Gregory of Nyssa fill out the threesome when three is the limit. But here I also include Macrina, their sister, who has recently drawn sufficient attention to be considered another important figure in this theological project.

Basil the Great (330–379) also came from an aristocratic Cappadocian family. His father had taught him at home but then sent him on to Cappadocian Caesarea where he may have met Gregory the Theologian. Their paths diverged as Basil went to Constantinople for the next part of his education, and where he most likely sat under the important Greek rhetorician, Libanius. When Basil traveled on to Athens in order to finish his education, he already had a remarkable reputation as an orator, one his friend Gregory thought deserved recognition from all the professors as well as the students.

Basil had a much stronger distrust of Hellenistic education than did his colleague, Nazianzen. Although his talents in Greek philosophy, rhetoric, and style were on a high level, as we can see from his orations and letters, he did not imbibe as deeply in the principles of investigation that marked Hellenistic paideia. He eventually turned all his energy to church service. His talent for both theology and administration caught the eye of Caesarea's Christian leaders. Basil was not fully admired by the bishop,

---

which the two systems do not fit well together, have tried to extend Bohr's sense of complementarity into a quantum logic that resists Aristotle's excluded middle. See Max Jammer, *The Philosophy of Quantum Mechanics: The Interpretations of Quantum Mechanics in Historical Perspective* (New York: John Wiley and Sons, 1974), especially chapter 8. John Polkinghorne notices how important John Von Neumann's quantum logic is for the discussion between science and religion (*Serious Talk: Science and Religion in Dialogue* [Valley Forge, Pa.: Trinity Press International, 1995], pp. 41-42). In a similar vein see the comments of Edward MacKinnon, "Complementarity," *Religion & Science: History, Method, Dialogue*, ed. Mark Richardson and Wesley Wildman (New York: Routledge, 1996), pp. 255-70.

Eusebius, and the circumstances of his selection as Eusebius's successor were a bit tainted; yet he did eventually follow him. In that office he comported himself well, at least to the satisfaction of the Nicene faction in Cappadocia. At times his administrative decisions remind one of a velvet claw. His effectiveness in shaping Nicene faith and its institutions, however, cannot be denied.

All Basil's ecclesiastical career took place in Cappadocia. He had left Athens early and returned to a stint of teaching rhetoric in Caesarea. Soon, however, he fully committed himself to his vocation and set out to visit monastic sites in Egypt and Palestine, perhaps even Syria and Mesopotamia, before he returned to his homeland.[14] His monastic rules, developed out of those visits and put in place at Caesarea, remain honored ones.[15] The liturgy that he reformed at Caesarea is still celebrated by churches of the Eastern rite on particular Sundays.[16] In a treatise written against the Eunomians, he sets many of the terms of the debate with this new Christology that viewed the Son's divine nature as less than that of the Father.[17] His nine homilies on the Hexaemeron show that he knew the natural science of his time well and could produce remarkably interesting interweavings of the Old Testament texts and the concerns of his era.[18] His treatise on the Holy Spirit has been retranslated in the twentieth century because it has so much to say about those burgeoning issues. He could not bring himself to refer to the Holy Spirit publicly as God, but he did hold that position and employed it in his private meditation and prayer.[19] His

14. Philip Rousseau, *Basil of Caesarea* (Berkeley: University of California Press, 1994).

15. *Regulae fusius tractatae, PG* 31, 1080A-1305B, and *Regulae brevius tractatae, PG* 31, 620A-625B.

16. *PG* 31, 1629A-1656D. There is little doubt that the substance of that liturgy comes from Basil himself.

17. *PG* 29, 497-669D; *SC* 299 & 305, ed. Bernard Sesboüé with Georges-Matthieu de Durand and Louis Doutreleau. Milton Anastos points up a series of difficulties in its arguments; see "Basil's *Kata Eunomiou*, A Critical Analysis," in *Basil of Caesarea: Christian, Humanist, Ascetic: A Sixteen-Hundredth Anniversary Symposium,* ed. Paul Fedwick (Toronto: Pontifical Institute of Mediaeval Studies, 1981), part 1, pp. 67-136.

18. *PG* 29, 4A-208C; *SC* 26, 2nd ed., ed. Stanislas Giet.

19. *PG* 32, 68A-217C; *SC* 17, 2nd ed., ed. Benoît Pruche. Ellen Charry, *By the Renewing of Your Minds: The Pastoral Function of Christian Doctrine* (Oxford: Oxford University Press, 1997), pp. 101-19, finds Basil, particularly in his work on the Holy Spirit, to be one of the primary examples for her case.

numerous letters provide remarkable glimpses not only of his own life but also of the contemporary political webs.[20]

Certainly one of his most engaging and unexpected accomplishments was the creation of a new city near Caesarea in Cappadocia. Taking advantage of his family's ownership of land just outside the municipality, Basil built a church, a bishop's residence, a monastery, and a hostel for pilgrims traveling to the Holy Land. The hostel soon turned into a hospital for the afflicted, with a section for lepers, and then during a difficult famine became a place of refuge for hundreds, even thousands, of homeless and starving people. Basil was able to cajole other wealthy people into offering assistance, perhaps even an emperor who did not like him very much. The overall influence of this new city was so impressive that it became the center of planning and activity. Three centuries later the old Roman city of Caesarea had fallen into ruin while Basil's new city had become the hub of urban life.[21]

In terms of the pattern noticed in Gregory Nazianzen's life, Basil had grown up in the midst of riches and, far from his homeland, had pursued education both in terms of Greek paideia and Christian monasticism. But he returned to Cappadocia and spent his lifetime vocation in Caesarea. Along with Gregory Nazianzen, he helped develop a theology from the outback that has had international consequences.

It is difficult to judge in what ways Basil's family made their decisions concerning education for their offspring. There were ten children, but not even all four of the males were sent abroad for study. Gregory of Nyssa (331/40–c. 395), Basil's brother, often seen as the darling Cappadocian by twentieth-century theology in North America and Europe, gained no education outside his homeland. Rather, like his brother Basil, he was able to

20. *PG* 32, 220A-112D; *Sainte Basile, Lettres,* 3 vols., ed. and trans. Yves Courtonne, Collection Guillaume Budé (Paris: Les Belles Lettres, 1957, 1961, 1966). *Saint Basil: The Letters,* 4 vols., trans. Roy Deferrari, Loeb Classical Library (rpt. Cambridge, Mass.: Harvard University Press, 1950-1953).

21. Brian Daly, "Building a New City: The Cappadocian Fathers and the Rhetoric of Philanthropy: 1998 North American Patristic Society Presidential Address," *Journal of Early Christian Studies* 7 (1999): 431-61. It is of interest to note that the sermons on the poor preached by Basil and the two Gregories often do not appear in the selected translations available in English. Even at the beginning of the twenty-first century all of them have not yet been translated. Susan Holman, "The Hungry Body: Famine, Poverty, and Identity in Basil's *Hom. 8,*" *Journal of Early Christian Studies* 7 (1999): 337-63, shows how important that homily and its themes are in any assessment of Basil.

acquire a number of the best books and pursue studies with frontier teachers. He became such a skilled rhetorician that for a time he considered making the teaching of rhetoric his main occupation. Both Basil and Gregory Nazianzen pushed him to think more seriously about a theological vocation, one that involved being a bishop. He married and did not remain celibate as did Basil and Nazianzen, yet he served as bishop in the small town of Nyssa.

In whatever way he acquired his education, some of it no doubt through discussions and correspondence with very fine theologians, its results were superb. His writings indicate remarkable wisdom about Scripture, sometimes at deeper levels than either his brother Basil or Gregory the Theologian. Of the three, Gregory of Nyssa demonstrates the greatest talent as a biblical exegete, one who followed in the steps of Origen. In his commentary on the *Song of Songs* he goes beyond Origen while considering the book's central theme as the love between God and the soul, an allegorical interpretation that even in our age brings considerable insight to both congregations and monastic communities.[22]

The profundity of his understanding, not only of philosophy but also of different disciplines of human understanding, is unexpected. One of his letters defines the technical vocabulary employed for distinguishing the threeness and the oneness of the Trinity, *hypostasis* and *ousia,* in ways not before made so clear.[23] He employed ideas from Galen and other physicians in order to work out various moves within trinitarian theology, particularly in the employment of the term *dynamis.*[24] His attack on Eunomian opponents is the last from the Cappadocians. It depends to a degree on both Basil's and Gregory Nazianzen's efforts, but represents the most sophisticated

---

22. *PG* 44, 756A-1120A; *Gregorii Nysseni in Canticum Canticorum,* Gregorii Nysseni Opera VI (Leiden: E. J. Brill, 1960); *Saint Gregory of Nyssa: Commentary on the Song of Songs,* Eng. trans. C. McCambley (Brookline, Mass.: Hellenic College, 1988). It is fair to say that the fifteen homilies, which cover chapters 1.1–6.8, represent the nearest thing to an extended commentary on a biblical book from any of the Cappadocians. The others usually treat Scripture as parts of their thematic arguments. They most probably did not write in that genre because they had access to and enjoyed Origen's numerous biblical commentaries.

23. *Ep.* 24, *PG* 46, 1088D-1093B; *Gregorii Nysseni Opera* VIII.2, ed. G. Pasquali, 2nd ed. (Leiden: E. J. Brill, 1959), pp. 75-79. This letter also appears in Basil's collected letters as no. 38, but now it is regularly ascribed to Nyssa because of his better attested philosophical skills.

24. Michel Barnes, *The Power of God:* Dynamis *in Gregory of Nyssa's Trinitarian Theology* (Washington, D.C.: Catholic University of America Press, forthcoming 2001).

analysis and persuasive response to Eunomius that the Cappadocians developed.[25] His vigorous rebuttal of Apollinaris, the friend who fought against Arius's denial of the Son's full divine nature but himself insisted that Jesus Christ did not have a full manhood, is the only extensive response we have from the Cappadocians.[26] Despite not entering the monastic life his mystical vision is one of the most stunning available from the early church. He constantly reflects on the life of God and the ways in which worshipers may not only grow through meditation and the practice of virtue but also actually may participate in God's perfections.[27]

In terms of the Cappadocian pattern, Nyssa differs from both his brother, Basil, and Nazianzen. His early marriage may account for the fact that he did not seek study abroad, although there may have been some other reason. He never darkened the door of a "major university," yet he was as responsible for the substance of Cappadocian theology as any. In his maturity he traveled outside Cappadocia to various councils, but he was a homegrown product who made a lasting contribution from the outback to world-class theology.

Usually the Cappadocians are considered to be these three. One of the gains from recent scholarship, however, has been the suggestion that Gregory of Nyssa is quite serious in insisting that his and Basil's sister, Macrina the Younger (c. 327–c. 380), was a significant figure in the evolution of Cappadocian theology.[28] Women were highly honored in that family. Macrina the Elder, a grandmother, had studied with Gregory the Wonderworker (c. 210–260), the best-known Cappadocian theologian of the third century. Macrina the Younger evidently never traveled much outside Cappadocia except to family holdings on the Iris River in Pontus. She certainly did not receive the formal educations abroad granted to Basil and

25. *PG* 29, 497-669D; *Gregorii Nysseni Opera*, vols. 1 & 2.

26. *PG* 45, 1123A-1270A.

27. Almost all his works reflect that set of interests. The collection *From Glory Unto Glory: Texts from Gregory of Nyssa's Mystical Writings,* selected with an introduction by Jean Daniélou, trans. and ed. Herbert Musurillo (Crestwood, N.Y.: St. Vladimir's Seminary Press, 1979), offers a group of texts helpful for understanding his mystical interests. Also see David Balas, *"Metousia Theou": Man's Participation in God's Perfections According to St. Gregory of Nyssa* (Rome: Herder, 1966).

28. Jaroslav Pelikan, *Christianity and Classical Culture: The Metamorphosis of Natural Theology in the Christian Encounter with Hellenism,* Gifford Lectures at Aberdeen, 1992-1993 (New Haven: Yale University Press, 1993), p. 8.

Gregory Nazianzen. She did, however, use her portion of the family wealth to set up a Pontus convent, something Gregory Nazianzen and Basil dreamed about but did not accomplish together. There she read and reflected on Scripture and the Christian tradition; she also offered both food and lodging to the poor. We know little about her except what Nyssa says in one treatise that reflects on her life at the time of her death and a second that speaks of their discussions on her deathbed concerning the soul and the resurrection.[29] He considered her an honored teacher of both himself and his brother, Basil. Their father had died about the same time as the birth of the tenth baby; thus she, as the oldest child, had spent much of her youth and young adulthood serving as a "parent" along with their mother. When Basil returned from Athens, full of himself and determined to sell his skills as a rhetorician, she confronted his arrogance and compassionately led him toward his life in the priesthood. On her deathbed, as Nyssa complained about yet another aching sorrow in his life, she insisted that God had been good to all of them, not the least to him. With the slight pin prick of a beloved sibling, she reminded him that although he had little natural aptitude for becoming an important theological figure, through the prayers of his family and the power of his God, he was often asked to serve the Church in many areas. And he did so quite well.[30] At her death, she was so calm in the face of her distress that Nyssa was struck yet again by her demeanor and her words. He also discovered that some nuns who lovingly served her in her final hours had been rescued by her from the severe famine during which Basil's new city hospital proved to be so helpful. If we read the piece *On the Soul and the Resurrection* rather straightforwardly, we hear him insisting that she offered him insights that he had not learned in his own studies and had not heard from the other two more famous theologians in the circle.[31] Her explanation began with a look at hu-

---

29. *PG* 46, 960A-1000B; *SC* 178, ed. Pierre Maraval; *Gregorii Nysseni Opera* VIII.1, ed. Virginia Woods Callahan, 370-414; *The Life of Saint Macrina by Gregory, Bishop of Nyssa,* trans. Kevin Corrigan (Toronto: Peregrina Publishing Co., 1987, rpt. 1989); and *Dialogus de anima et resurrectione qui inscribitur Macrina, PG* 46, 12A-160C.

30. *Life of Saint Macrina,* trans. Corrigan.

31. *PG* 46, 12A-160C. In a sensitive postmodern reading, Elizabeth Clark uses the material about Macrina to warn that we do not have her words and thus her views. The treatise itself may be wholly from Nyssa. We might discover aspects of her life if we become more sophisticated historians ("The Lady Vanishes: Dilemmas of a Feminist Historian after the 'Linguistic Turn,'" *Church History* 67 [1998]: 1-31). I have chosen to emphasize Macrina's contri-

man life from the vantage point of natural phenomena, but she went on to speak of the hidden hand of God within human tragedies and then moved to talk about life hereafter. In Nyssen's view, she seemed to be inspired by the Holy Spirit. Gregory notes that if he had extended the small tract to include everything she logically and systematically discussed on her deathbed, he would have had to report her entire "philosophy of the soul."[32]

Macrina offers yet a further variation on the pattern of theological life in the outback. As a woman she did not receive the access to formal education that some of her brothers did. But in the hinterland she learned to read, to contemplate, and to talk about important topics in ways that permanently influenced her family and those in her convent. The insightful Nyssa appears to be happy to serve as her scribe and thus offer the world her views.

All of these fourth-century figures suggest that the plight of many twenty-first-century theological teachers does not necessarily entail the death of their theological contributions. You need neither stay in the famed city, never occupying a full-time position, nor resign yourself to the outback as if sentenced to total obscurity. There is no ultimate reason to take the decision of a great university not to grant tenure as the final judgment on your possibility of pursuing a productive career as theological teacher, either in the classroom or through publication. The history of theology makes it abundantly clear that the best efforts of any era have not always come from the most prestigious educational or theological centers. We would never think of Nazianzus, Nyssa, Annesi in Pontus, or even Caesarean Cappadocia as important places had we not had the contributions of the two Gregories, Macrina, and Basil. For that matter, what is Hippo without Augustine, Cluny without Bernard, Bingen without Hildegard, or Wittenberg without Luther? Every published history of Christian doctrine or practice is forced to rely heavily on people who did not live in the "recognized" centers of learning and power during their given eras. And each printed history that now informs such study in departments of religious studies or theological seminaries can be shown to have overlooked impor-

---

butions through the stories about her relationships with her brothers and her work in the convent/monastery. The entire Cappadocian project should warn us about thinking that we always get the exact words from any one of the participants. The church historian Socrates (*Historia Ecclesia* 4.26; *PG* 67, 528B-536A) says that after Basil's death Gregory Nazianzen polished the text of Basil's *Hexaemeron*. Then whose words and thoughts are they?

32. *PG* 46, 976D-977D; *The Life of Saint Macrina*, pp. 42-43.

tant developments in the hinterlands. Christian theologies developed along the Silk Road to China in the first millennium are seldom given attention in courses on historical theology. This is so in spite of the fact that their originators knew religious pluralism first-hand and formed some of the best available approaches to other world religions. For example, some ancient Chinese documents found in a Buddhist monastery at Dunhuang, China, display a contextualized Christian theology that has come to terms with a series of Confucian and Buddhist insights without totally sacrificing the Christian gospel.[33] Recorded discussions between Christian bishops and Muslim leaders, available in Syriac or Arabic, show ways in which indigenous Christians could accept the dominant Arabic culture without abandoning their faith for Muslim belief. The best-known, but not necessarily the best treatise, is the discussion between Timothy I of Damascus and the caliph.[34] It is astoundingly odd that such works from the outback, so clearly valuable in facing the challenges of contemporary global religious pluralism, remain widely unknown in standard religious studies and theological curricula. This normative Western myopia has proved to be difficult to cure. Even in surveys of the modern period, African, Asian, and South American works have only recently begun to dent the dominance of the European-North American partnership.

To live in the outback and teach theology you must look for the footprints of God imbedded in a (sub)culture perhaps unknown to you or left behind for your advanced studies. The Cappadocians were able to return to their homeland or stay within or near it because in many ways they loved it. Basil was never certain that all his Greek education was of ultimate value. Gregory Nazianzen was estranged from some of the cultural values that formed the core of Constantinopolitan society. In response to those citizens

---

33. P. Yoshiro Saeki, ed. and trans., *The Nestorian Documents and Relics in China*, 2nd ed. (Tokyo: The Maruzen Company, 1951).

34. Timothy I, *Apology for Christianity*, trans. A. Mingana, Woodbrooke Studies 2 (Cambridge: W. Heffer & Sons, 1928), pp. 1-162. Sidney Griffith has a series of articles that deal with this literature, "'Ammar Al Basris *Kitab Al-Burhan:* Christian *Kalam* in the first Abbasic Century," *Le Muséon* 96 (1983): 145-81; "The Arabic Account of 'Abd al-Masih An-Nagrani Al-Ghassani," *Le Muséon* 90 (1985): 331-74; "Muhammad and the Monk Bahîrâ: Reflections on a Syriac and Arabic Text from the Early Abbasid Times," *Oriens Christianus* 79 (1995): 146-74; "The View of Islam from the Monasteries of Palestine in the Early 'Abbâsid Period: Theodore Abû Qurra and the *Summa Theologiae Arabica*," *Islam and Christian-Muslim Relations* 7 (1996): 9-28.

who laughed at his looks, snickered at what was probably his Cappadocian Greek accent, and ridiculed his bad clothes, he warned that the citizenship of Christians is in the heavenly Jerusalem, not the empire's capital metropolis.[35] Gregory of Nyssa reflected brilliantly on the Christian faith from within that small town, and Macrina, who could plumb the depths of various Christian doctrines and practices, found her place within a small community in Pontus. They all had worldviews that encompassed more than their specific localities but were well rooted within them.

Their most profound vision regarding the vocation of a theological teacher emerged from their sense of the priesthood. Gregory of Nyssa referred to his sister, Macrina, as "The Teacher." Although we would probably be wise to think of Macrina as an abbess, it did not occur to Nyssen to restrict teaching to ordained priests.[36] Gregory Nazianzen perhaps says it best for all of them: their vocation is the "care of souls": "The scope of our art is to provide the soul with wings, to rescue it from the world and give it to God, and to watch over that which is in His image. If it abides, we are to take it by the hand; if it is in danger, to restore it; if it is ruined, to make Christ dwell in the heart by the Spirit. In short our task is to deify, and to bestow heavenly bliss upon one who belongs to the heavenly hosts." The responsibility is weightier than that of medicine, indeed a humiliating and depressing one from which more people than Jonah have run. Without the grace of God, long philosophical training, and the practice of looking upward, it is never safe to undertake a vocation that is like the mediation between God and man that Christians see in Jesus Christ. Only the example of biblical heroes as well as the prayers, words, and spirit of the local church can empower the priest to undertake such an impossible duty.[37] None of these four Cappadocian theologians would ever think of the vocation of a theological teacher outside the activity of God and the support of the faithful within the church.

35. *Or.* 33.8, *PG* 36, 224C-225A; *SC* 318, ed. Claudio Moreschini and Paul Gallay, 172-74.

36. In his treatise *On the Soul and the Resurrection, Dialogus de anima et resurrectione qui inscribitur Macrina,* he seldom refers to her with any other title than "The Teacher."

37. *Or.* 2, *PG* 35, 461B, 432A-B, 493B-C, 513A-B; *SC* 247, 158-60, 118-20, 206-8, 238, 52, 22, 91, 116; *NPNF* 7, 216, 209, 223, 227. [The translation of section 22, p. 209 is adapted.] No reader should assume that this "care of souls" implies a disdain for the body. Basil and the two Gregories worried deeply about poverty and famine as well as the plight of the sick, especially lepers.

In our present setting, some teachers may not have been able to study at the university of their choice. Others may not have gotten the jobs they most desired. Still others may not have received tenure in the university whose reputation was going to ensure their careers. But should any of us decide to take advantage of the outback, of places we did not know or have rejected, ones our advisors have never heard about, we need not think that all is lost. The Cappadocians have taught us a series of lessons that are still worth learning today. (1) Each of these people understood rather fully that prayer, meditation, and worship were basic components of their theological vocation. During each day they tended to have various periods of prayer, study of Scripture, and probably one celebration of the Eucharist. The spiritual formation of the soul was the purpose of their ministry. It led to lives of devotion and service. That can be undertaken in any setting. (2) These four, and a number of others such as Basil and Nyssen's brother, Peter, formed a critical mass that was sufficient in number and in scope to encourage the emergence of nearly the best from each. They sent letters to many others, thus enlarging their circle. The Internet now provides contacts never dreamed of by scholars even thirty years ago; it is certainly better than the slow letter traffic and slower travel available to the Cappadocians. Critical mass need not be confined to a small locale. (3) The Cappadocian circle shared work with each other that is now available to us quickly and in much larger quantity than they ever possessed. Gregory Nazianzen notes that some had studied the uses of "holy" in Scripture, others "spirit," and still others "Holy Spirit," all of them investigations that assisted his efforts.[38] Our critical texts and concordances, not only of Scripture, but also of many significant theologians throughout history, are much more accessible than anything they ever possessed. Interlibrary loan does strike us as slow but it is usually efficient. One distinct advantage it provides is the need to question whether one really needs the new title that has appeared in the footnotes of other works or in a list from some publishing house. Furthermore, the time of reflection during the wait for an ordered volume can create the opportunity for deeper insight into the project. In addition, some outback institutions may provide funds for travel to larger libraries. Sometimes administrative support for lexical aids, dictionaries or commentaries, and research projects that take considerable time, is more easily found in a good backwoods setting. (4) The

38. *Or.* 31.2, *PG* 36, 133D-136A; *SC* 250, 278.

Cappadocians seem to have breathed the local air deeply and made the different character of the hinterland serve as a creative component of what they did. None of them was so taken in by dominant Hellenistic culture that they could not see places in which it adopted anti-Christian stances. They appropriated that heritage with incisive care. For example, they could talk about the passibility of the impassable as a marvelous, mysterious phrase. They knew that only a conundrum could picture the total truth of Jesus Christ; the overpowering witness of Hellenistic philosophers and theologians to deity's impassibility was only partially correct. They also looked carefully at developing Christian views and practices. Precisely in the midst of his deep spirituality, Gregory of Nyssa questioned the growing sentimentality of pilgrims traveling to sacred sites in the Middle East.[39] Sometimes the backwater provides critical distance just by being what it is.

Moving farther away from the extended example of the Cappadocians to more personal observations after nearly a quarter century teaching in the outback, I note that aspects of spiritual formation become a necessity in the provinces. Obviously evil is never absent. Jealousy, irritability, infidelity, and many other vices irrupt here as forcefully as they do elsewhere. Yet I suspect that nearly any seminary or religious studies professor in North America is struck by the vital spirituality of international students who come from out-of-the-way Christian fellowships. There they experienced the power of grace and virtue, the significance of prayer, study, and communities of friendship. Their towns and regions, like those of the Cappadocians, are seldom known. But their faith and life often seem much more advanced.

To focus directly on the vocation of twenty-first-century theological teachers, laboring in the hinterland entails a pervasive humiliation. That can lead to deep-set anger or it can lead you to accept grace and develop humility. According to the canons of the time, where you teach in the provinces is neither the best school with the best students, the best curriculum, nor the best resources. That means that we who teach here are anything but the best. Therefore we have no discussions marked by the fact that our university is definitely the finest. Among the elite I have heard claims that a particular university's doctoral robes have the most magnificent design and fabric, one more indication that it is the best in the world.

---

39. *Ep.* 2, *PG* 46, 1009B-1016A; *Gregorii Nysseni Opera* VIII.2, pp. 13-19.

A context from which such idiocy can never emerge tends to encourage good sense, to weaken pride mortally, and to offer an opening for gracious healing in many areas. God works where God wills. God is not limited to great cities and outstanding institutions. Teachers anywhere can concentrate more clearly on God when their own reputations are not continually in the way.

Outside the confines of modern European/North American university culture, outside the cities that provide endless stimulation, entertainment, and bustle, there is time to consider other things. A place where they roll up the sidewalks at ten often provides the dirt where goodness grows. In the outback there are certain habits of the heart, virtues of life and vices of death, that are especially needful to develop or to restrain. Early Christian theologians spoke of *acedia* as a vice to be avoided. It is that ennui that saps anyone of vision and energy. At low times in a day, you can easily and unhelpfully become fixated on what conventional wisdom would regard as your unfortunate circumstances, reminding you repeatedly that you are not in a place where colleagues are ever so interesting and resources ever so available. This really is the hinterland. The lives of desert saints seem far too similar to your own. And then you reconsider the fact that such similarity is desirable because those saints' insights have been found fertile by generations of theologians striving in many locations to understand their own vocation. Could those desert monks, or those involved in other kinds of orders, have attained the wisdom we recognize, if they had not lived in the outback?

The amount of determination needed to stay with the tasks that mark your vocation can often be more than you possess at a given moment. Sheer cussedness can mark your reaction to the situation: just watch me and see what a mistake you made in not recognizing my talents. That vice can make life utterly miserable. Or perhaps you can muster up the courage required because your sense of the contributions you might make with God's help remains an important part of your own self-image. Persistence in slow and steady work still produces results; indeed there are some scholarly tasks that respond to nothing other than that. A heavier teaching load than that of your colleagues in the great universities can mean that you are becoming more entwined with your students and thus are being offered a better understanding of the audience you hope to engage.

From a different look at the provincial work load, it is probably easier to carve out moments for prayer in an outback culture where the demands for research and publication are not quite as heavy and the speed of the culture is not quite as fast. Meditative study of Scripture and classics of spirituality can more readily become a part of daily life, not in the sense that such hours are demanded in a monastic setting, but that they appear in a place more amenable to such significant monastic practices. Hinterland teaching that so depends upon these lifestyles just might provide the richest environment for what you want to teach, research, and write.

For people pursuing their calling with vigor in the provinces, patience is a difficult virtue to acquire. You wait for the inter-library loan, for the outdated local server and the local Internet provider to get you back online. Overseas you pay exorbitant prices for Internet access and thus are thoroughly frustrated with messages that don't get to the point. Yet the strengthening of that virtue makes daily life fruitful. Waiting is an aggravating part of most people's existence. The larger audience you want to reach with the possible words of wisdom that your vocation evokes often sits in doctors' offices, in cars at stoplights, in front of schools, in the checkout line or even at the copying machine. You can speak more forcefully to them about patience if you are not so pampered by assistants and secretaries in a large university.[40]

A community of local friends with whom you worship, teach, play, serve, etc. can reinforce the purpose that frees both the intellect and the spirit for growth. In the provinces, you get to know faculty and staff spouses and children as real people and thus as those who must be considered seriously as potential audiences for any scholarly project. Thus the focus of written work is larger; the best is not always thought to be the technical investigation important to the other dozen people in the world who labor in the area. In the hinterland, friends and families form the crucible in which theology is brought to a boil. Worshiping congregations are often an extension of this community, remarkable participants in your life as well as any project you might undertake. They form that audience that enlivens your efforts.

A different community of friendship, both with those met at conferences and pursued over the Internet, is not the best route for finding comrades, but it does allow specialists to talk with each other at length about shared issues. Scientists used e-mail for these purposes long before it became a tool for theologians. Those who have been engaged in such ex-

40. See the chapter by Bonnie Miller-McLemore.

changes know that they participate in their mutual work more as friends than acquaintances.

One last point needs strong emphasis. None of these habits of the heart, which invigorate the vocation of theological teachers, arise only in the boondocks. I find those mentioned above to be absolute necessities for continued provincial life. But the focus of this chapter is not on portraying universities and cities as strongholds of the demonic, incapable of providing any soil for spiritual formation. I would be quite surprised if you, the reader, could not suggest grand examples of virtue you saw practiced in great metropolitan universities. I have my own inspiring memories, some not very old.

Rather, the ruminations of this essay are meant to accentuate the good that can emerge in the provinces, a reality too often overlooked as teachers search for places in which they may pursue their theological vocations. Readjusting our search to include the outback, whether it be a mission college in Malaysia or a small college in Montana, makes sense. Putting our energies into efforts that can be done where we are encourages remarkable insights. Theologies and theological teachers now popping up outside Europe and North America clearly indicate that the outback produces world-class accomplishments. If we look more carefully we may even find this true within unexpected places in Europe and North America.[41]

41. I gained much from conversation with Phil Kenneson, who also teaches here in the northeast Tennessee province.

Negotiating the Tensions of Vocation

L. GREGORY JONES

How DO PEOPLE LEARN to negotiate the different, overlapping, yet also often conflicting senses of the vocation to which we are called? Entailed in that question are some presumptions that ought to be identified: (1) that vocation is a fundamental description for how Christians understand our lives in relation to God; (2) that, since the Reformation, it is a description that both lay people and clergy deploy to make sense of their lives; and (3) that there are competing claims for our vocation that we cannot definitively resolve but must learn to negotiate as we struggle to make sense of our lives in relation to God.

I will not take up the first two presumptions, which would require a very different sort of essay to treat them adequately. Rather, I want to focus on the third presumption, which in some ways arises particularly out of the first two. That is, people struggle with the conflicting senses of vocation because we believe there is a claim on our lives, and a vocation to which we are called, in relation to God that is deeper than just doing a job or developing a career. Further, if vocation does not refer strictly to the calling of particular individuals to vowed lives within a clearly identified community and institution, we are frequently faced with conflicts or at least tensions that arise as we seek to fulfill our vocational commitment amidst diverse communities and institutions.

The primary thrust of this essay is to suggest that Christians negotiate our sense of vocation by continually narrating and re-narrating the dramas of our lives in relation to God, dramas in which there are various choruses we are summoned to hear and other voices we ought to resist. The dramas will often involve difficult and sometimes tragic choices; however, whether they entail tragedy in the strong sense is significantly dependent on the health and well-being of the communities and institutions to which we have devoted our critical allegiance. But that summary claim moves us too far too quickly.

Before turning to the steps necessary to justify my summary claim, I begin with an autobiographical note. In one of our first consultations at the Wabash Center in 1998, I observed that I was struggling with a gap between what I think I am called to be doing, namely serving as a theological administrator, and the loss of time to do other activities I enjoy doing, such as teaching, reading, and writing. In late May of 1999, as I was working on the first draft of this essay, my struggle intensified in the wake of a good friend's unexpected and untimely death. Dr. Charles Putman, Senior Vice-President for Research at Duke, suddenly died of a heart attack at the age of 57. His death recalled all too realistically the circumstances of my own father's untimely death of a heart attack at 53, while serving as one of my predecessors as Dean of Duke Divinity School. As I moved through the conversations, visitation, and memorial service for Charles Putman, reliving in some ways the week of my father's death, I remembered quite poignantly that during the week after Dad died, I had resolved quite strongly not to accept any positions that would involve the stress of my father's "job."

How, then, did I end up serving in precisely the same position that he held? Put oversimply, it was a sense of vocation. When the chair of Duke's search committee called to ask if I would be willing to be considered, my initial internal reaction was simple and straightforward: "No way." This was in part because of my father's death, in part because I was quite happy teaching theology at Loyola College, and loved my colleagues there, and in part because I wanted to continue to honor a clear sense of my wife's vocation as a parish minister. She had just been invited to serve as the senior pastor of a large United Methodist congregation in Baltimore, an affirmation both of women in ministry and of her particular gifts. Even so, all I told the search committee chair was, "I will need to talk with my wife."

Much to my surprise, Susan's initial reaction was quite different from mine: "I think this may be a call from God. You need to be open to the discernment process." I was shocked. She knew all of the things I mentioned above — the complexities of my father's legacy, my happiness at Loyola, her own vocation — and yet she thought I ought to discern very carefully whether this might be a vocational pull. She observed to me: "After all, you are a United Methodist elder, and Duke is one of the primary places in which United Methodists are prepared for ordained ministry." Could it be that the community that had ordained me was calling me to a different expression of my vocation?

To be sure, there were also flattering lures in the invitation: a tenured faculty position at a major research university, the opportunity to help shape a faculty for both professional and graduate education, financial security for the education of our children. Even so, none of those seemed sufficiently appealing to override the other considerations — except Susan's sense that it might be integral to my vocation.

To make a long story short, several others affirmed Susan's sense that this opportunity might be important for me to consider vocationally. These others included people whom I expected to be encouraging, but also people whom I expected to say that my scholarly and teaching vocation was more important. Over time, and the vagaries — political and otherwise — of the search process, I was invited to accept the position. By that point, it seemed clear to both Susan and me that we could and should accept this position. We reached this conclusion by narrating our vocations in relation to communities and institutions that we care about, by seeking a sense of what we might find fulfilling, and by reminding ourselves of the need to take risks of sacrifice in faithful discipleship.

It has been a good vocational move, and yet I continue to sense that gap between what I think I am called to do and the loss of time for other aspects of my vocation. There is nothing particularly illuminating, or interesting, about the details of my own vocational struggles. Indeed, I have been fortunate to be able to discern vocational choices that were quite desirable. I also recognize that many talented colleagues never get the chance for such choices, and often feel blocked by circumstances from being able to discern their vocation.

Even so, I hope that reflecting on my struggles, and the costs to the choices I have made, have enabled me to tease out some broader themes that face any of us in the discernment of vocational choices. Indeed, I hope these themes can help illumine what it means for people to negotiate and narrate their vocation in service to the God of Jesus Christ amidst the tensions of diverse and often conflicting commitments and desires.

211

Each of the following sections is framed by a quotation that I have found provocative in thinking about vocation. Taken alone, however, I find each of them only partially adequate and potentially destructive. Taken together, they offer the kind of creative tension that can help us negotiate, narrate, and discern more faithfully the intersection of our loyalties to institutions, communities, and our own integrity.

I

"Something's your vocation if it keeps making more of you."

Gail Godwin, *Evensong*

We typically are drawn to vocations in which we will find fulfillment. Part of what distinguishes vocation from simply a job is the conviction that, far more than a task that needs to be done, what I am doing is ingredient in a faithful, flourishing life. We ought to aim for a commitment that continually makes more of us, that generates and disciplines our passion, than would be the case if we failed to engage in that way of life.

The focus in Godwin's description is on the vocation, not the self. I am to search for a vocation that will make more of me, not a job in which I can make more for myself. There is an asceticism to vocation, a recognition that I will ultimately find fulfillment by attending to, even submitting to, standards and expectations larger than myself.

Our vocations shape us as much as, if not more than, we shape what we do. This is particularly important to recognize when we go into a profession with the aim of reforming or transforming it. There is much to commend such desire, especially when it involves deepening its possibilities by opening it to persons heretofore excluded from the profession (e.g., women entering into theological teaching over the past couple of generations). However, if people fail to recognize the ways in which the vocation will shape them as much as they seek to shape it, they are likely to be doomed to frustration and, perhaps, despair.

How does a vocation make "more of you" over time? In Godwin's novel, the comment is offered as one Episcopal priest's advice to another, suggesting that the "more" is to be understood theologically. That is, for Christians — people whose way of life is shaped by the God of Jesus Christ — the aim to be "made more" by a vocation should shape our desire and enable us to know and love God more truly (as we have already been known and loved by God).

Hence, from this perspective, the vocation to a scholarly life, understood as embracing theological teaching and learning, research and scholarship, service and engagement, is undertaken by persons whose knowledge and love of God will be enhanced by the disciplines of study. This is not a vocation for all people, nor is it one that can fruitfully be undertaken in isolation from a wider community of inquiry. But it is a vocation in which more can be made of you through practices of attention and study, teaching and learning, reading and writing, serving and engaging others.

For example, I have discovered that my scholarly vocation has made more of me through an enlarged ecumenical vision, more socially engaged reflection, a deeper knowledge of God, myself, and the Church, and a more profoundly Christian life through research, teaching, and living with the obstacles to, and opportunities for, authentic forgiveness. Central to my own self-understanding is a conviction that my vocation to theological teaching ought to continue to make more of me.

Yet, in discerning whether our vocation is likely to make more of us, there are also clear contrasts that we ought to avoid. We ought to avoid a vocation, or those aspects of a vocation, that will make "less" of us, particularly if that is because we find ourselves being shriveled by one or another form of sin. We can be made "less" by our own temptations, by a particular mismatch between what we are doing and the gifts we have been given by God, by contingent events that overwhelm the possibilities of continuing a particular vocation, or by the corrupting practices or institutions that currently shape our vocation. For example, some of us may need to avoid the temptation to live out our vocation to a scholarly life in a highly competitive, highly charged environment precisely because such a context will make less of us. Conversely, others may need to avoid the temptation to find a context in which fewer demands and expectations will make us both physically and intellectually slothful. People may also need to grapple with the ways in which contemporary institutions and power dynamics may block them from exercising their vocation, thus making less of them.

How, then, do we test whether a vocation is likely to make "more of you" by undertaking it? Once we are in a vocation, how do we discern whether it is continuing to do so? We rely on the truthful judgments of friends and community as well as — to some extent, for both good and ill — external arbiters to determine these things. In the first instance, we are

213

searching for fitness between a vocation and our particular gifts and temperament, our personal histories that have shaped who we have become, and the specific needs and opportunities of discovering meaningful work.

We rely heavily on friends and, hopefully, a truthful and discerning community in this process. We ought to search for others who will challenge the vices we have come to love, and to affirm the gifts that we are afraid to claim. After all, it is not difficult to find people who will overlook our vices, or only challenge those vices we already despise. Nor is it difficult to find people who will affirm what we already love about ourselves. What we need are people whose support and challenge will genuinely enable us to discover a vocation, and ways of living that vocation, that will make more of us over time.

However, apart from the existence of an ongoing, stable community that defines and enables each participant's vocation, difficulties will arise through the existence of other arbiters of fitness for a vocation. This may be, for example, the admissions committee for a particular degree program, the search committee for a particular job, the examining committee for receiving a license to practice a particular profession, or the bank officers whose loan decision will either make it possible or impossible to pursue the training one needs. A person may become absolutely convinced that a particular vocation will make "more of you," and feel confirmed in that decision by well-intentioned (and perhaps even well-informed) friends. However, other arbiters may preclude one from fulfilling that vocation by their decision, sometimes for understandable reasons and sometimes for pernicious ones.

Even more, the social and political conditions may not exist to make the vocation that seems clear to you possible. For example, you may belong to a church that does not ordain women; you live in a time when theology positions are largely eliminated from undergraduate departments of religion; you live in a country where the universities are being closed by an oppressive regime; or you live in the midst of social conditions where people cannot afford to offer theological teachers and pastors an adequate income to sustain a life.

These latter remarks suggest some of the dangers in Godwin's phrase. While it rightfully points to the need to find a vocation in which we can flourish, and the ways in which our vocation will shape us, it fails to account either for the roles that communities ought to play in helping us discern what might make more of us on the one hand, or the constraining

214

effects of sinful tendencies in our own lives, communities, and social and political contexts on the other.

Further, while I have offered some theological specificity to Godwin's phrase, left on its own it can easily be co-opted by a culture of self-fulfillment. Admittedly, it echoes biblical sentiments that Jesus came that we might have life, and have it abundantly. However, taken out of context there is little sense of the cross in such descriptions, at best a dim awareness that my vocation may actually only make "more" of me indirectly because its direct claim is to require an enormous sacrifice. What might that mean?

II

"When Christ calls [someone], He bids him come and die."

Dietrich Bonhoeffer, *The Cost of Discipleship*

Even as we recognize the potential for fulfillment and abundant living, Christians also recognize that the God we worship is the God who tells us that only those who lose their life will find it. Further, the Jesus we follow dies on a cross, and Christians have long recognized martyrdom as a sign that, when called for, indicates not only faithfulness but also sanctity.

Bonhoeffer himself offers a rich example of the ways in which our particular vocation to theological teaching, or to law, or medicine, or anything else must be set within a more fundamental vocation to discipleship in and through Christian community. By any standard, Bonhoeffer had a rich vocation to the scholarly life. His early scholarship, written while he was still astonishingly young, has withstood the test of time and offered a significant contribution to a variety of fields of study. He was on a remarkably high career trajectory as a theological scholar and teacher. Yet he left that track because the social and political conditions, and his own Christian convictions, required it of him.

For several years, his vocation continued to make more of him as he faced head-on the challenges of Nazi Germany. It made more of him as his theological work deepened and his discipleship became more second-nature. During the mid-1930s, his writing on the nature of Christian community and the need to be in solidarity with the Jews was reflective of, and continued to shape, his concrete pastoral and political activities.

Yet, paradoxically, more was being made of Bonhoeffer only as his vocation was requiring intensifying sacrifice. In some ways, this was simply a manifestation of his vocation to discipleship; yet it was also a crucial ingredient in his vocation to a scholarly life. This is so in at least three ways. First, he recognized and embodied the attention, and asceticism, of effective scholarship that ought to continually open us to the other — whether that other be the uncompromising demands of Truth, the difficult puzzles of mastering a discipline, or the persons whom that scholarship ought to serve. Second, the specific character of Bonhoeffer's writing opened him to the discovery that his identity as scholar/teacher and as Christian required, in his specific circumstances, sacrifice that he clearly had not anticipated when he embarked on his vocation. Third, Bonhoeffer recognized that, for Christians, our vocation invites paradoxes that create tensions between that which gives us fulfillment and the self-emptying we are called to offer in service to others.

Hence, Bonhoeffer struggled to discern whether he ought to continue to create spaces for teaching and learning — at Berlin, or Finkenwalde, or ultimately, in 1939, Union Theological Seminary — or whether he was called to take even greater risks of sacrifice for the sake of the gospel. If his only guidance was what would make more of him as a person created and loved by God, I suspect his life would have unfolded quite differently — perhaps along the lines of other émigrés who quite faithfully undertook their vocations in the United States. Yet Bonhoeffer discerned, in the midst of chaos and complexity, that the risk was necessary and integral to his vocation.

My study of Bonhoeffer's life and scholarship has been pivotal in shaping my vocation as a scholar and teacher. I have admired his passion for the creation and sustenance of specific forms of community, his willingness to revise or reject views he concluded were wrong, and his openness to have both his ideas and his life shaped by the God of Jesus Christ. I have also recognized in him a challenge to my temptation to detach the scholarly life from the concrete needs of others and from wider political issues. Bonhoeffer has been a significant mentor in helping me understand the vocation of teaching and learning as involving a mutual apprenticeship in which, as Augustine puts it, Christ is the only true Teacher.

It would seem, then, that there are checks internal to a Christian sense of vocation to guard against it being co-opted by a culture of self-fulfillment. We ought to be wary of a life in which I, as an individual, find my opportunities or external rewards continually expanding without any sacrifice — particularly when those rewards come at the expense of others. This ought to be especially poignant for those of us whose teaching and scholarship is in theological areas of inquiry, but it ought to be no less apparent to Christians involved in law, medicine, business, social work, or other vocations. Ultimately, my vocation should be shaped not so much by whether I find it fulfilling, or whether it makes more of me, as by whether it enables me to be faithful to the God of Jesus Christ and to particular communities of people.

To be sure, we ought also to be wary of those who are too ready to make sacrifices, too unwilling to insist that their vocation ought to be making more of them as persons. After all, Christians have been wary of those who seem too eager for martyrdom, those who are incapable of recognizing the difference between an acceptance of suffering and a perverse love of it. But we ought also to recognize that, while we may need to accept seasons in which we sacrifice for the sake of God and particular communities, we need also to discover seasons and arenas in which our vocation will continue to make more of us over time.

The call to wariness about sacrifice carries with it significant gender implications, especially as women in our culture are given explicit and implicit messages to sacrifice rather than to find fulfillment in their scholarly vocations. There are persons who need to be as worried about being coopted by a destructive culture of self-sacrifice as by one of self-fulfillment.

More generally, fidelity to the God of Jesus Christ involves, vocationally, a multitude of tradeoffs and contingent costs. How does one undertake a vocation to theological scholarship in the midst of competing loyalties to family and children, to church and other communities, to the institution where one teaches, to the guild, and to one's own internal rhythms of work, rest, and playfulness? How does one sustain a vocation when blocked by a lack of opportunities or by political dynamics from securing a teaching job in order to exercise that vocation? How should one understand the seasons of a vocation, including especially the potential cost that sacrifice may be required at precisely the time one most needs to discover a sense of fulfillment? Ironically, for theological scholars, the demands of family and children often are most pressing at precisely the time when our vocational investment as scholars is most intense — learning to teach, to write and publish, both in order to earn tenure and to establish one's scholarly identity in a multitude of communities.

217

More perniciously, at least potentially, how should one understand and live out a vocation that requires sacrifice if one inhabits a community, or an institution, that is unwilling to acknowledge any flexibility, much less sacrifice, in the ways it deals with its employees? Vocations become destructive when communities require sacrifice always to be unidirectional rather than mutual, especially when the direction usually is sacrifice by the relatively powerless in ways that benefit the powerful.

Once again, we need friends and a discerning community to help us narrate and negotiate the tensions of our vocation, especially as we seek to understand the tradeoffs that are, in some sense, inevitable for us as contingent creatures, as well as the sacrifices that become necessary because of the sinful personal, social, institutional, and political constraints that afflict our discernment. Such friends help us with discernment, sustain us amidst the frustrations and discouragement we inevitably encounter, and can even begin to offer new resources to deepen our sense of vocation even as we find it requiring sacrifices for them and others.

However, what if one of our pressing vocational needs is for persons to undertake the practice of sustaining scholarly communities for the sake of others?

III

"The place God calls you is the place where your deep gladness and the world's deep hunger meet."

Frederick Buechner, *Wishful Thinking: A Theological ABC*

Buechner's statement focuses our attention on the need for discernment. How do you understand the world's deep hunger? How do you come to recognize what provides your deep gladness? How do you come to recognize where they meet? How might we discern the vocation to theological teaching as a convergence of our deep gladness and the world's deep hunger?

Given our nature as human beings and the ways in which we learn to navigate the world and to come to know and love God, there will be an ongoing need in the world for effective teachers and scholars. Further, many of us have a talent for teaching, research, and writing, perhaps a talent so clear that it ought to shape our lives. But what ought we to teach? Perhaps there is a greater need in the world for teaching young children, or for

218

teaching in Russia, or for teaching economics, than for teaching theology to undergraduates at a midwestern church-related college. Or perhaps there is nothing more urgent than doing the latter — for the flourishing life of the teacher, for the long-term well-being of the church and the students who are taught, and for the scholarship that the teacher will develop and publish for others. Obviously, such a long-term view is crucial to understand the complex relationship of vocations and the needs and hungers of the world. For example, it is necessary in order to understand the powerful witness of monastic vocations, where what seems to be a rejection of the world is precisely a life lived for the sake of the world through contemplation and prayer.

To be sure, we need a richer and more expansive sense of what people *need* than is found in much modern discourse. As Michael Ignatieff has beautifully characterized the issues in his book *The Needs of Strangers*, too much of our discourse focuses on what strangers need to survive rather than what they need to flourish. The needs of the world include issues of beauty and truth as well as goodness and mercy, of love as well as justice, of gracious rest and playfulness as well as the fulfillment of duty.

Buechner's saying clearly implies a need for ongoing discernment of the world's needs and hungers (including the very particular needs and hungers of others on whom we depend and who depend on us), a person's gifts and deep gladness, and places and spaces where they may converge. This discernment involves ongoing negotiation of how we manage to hold together our significant, diverse, and overlapping yet conflicting identities as parent, pastor, professor, parishioner, partner, player, citizen.

Even so, there may be times in which we find ourselves in situations where the normal identities are threatened, where the ordinary complexities of our lives are endangered by a cacophonic chaos. What do we do when we find ourselves in social, political, or institutional contexts in which space for such discernment has been occluded? This was what Bonhoeffer faced in Nazi Germany, a situation where he witnessed the collapse of any meaningful Christian community, indeed the collapse of any critical intellectual community.

Or, what if we find ourselves in situations where the communities necessary to sustain meaningful vocations are increasingly fragile or, perhaps, occluded? In such times, then perhaps more of us than usual are called particularly to devote ourselves to fostering the sustenance of communities of discernment. Indeed, one of the world's deep hungers is to mend the fabrics of our relations with one another in order to enable not only my flourishing but others' as well.

Might it be that, in a time such as ours where we find ourselves and our institutions in the midst of great transition, and our church and institutional communities threatened from within and without, we need people whose vocation is to enable others' vocations? I suspect that, in no small measure, such a sensibility was behind some of my friends' insistence that I consider becoming a theological administrator. It was not that my deep gladness and the world's deep hunger couldn't converge in a life as a teacher of undergraduates; that seemed to be working rather well.

Rather, it seems that a particular reading of "the world's deep hunger" — in the context of my own particular discernment, such a phrase is unnecessarily grandiose — and of my talents suggested to a number of friends and acquaintances that I should devote this time in my life to an embodiment of my vocation shaped by the work of enabling others' vocations. In part, this was because my vocational commitments encompass a peculiar combination well-suited to Duke's own institutional vocation: the United Methodist Church and the preparation of its ministers, research and scholarship suitable to a research university, interest in interdisciplinary work.

As one of my friends put it to me when I objected that I could fulfill a sense of vocation, even understood in Buechner's terms, by bearing witness to the need for effective church-related undergraduate education: "You ought to go not simply where you are needed, but where you are needed most." There is a part of me that resonates to such a description, recognizing that there are other people who can do well many of the things I can do — even those I do well. Perhaps we ought to serve wherever there is the closest match we can find between our own vocation and the vocation of a particular institution. Such a match is obviously subject to various personal, political, and institutional constraints. But it is even more difficult to find in a time and context, such as contemporary American higher education, where graduate education, the job market, and the failure of many institutions to be clear about their own vocation and mission converge to encourage theological teachers to be entrepreneurial free-agents unwilling to commit to anything other than their guild.

In the midst of such complexities, we are called to narrate and re-narrate the dramas of our lives in relation to God. People need a deep and renewing sense of God's grace, and of God's love, in order to sustain the twists and turns that shape the dramas of our lives. If we encounter deep frustration in having our vocation blocked by political power-plays, institutional constraints, or perhaps our own misdirected hopes, we need to find ways to re-narrate our vocation in a renewed discernment. Alternatively, if we encounter unexpected joy by the flattering lures of prestigious positions, we need to test that joy by narrating how this-worldly success fits into our vocation in relation to God.

These first three sayings point, I hope, to the necessary tensions and complexities involved in discerning and living a Christian vocation. These tensions and complexities take particular shape in relation to demands of theological teaching and the need for administrators to serve communities that make theological teaching possible. But we learn to narrate and negotiate such tensions and complexities of vocation in the context of a journey where, we hope, we have both a sense of direction and a capacity for surprise.

IV

"Do you want to make God laugh? Tell God your plans."

Familiar Saying in Divinity School

We need some clarity of direction as we are in the midst of the ongoing process of discerning our vocations, and narrating and negotiating its tensions, throughout the seasons of our life and those of the communities and institutions we serve. If we lack that direction, we are likely to take (or to be confused by) any road that comes along. We know from painful experience that shortsighted judgments are unlikely to provide the sustenance and growth we look for from longer-term vocational direction. At times, we might unpredictably discover that a chance opportunity turns out to provide lifelong direction. More likely, however, we make wise discernments when we have a compass that provides us clearer direction. For Christians, that direction should be given its shaping orientation by our destination to know and love God faithfully.

To be sure, this destination offers us a *telos* that we identify with some clarity at the outset but grasp at best partially as we begin to explore what it might fully mean. To adapt an image deployed by Sabina Lovibond, we seek a description of our vocation broad enough to offer us direction

221

while also providing "semantic depth" sufficient to enrich our commitment over time. Or, to mix the metaphor, the journey is crucial as we learn to understand more fully and faithfully our destination. It is a journey filled with conflicts and tensions, unexpected joys and griefs, a sense of self-fulfillment as well as self-sacrifice, opportunities to serve others and to resist injustice.

It is also a journey where I am not exclusively in control. This is partly because of constraints we face — social, political, and institutional as well as personal — and partly because of the ways in which friends, families, and communities help to shape our discernment. Yet for Christians it is more determinative than that, for ultimately we believe that God is the primary guide in the discernment of our vocation. How we understand that process is a complex and controversial matter, though clearly not to be separated from the conversations we have with friends, families, and communities.

Even so, this openness to the guidance of others, and even of a determinative Other, suggests that we need both a sense of direction and an awareness that we are often led to places we did not plan to go. This is typically a retrospective judgment as we seek to make sense of our lives, but it also ought to shape our prospective sense that God is with us even amidst the perplexities of our present and future. If we live in the confidence of God's providential care, a providence that admittedly is clearer to us retrospectively and will only finally be clear eschatologically, then we can move forward in the journey with a sense of direction but without a set of predetermined plans.

Obviously, this is easier said than done. But it ought to enable us to have fewer anxieties about the future, as we recognize that our plans are not as important as remaining faithful to our vocations. Careful discernment about the future, and clarity about our vocation, are crucial. So also is knowing to whom we are accountable (in all of that complexity) and whom we trust for guidance in challenging the vices we have come to love and affirming the gifts we are afraid to claim. This is, admittedly, a process in which times of clarity and contentedness will undoubtedly alternate with times of messiness and chaotic uncertainty. But as we narrate and negotiate the tensions of our vocation, we also discover the gifts we receive from others in calling us to deeper and richer commitment.

Fidelity to our vocation might mean, even in the best of circumstances, a gap between discerning what we think our vocation is calling us to do and what we would like to be doing. Or, put in the language I used above, it might mean a gap between what we think is likely to require self-sacrifice from us and what we believe will make more of us. We would hope that the gap is temporary, that over time we will begin to discover an increasing convergence between what we are called to do and what we want to do. But, regardless of how short or long the period might be, we need that long-range vision of growth in the knowledge and love of God that envelops and sustains us in all that we are and do.

The gap may indeed be a gracious sign of God's patient, forgiving love, continually receiving us back even amidst our own confusion or even sinful rebellion. After all, Jonah was clear about what God was calling him to do; he just didn't want to do it. But even though he failed to do what he was called to do, the gap is gracious because it kept Jonah thinking about his vocation. After all, Jonah did not distort his understanding of God in order to create a vocation more suitable to his desires. He maintained a sense of the gap between his calling and his desires, a gap whose gracious character enabled him to understand and obey God more truthfully (even if not yet to love God more faithfully).

I trust that, at least thus far, I am living with the gap more by struggling with what God is calling me to do rather than running in sinful rebellion from it — though, to be sure, there are always signs of sinful rebellion even in the midst of my struggles to be faithful. Even if I am not headed off to Tarshish, however, there is little room for me to sit smugly in judgment on Jonah. After all, I have not heard as clear a voice from God as Jonah did, nor is what I am doing anywhere near as difficult as what Jonah was called to do. Even so, I live trusting that the gap that I experience is a gracious sign of God's providential care, and that it will become clearer to me over time how to discover a closer convergence between what I sense I am called to do and what I would otherwise like to be doing. The paradigm here seems to be Abraham's willingness to follow God's call, even though God did not offer a clear "plan" for where Abram and Sarai would be going. At various points in his journey, Abram clearly sensed a gap, and even some sinful rebellion — but he continued to trust in God's providential care.

Ideally, we will not experience a sharp sense of the gap between our calling and our own desires, regardless of how we negotiate the challenges of faithfulness and rebellion. Rather, we will hope to discover an increasing convergence between what we are called to do and what we find fulfilling and desirable.

But on this side of the fullness of God's Kingdom, we are not likely to experience such idyllic bliss. More likely, we will continually struggle to narrate and negotiate the tensions of our vocation as we seek to be faithful to God, to serve effectively communities and institutions, and to honor our own integrity and truthfulness. At times, we may even discover that we have misdescribed our vocation, and thus need to make a significant shift in what we do and for whom we do what we do. At other times, we may discover that contingent personal, social, political, and/or institutional circumstances compel a broader description of our vocation, or a redescription of the particular tasks that enable us to fulfill that vocation.

Throughout the seasons of our lives, we are called to negotiate our sense of vocation by continually narrating and re-narrating the dramas of our lives in relation to God. These are dramas with numerous twists and turns and calls for discernment, and they are dramas in which sometimes we have to come to terms with a recognition that we are called not to our own grandest dreams but perhaps to a smaller, less dramatic role. They are dramas in which there are various choruses of trusted friends and communities that we are summoned to hear and other voices we ought to resist. Sometimes those voices will call us to find spaces that make more of us, while at other times we will be called to come and die (figuratively and sometimes literally). These voices will help us discern where the world's deep hungers are, what sustains our deep gladness, and how the world's hunger and our gladness might converge. They might even help us understand the vocation of helping to nurture the care and sustenance of communities and institutions so that others might fulfill their vocation.

Most of all, we hope and pray that the voices of these friends and communities will help us develop and maintain an ironic sense of humor as we discover the surprises that God seems continually to have in store for us. Who would have thought that a part of Abraham and Sarah's vocation would be the discovery of a pregnancy when Sarah was ninety and Abraham a centenarian? Yet Sarah laughed.

I suspect that we will be able to negotiate the tensions of our vocation most faithfully if we are able not only to appreciate the ways in which we make God laugh, but also to embody the richness of learning to laugh with God. To be sure, there will be times when the laughter will emerge only in the wake of pain and tears, but — if we are able to trust in the goodness and providence of God — it will nonetheless be laughter.

The Formation of Vocation —
Institutional and Individual

LEANNE VAN DYK

EACH MORNING, AT THE SEMINARY where I teach, in between two scheduled class times, there is an hour of community ritual that represents the particular ethos and core values of the seminary. First we worship. Chapel is well attended by students, staff, faculty, and visitors, with the exception of exam weeks, when attendance drops off somewhat. Then there is a coffee break, a sacred time and space in its own way. Again, the entire community is there, sitting at round tables, sharing in conversation and laughter.

An identical routine is played out at the end of the coffee break. The president of the seminary stands and rings a bell, signaling quiet. First, he asks if there are any guests to introduce. Prospective students, spouses or parents of students, local clergy mentors, or visiting lecturers are introduced by a student host and welcomed with applause. Next, he asks if there are any announcements. Information is given on seminary sports teams, special lectures, and opportunities for service or giving. Last, he asks if there are prayer requests. The community is asked to pray for a wide spectrum of needs — illnesses within the extended community, unemployment, family stresses, global disasters, and any other matters of concern. This daily ritual at Western Theological Seminary, in Holland, Michigan, a ritual of worship-fellowship and welcome-prayer is a visible "mission statement," one that is highly revealing not only of the quality of community life at Western, but also of the identity of the institution as a place for the formation of pastors.

This essay explores a set of issues that cluster around institutional identity, ethos, and vision in the theological seminary. The issues include the relationship between the corporate vocation of a theological seminary and the individual vocation of the theological educator. What is this relationship? Does corporate identity shape individual identity? Do the vocations of each professor combine to form a coherent corporate identity? Is the relation more complex and varied?

In addition, the issue of how a corporate identity is fostered will be explored. Again, the complexities of this issue are imposing. Each theological school's history, context, faculty, staff, board, finances, students, relationship to wider academic and/or denominational entities — all these impact corporate identity. By reflecting on these questions from the context of my own institution, Western Theological Seminary, a denominational seminary of the Reformed Church in America (RCA), this essay will suggest that a theological school's corporate identity can be a conscious, considered, yet complex reality. In recent years, Western Seminary has undergone just such a conscious and considered reflection on identity. The essay will further suggest that such an institutional reflection of corporate vocation has an unmistakable, though varied, impact on the vocation of each theological educator.

Because this essay reflects on the interactions of the identity of a theological seminary and the identity of individual theological educators, some brief account of my own entrance to Western's ethos is helpful. I came to Western Seminary after six years of teaching at San Francisco Theological Seminary. During the series of interviews, the dean explained that a new curriculum had just been instituted, one that required significant changes for the faculty, but one that also had the full support of the faculty. Far from a slate of minor adjustments, this curriculum was the result of an extensive process of articulating the vision of the seminary — not only for theological education, but on the very nature of the gospel, the church, and the culture. When I arrived at Western in 1998, I had little awareness of how the institution's vision of its vocation would fundamentally alter my own vision of identity as a theological educator. These last few years of immersion in the ethos and values of Western have shaped me in significant ways that I judge to be both deepening and expanding of my understanding of both the Christian faith and the formation of students for ministry.

Some brief account of the character of Western as a denominational seminary is also warranted. Western Theological Seminary is one of two seminaries of the Reformed Church in America. The RCA is a denomination of just under a thousand congregations. It is organized by eight regional synods under which are forty-six classes. Originally a denomination primarily of Dutch immigrants, the RCA has become "Americanized" in the past half-century, losing many, although not all, characteristics of an ethnic immigrant subculture. The denomination is now very diverse in several respects: there is theological diversity, diversity in worship styles, some ethnic diversity, and geographical variations that might best be described as ethos differences. The RCA congregations in upstate New York, for example, have a character quite different from those in Iowa, which, again, are different from those in Southern California.

The RCA is experiencing the same stresses and strains that have impacted other mainline denominations in recent decades, including declining or stagnant membership numbers, clergy shortages in rural communities, and a growing "congregationalism" that parallels a declining "denominationalism." The challenge for the seminary, in the face of these variations, is to forge a theological vision that is open and hospitable to difference as well as united in mission, worship, and service.

This essay will account for recent developments in Western Seminary's self-awareness of institutional vocation by examining the *influences* on identity reflection, the *process* of this reflection, and the *impact* that it has had on both the institution and individual faculty members. The essay makes no claims that this is a universal, or even a typical, account of institutional vocation formation. It is one specific way that institutional vocation and individual vocation have unfolded. What is unique about Western Seminary's experience, I believe, is the deliberate process of institutional reflection on the basis of a particular theological framework, a framework that inevitably has shaped my own vocation as a theological educator, as well as that of other faculty members.

Influences

Western Seminary is situated in one of the strongholds of the RCA. Located in Holland, Michigan, the seminary is an important resource, most directly, for the fifty or more RCA congregations in the immediate area,

227

but also for the entire denomination. Clearly, its identity as a denominational seminary is a key factor that informs institutional vocation. The
seminary explicitly wishes to serve the RCA and to address the challenges
of denominational health and growth.

Other clear values come into play as well, however, including ecumenicity and diversity. Tensions around a perceived clash of values that affirm
both denominational particularity and a wider ecumenicity sometimes
arise. As one way of recognizing this tension, the worship committee recently asked the faculty to address the "core values" of Western Seminary
in their chapel homilies, including openness and welcome to all students,
willingness to listen carefully to others, support to women in ministry and
sensitivity to gender issues, and a lively and contemporary Reformed theological perspective.

The clear identity of Western Seminary as a denominational seminary plainly impacts faculty vocation. It is the responsibility of the faculty,
for example, to evaluate each student's "fitness for ministry" throughout
his or her seminary career, a process that is time and energy intensive. Not
only do faculty members evaluate the students' academic abilities and
skills for ministry, but we reflect carefully on each student's maturity, ability to engage in constructive conflict resolution, spiritual health and psychological health. We look for any indications of unresolved anger or hos-
tility, inability to collaborate, or difficulties in quality relationships. For
students that are identified with any concerns, a special faculty committee
is formed and is responsible to formulate and carry through appropriate
intervention. This evaluation procedure is one example of the denomination's expectations for seminary faculty involvement in the ordination
process. These expectations exert significant influence on both institutional vocation and individual faculty formation.

The influence on the seminary in recent years that will be highlighted in this essay is the Gospel and Our Culture Network (GOCN), a
coalition of theological educators and pastors who are committed to articulating the implications of "missional" ecclesiology. Missional ecclesiology, drawing its resources from several seminal thinkers, including the
late Lesslie Newbigin and the late David Bosch, is not limited to one denomination or theological tradition. It is comprised of a wide range of traditions, including Reformed, Lutheran, Methodist, Episcopal, Catholic,
Mennonite, United Church of Christ, and others. The coalition was begun
in the late 1980s and has a present mailing-list membership of over three

thousand people, a newsletter, and a small but growing body of literature published mainly by Eerdmans Publishing Company.[1]

The coordinator of the GOCN is George Hunsberger, Professor of Missiology at Western Seminary. His leadership role in the GOCN has shaped not only that network of pastors and theologians but also the vocation of the seminary. A number of other faculty also, as well as the dean and the president, have continually asked probing questions on institutional identity and vocation along missional lines. For example, the new curriculum, inaugurated in 1998, is fundamentally guided by the principles of missional ecclesiology.

Further description of the character of the GOCN will clarify how Western Seminary has developed its institutional vocation. What unites the GOCN is an interest in articulating the gospel in a way that takes seriously the post-Constantinian realities of much of the Christianized West. Such a reality must impact the way the church understands its call and its mission. Much more than ecclesiology narrowly considered, a missional approach in a church influences cultural critique, congregational life, theological education, missiology, discussions of the common good, small Bible study groups, preaching, exegesis, and every other practice of ministry. It also influences one's fundamental understanding of the Christian faith.

The mission statement of the network reads as follows: "The Gospel and Our Culture Network is a collaborative association of Christian leaders from diverse communions, working together to help the church explore and engage the newly emerging missionary encounter of the gospel in the cultures of North America." The network came together as a response to cultural realities that demand the attention of the church. Such cultural realities include increasing pluralism and diversity in what once was a Christianized West; the dislocation of the church from what was its

1. These titles include: Robert Banks, *Reenvisioning Theological Education: Exploring a Missional Alternative to Current Models* (Grand Rapids: Eerdmans, 1999); Darrell L. Guder, ed., *Missional Church: A Vision for the Sending of the Church in North America* (Grand Rapids: Eerdmans, 1998); George Hunsberger, *Bearing the Witness of the Spirit: Lesslie Newbigin's Theology of Cultural Plurality* (Grand Rapids: Eerdmans, 1998); George Hunsberger and Craig Van Gelder, eds., *The Church Between Gospel and Culture: The Emerging Mission in North America* (Grand Rapids: Eerdmans, 1996); and Craig Van Gelder, ed., *Confident Witness — Changing World: Rediscovering the Gospel in North America* (Grand Rapids: Eerdmans, 1999).

assumed place of influence and power; the secularism, commercialism, and individualism of popular culture; and an expanded awareness of how cultural particularity shapes both understanding and articulation of the Christian faith.

The issues that the GOCN has identified that need research and articulation range across broad cultural questions, including the function of civil religious symbols and popular religion. How, for example, has the gospel been "domesticated" in North America, in a setting of cultural dominance? The big questions of power relations within society, especially as they impact the poor and disenfranchised, are also targeted for analysis. The contemporary interest in postmodernism, technology, and diversity are also relevant to the range of interests among the network.

The vision that infuses the thinking and writing of the GOCN is a prophetic vision concerning the call of the church in contemporary society. Convinced that the church is now in a cultural setting radically different from old paradigms of Christian cultural hegemony, the network wishes to articulate a vision of the church that challenges those old assumptions and summons the church to be an alternative community, a gospel community, an authentic witness to contemporary cultures.

A network author summarizes this vision:

> Two realities are readily apparent to Christians as they examine the present situation of Christianity in its North American context. First, the increasing marginalization in North American culture of Christian faith in general and of the Christian church in particular must call forth from Christians a fresh vision of what it means to be a Christian and to be the Christian church in our post-Christian setting. Second, Christians also believe that the Christian faith offers good news and hope for our situation, good news that must be lived out and proclaimed with courage and wisdom.[2]

Douglas John Hall, whose work has consistently addressed the particular cultural realities of a North American context, suggests a threefold

---

2. James V. Brownson, "Speaking the Truth in Love: Elements of a Missional Hermeneutic," in *The Church Between Gospel and Culture*, p. 228. James Brownson is the academic dean at Western Seminary and the primary architect of the new curriculum which attempts to put into practice a missional model of theological education.

analysis of Christian witness in a post-Christendom age. He says, first, we are in a state of *metamorphosis,* a state of enormous change. Second, we must approach this change with *intentionality,* with understanding and careful reflection. Third, we must be clear about our *theology,* so that we can engage culture, not uncritically absorb it or defensively reject it.[3]

The metamorphosis of North American culture is documented in the growing literature of cultural analysis, which attempts to account for the profound changes in North American culture in the past few decades. The characteristics of so-called Generation X, for example, are carefully measured and interpreted. Such analysis records attitudes in Gen-Xers, who are suspicious of tradition, of authority, and of commitment.[4] Church leaders sometimes interpret this data as a call to launch programming and worship experiences that will attract, dazzle, impress, and entertain Gen-Xers. Out with the old. In with the "new and the next."[5]

This is not the intentionality that Hall and the missional thinkers of the GOCN propose. For them, Christian witness in a post-Christendom age requires a keen sense of who the church is and what its call is in a culture that has radically de-centered the church. The theology of the missional church perceives the church not as the master of culture, the central power that arbitrates mores and values, but as the people of God called to serve the kingdom of God by living in gospel-shaped community. Missional ecclesiology means "embodying a particular way of life that exemplifies the ontological reality of the eschatological future brought into the present by the incarnational reality of Jesus Christ."[6]

---

3. Douglas John Hall, "Metamorphosis: From Christendom to Diaspora," in *Confident Witness — Changing World,* p. 68. It is interesting to note that in this essay, Hall identifies themes in Karl Rahner's 1963 book *Mission and Grace* similar to the contemporary missional theology conversation. Rahner was convinced that radical self-knowledge is necessary for the church in order to engage in authentic mission based on grace rather than based on uncritical Christian expansionism.

4. Tom Beaudoin, *Virtual Faith: The Irreverent Spiritual Quest of Generation X* (San Francisco: Jossey-Bass, 1998), p. xvii. Other literature which analyzes Generation X includes G. Barna, *Baby Busters: The Disillusioned Generation* (Chicago: Northfield, 1994); K. Bergeron, "The Virtual Sacred," *New Republic* 212, no. 9 (1995): 29-34; D. Coupland, *Generation X: Tales for an Accelerated Culture* (New York: St. Martin's Press, 1991); W. Mahedy and J. Bernardi, *A Generation Alone: Xers Making a Place in the World* (Downers Grove, Ill.: InterVarsity Press, 1994).

5. This is Alan Roxburgh's phrase from his article "The Church in Post-Modern Context," in *Confident Witness — Changing World,* p. 258.

Echoing the language of Vatican II's *Lumen Gentium,* such a perspective will "recover the call to form a pilgrim people who are strangers and aliens in the land."[7]

An article from Western Seminary's journal, *Reformed Review* (1998), written by George Hunsberger, gives a clear and concise summary of the theological principles of missional ecclesiology. These principles make it clear that this conversation reaches far beyond ecclesiology as a separate and distinct theological locus; they implicate all arenas of Christian activity, within the church and in the wider culture.

The first principle states the fundamental perspective that the "charter story" of the church's life together is the action of God in the life, death, and resurrection of Jesus Christ. The church is not, at base, a volunteer organization or a service provider. It is the gathered people who together confess, enact, and herald the reign of God. The church exists as a "tangible option" for people, an option that exists in embodied and concrete form. It lives out what it proclaims. Thus, the qualities of peace, hope, and joy are not only anticipated in the full realization of God's reign, but are, in partial yet still significant ways, present in the community's life now. These virtues-in-practice characterize the community as they gather together in worship and service; yet they are also lived in "full view of the world." In briefest form, these are the contours of a missional theology.

These theological affirmations that describe the approach of the GOCN are the guiding principles for the institutional vocation of Western Seminary as well. The seminary faculty, in extended conversations over the past six to eight years, has come to a common mind on both the accuracy of the cultural critique proposed by missional theology and the vigorous call to the church posed by it.

Of course, missional theology is not an innovation. It finds deep roots in many streams of the broad Christian tradition. It draws on biblical sources, is deeply consonant with social justice ethics, echoes much of the language of narrative ethics and reflections on Christian practices, emphasizes the formational potential of liturgy and sacraments, employs key metaphors from Vatican II, and reaches across denominational barriers to express a common vision of authentic Christian existence in the world.

The challenge for the seminary has been in finding concrete and visi-

6. Roxburgh, "The Church in Post-Modern Context," p. 258.

ble ways to embody these principles in the curriculum, community life, teaching relationships, and the numerous encounters between students and faculty. This challenge shapes not only institutional vocation, but individual faculty vocation as well.

Process

Although brief, the above summary of the themes of the missional church conversation developed in the Gospel and Our Culture Network can now be applied to the question of the process of institutional vocational formation at Western Seminary and individual vocational formation of faculty members. There is no question that the convictions of missional church thinkers, especially those on the Western Seminary faculty, have had a central role in an explicit formulation of institutional vocation.

Any description of process with respect to institutional identity and formation is highly complex. All the factors that make up an institution are included. Faculty, staff, students, administration, board of trustees, physical plant, financial stability, donor loyalty, denominational vitality, and trust in the seminary — all these factors, and more, must be considered in a reflection of process. For the purposes of this essay, however, I attempt to make some manageable generalizations. The vocation of Western Seminary as an institution has developed in the past few years by a roughly discernible threefold process: *guiding vision, convergence, and implementation.*

The first part of the process, which has clearly been the guiding vision of missional church principles, has been particularly important. The leadership of Professor of Missiology George Hunsberger, Academic Dean Jim Brownson, President Dennis Voskuil, and other faculty members to make these principles integral to the life of the seminary shaped the curriculum from beginning to end. What Western Seminary has experienced in recent years is how key faculty voices can deeply influence the entire institution's understanding of itself and its purpose. The influence of these faculty members has been remarkable. Many institutions, perhaps most, would respond with resistance to a clear, strong faculty member's voice. Such clarity of vision would be considered in some way threatening to the diversity of other faculty members' values. Although the process of new curriculum planning inevitably and always involves some conflict, the faculty did not respond with strong resistance and rejection. The vision, terminology, and goals of missional ecclesiology have been taken up by the entire faculty not as a threat or incursion but as a clarification to their own work and their sense of call.

The second part of the process of institutional vocation formation at Western is convergence. Because missional ecclesiology has been understood as a rich and fruitful vision of Christian existence in the world, the process of institutional vocation formation has included the convergence of key faculty voices with the entire institution, including the rest of the faculty, the administration, and the board. Missional perspectives have clarified the M.Div. curriculum, the Th.M. program for international students, and the D.Min. degree for pastors in congregational settings.

Specifically, the missional perspectives that shaped the curriculum can be articulated as follows: The *contextuality* of all theological expression is emphasized. There is no neutral or value-free theological utterance. This is a crucial first awareness for theological education. Some students initially are dubious of such an insight. In a variety of settings — classroom, peer groups, ministry assignments — students learn to see their own contextuality, their own particularity, their own situatedness.

In addition, and as an implication of contextuality, the *multicultural* character of contemporary theological discourse is modeled. Not only in required class reading assignments, but throughout the curriculum, the faculty attempts to present a wide array of theological voices and perspectives. A multicultural immersion experience during the January term is required for second-year M.Div. students. These immersion groups have recently traveled to Chiapas, Mexico, the border regions of southern Arizona, and Guatemala. Students return with a far richer and more nuanced understanding, for example, of the political pressures on Christian believers in Chiapas; they also witness the vitality and joy of the church there, and the political and economic realities of migrant workers along the border. As a result, students report growth, transformation, and clarity to their sense of call to gospel ministry.

In an effort to bring practical ministry skills and theological reflection together, the curriculum aims for *integration* in all the disciplines. This means that students are linked with area pastors as mentors, and they form peer groups in order to reflect theologically on ministry and reflect practically on theology. It also means that the faculty plans courses with integration as a key course objective. Faculty members accustomed to a "research model" of theological education have been stretched to think through course objectives more concretely. But the goal of integration is central to a missional perspective; because the missional church seeks to embody the gospel in a particular place at a particular time, active reflection on how that embodiment ought to be visible is required.

Another perspective of missional ecclesiology that has impacted the new curriculum is the importance of a *collaborative approach.* The church is a community of mutual discernment and discipline. Hierarchies of specialized clergy are not the center of ministry; the whole body of the gathered people is the center of ministry. This means that seminary education must model for students those collaborative values. Every week, resource people from a variety of ministry settings and denominations come to the seminary for mentoring interaction with students. The quality and effectiveness of these groups are not easy to measure at this early stage, just three years into the new curriculum. But the effort to bring the wide resources of the church into the seminary models the value of a collaborative approach.

One further missional perspective is the *articulation of core values.* Because the church is the embodiment of the reign of God, virtues and core values must be visibly expressed. Acceptance, mutual forgiveness, accountability, and love are among the values that the seminary community attempts to reinforce in specific ways. The worship committee, for example, reminds the community to use language in worship that consistently includes women and that employs the wide range of biblical language with respect to God. The coffee time ritual of introductions and prayer requests is another place where values find visible form. Led by the example of the president, the community genuinely bears each other's burdens in prayer and expressions of support and concern.

The process of convergence between key faculty voices influenced by missional ecclesiology and the development of the new curriculum has not been without struggle and conflict. Healthy institutions must be able to withstand disagreement. But the adoption of the new curriculum, after several years of debate and meticulous planning, was with the full support and ownership of the whole faculty. Thus, the final stage of the process of formulating a sense of institutional vocation has been the *implementation* of the curriculum. We are presently in the third year of its three-year cycle. Already adjustments and corrections are being made to the first and second year, but the faculty's commitment to the overall design and goals of the curriculum remains high.

Impact

Institutional Impact

The impact of missional church perspectives on the *curriculum* has already been indicated. The impact has extended beyond the curriculum, however. There is a noticeable emphasis on the *community* of students, faculty, and staff together. If the missional church is called to embody the reign of God, then that sense of community and accountability is appropriate in the theological seminary as well. This is why the morning routine of community worship and then community coffee time and prayer requests stands as a concentrated paradigm of the institution's identity and vocation — it is an opportunity for the community to embody in concrete and visible ways their identity as the people of God.

Increased *collaboration with area churches* has heightened the visibility of the seminary in the community and has resulted in an increase of community appreciation and support for the seminary. There seems to be a growing awareness that the seminary is not a remote center of intellectual activity but an institution deeply interested in and committed to the health and witness of congregations.

Because the seminary is committed to partner with congregations in the area, to challenge them to a greater awareness of their own cultural particularity and their call to be the church in a gradually de-churched society, the seminary is planning to expand its offerings of *continuing education* opportunities. Such education opportunities will be geared not only toward area clergy but lay people as well. Convinced that the witness of the missional church is most authentic when the gospel is concretely embodied in community, the seminary hopes to provide times and places where this prophetic call to the church can be discussed, imagined, and practiced.

Faculty Impact

The impact on the seminary of the process of reflection on institutional vocation has been amply demonstrated. It now remains to be asked what the impact of a conscious and careful reflection of institutional vocation has been on individual faculty vocation. The implications for the faculty are clearly significant, perhaps in ways that the faculty is only gradually be-

236

ginning to sense. Implications range over three general, though overlapping, areas: teaching, research/publication, and student involvement.

One way to recognize the impact on teaching would be to contrast the ways the new curriculum has shaped faculty teaching responsibilities with what might be called the "classic" understanding of the theological professor as a research specialist. The "classic" model highly values opportunities to teach focused elective courses to advanced students. It seeks out teaching settings that might advance research projects and result in recognized publication. It might also, and conversely, judge introductory courses and integrative seminars as a diversion from one's primary vocational goals.

The new curriculum at Western Seminary turns this "classic" model of teaching and research upside down. Courses that integrate, that are interdisciplinary, that cross traditional boundaries of academic field and specialty are the norm rather than the exception. My own teaching responsibilities extend far beyond my field of systematic theology and include integrative courses with my colleagues in homiletics, pastoral theology, congregational studies, and practical ministry studies.

It must be emphasized that this sort of collegial approach and interdisciplinarity is not just an accidental outcome of the new curriculum. It explicitly fosters, models, and promotes the values of a missional, contextual approach to theological reflection and ministry. The impact on teaching responsibilities for each faculty member is a concrete implication of the dramatic critique of missional ecclesiology on North American religious culture. "Business as usual" is simply not possible. The post-Constantinian, pluralist realities of North America demand not only that churches change their programs and priorities but that theological seminaries change their curricula and faculty teaching responsibilities as well.

Another impact of institutional vocation on individual vocation is the area of research and publication. It is reasonable to assume that faculty members who teach courses that integrate disciplines and cross disciplinary lines will explore new genres of publication. The full extent of the impact of the new curriculum on faculty publishing remains to be seen. But as new connections are made, as fresh insights are seen, as previously unexplored literature is encountered, it is not unrealistic to suppose that faculty members will write in different sorts of ways than they wrote before. Collaborative projects, interdisciplinary projects, contextual and local theologies, articles or books that consciously take into account both academic theological reflection and lay resources — all these are possible, given the impetus of the new curriculum.

The potential impact on faculty research and publication is not limited to the *sort* of publishing projects undertaken. One of the unique features of Western Seminary's institutional vocation discussion of recent years, as already noted, is the emergence of a common commitment to a missional perspective. Such a common ownership of a guiding perspective shapes the very presuppositions, methodology, and purpose of writing, research, and academic identity. For example, the emerging ethos and values of the seminary encourage sabbatical activity that reflects the contextual character of all academic work. Although there are no institutional requirements for this particular kind of research and publication, clearly the encouragement is there. In addition, the guidelines for sabbatical leave in the faculty handbook validate not only traditional sabbaticals for research and writing but also suggest ways of integration of academic goals with ministry experience, including the possibility of engaging in part-time or full-time congregational ministry for a period of time.

Finally, the reflection of institutional vocation has impacted individual faculty interaction with students. Because missional perspectives on community include the perspective that Christian believers are called authentically to embody the gospel, are called to exhibit and inhabit virtues that identify them as the people of God, community has become important in the life of the seminary. This means, inevitably, increased expectations on faculty for faculty-student interaction. The task of student advising has expanded to include not only academic advising but also chapel advising, vocational advising, crisis counseling, and the support of friendship. Faculty members are expected to model and facilitate the cluster of virtues that make Christian life concretely visible and authentic. This takes time and emotional energy. More traditional professional responsibilities of research, teaching, and writing must make room for additional responsibilities that support and further the vocational identity of the seminary.

The tensions of the new curriculum hit many faculty as a reduction of available time for the passion of their discipline. After all, biblical scholars are biblical scholars partly because they love biblical studies. I am a theologian partly because I love theology. There are times when the multiple demands of an integrated curriculum are frustrating. On balance, however, the benefits have outweighed the costs. I believe the emphasis of Western's vocational identity as a seminary for the sake of the church, in the particular time and place where God has placed it, has made me a better theologian. Institutional vocational identity has shaped my own individual vocational identity. In this case, the influence of the institution on me has been fruitful. It perhaps remains to be seen whether the benefit extends the other way as well.

The first three years of the new curriculum have demonstrated that a missional theology has broad implications for institutional vocational identity and individual vocational identity. It is impossible, if not foolish, to attempt a "cost-benefit" analysis of the process Western Seminary has engaged in in recent years. As we move forward, issues of faculty load, research and publication, student involvement, denominational commitments, and area church expectations all arise on different fronts. These issues impact faculty in widely different ways. The faculty continues to express a commitment to working through the implications of the cultural critique, the theological perspective, and the prophetic call of missional theology.

Attending to the Collective Vocation

GORDON T. SMITH

Finding Affinity with a Collective Vocation

In the 1996-1997 academic year I was involved with a colleague, Ken Badley, in a qualitative study of long-term vocational vitality of faculty in theological schools in Canada (Roman Catholic, Evangelical, and Mainline Protestant). The project sought to identify the factors that would determine, or at least foster, long-term vocational vitality. To this end, Badley and I interviewed faculty who in their senior years were generally viewed to be highly engaged and alive in their teaching and research. We asked them questions designed to determine if there was any consistent pattern to the choices they made in their life and work in mid-career. From this we hoped to identify the elements in the life and work of theological teachers who would likely thrive in their vocation.

The results confirmed what we suspected: those who were alive and vital in their senior years were individuals with a love of teaching, a love of students, and a well-developed capacity to adapt their teaching to the changing character and needs of their students. However, our research also highlighted elements that we had not anticipated. A theme that came up again and again in the interviews was the relationship between individual theological teachers and the institutions where they had taught or were teaching. In this regard, two things stood out to us.

In some cases the professors we interviewed had been mistreated,

240

sometimes in ways that were astonishing, by the schools where they taught, either by their colleagues acting in concert, or by the administration. Some were forced to resign and leave to seek a position elsewhere. What was striking in each of these interviews was the lack of resentment. They had each moved on in their careers with passion, commitment, and joy without allowing their spirits to be derailed by the setback.

We were also impressed with the degree to which these individuals found themselves, by the time they reached their senior years (which we defined as 55 and older), in institutions where they could enjoy a high degree of congruency between their own vision and values and those of the institution where they were teaching. They were at home vocationally.

Our conclusions have been reinforced by the work of the Auburn Center, particularly Barbara G. Wheeler's findings in her study on the cultivation of effective theological school faculties. She stresses that "the most effective forms of faculty cultivation are those that are deeply and permanently enmeshed in the policies and everyday practices of the schools."[1] And further, that "The most important steps that a school can take to cultivate its new faculty are those that promote their integration into the institution's culture."[2] It only follows, then, that faculty "should be chosen with the greatest care for their fit with the purpose and mission of the school."[3] In other words, integration with the culture, mission, ethos, and values of the school is a profoundly significant indicator of likely success as a faculty member.

Both of these studies highlight the obvious reality that schools are different. There is no such thing as a generic theological school. And I would suggest that the most helpful way to think of these fundamental differences is through the lens of *vocation.* Just as it is possible to speak of the vocation of the theological teacher, one of the most helpful ways to think about theological schools is to consider the matter of a communal or corporate vocation. The assumption behind such a suggestion is that from a theological perspective, we cannot speak of the individual vocation except in the context of the community. All vocations are fulfilled in solidarity with others; each person fulfills an individual vocation in partnership with

---

1. Barbara G. Wheeler, *Tending Talents: The Cultivation of Effective and Productive Theological School Faculties,* Auburn Studies, No. 5, March 1997, p. 3.

2. Wheeler, *Tending Talents,* pp. 20-21.

3. Wheeler, *Tending Talents,* p. 21.

another. In the Epistle to the Romans St. Paul uses the image of the body to capture the principle that we do our work and fulfill our vocations with a high degree of mutual interdependence. Our individual potential is achieved in collaboration and partnership with others, whether it is our potential of personal transformation or the potential of making a differ ence in the world. Therefore it follows that we must determine that we will do our work not merely as individuals with particular and unique commitments, but also as a collective, as a community of scholars who in our work with administrators and trustees embrace and actually serve something that is bigger and more all encompassing than the sum of our individual vocations. Indeed I would go so far as to say that we will only be effective in the fulfillment of our individual vocations if we do so in the light of and in a manner that is congruent with the collective vocation.

I would propose that this will, at the very least, require three commitments: (1) that we discern and do our work in a manner that is congruent with the distinctive vocation of the school where we teach; (2) that we develop the organizational competencies to work with others toward a common goal, a capacity that at heart is the ability to work within a system of shared governance or power; and, (3) that we sustain a healthy distinction between our individual vocations and that of the school in which we serve.

Discerning a School's Vocation

We will thrive in our institutional context if we discern the distinctive vocation of the collective of which we are a part — the communal or institutional vocation of the school where we teach. When I joined the faculty of Regent College in the summer of 1998 as Dean and Associate Professor of Spiritual Theology, I was confronted once more with discerning the unique vocation of a theological school.

I had been the Dean and taught at three previous schools: the Alliance Biblical Seminary in Manila, Philippines, and both the Canadian Bible College and the Canadian Theological Seminary in Regina, Saskatchewan. One was an undergraduate college; the other two were denominational seminaries. When I arrived in Vancouver, I came with a growing conviction that vocation is not merely something that applies to individuals but also to the schools in which we fulfill our vocations as theological teachers. I accepted the invitation to Regent College largely because I observed or at least had a preliminary sense that my own values and vision were congruent with those of the school; I suspected that I had found a place in which I could be faithful to my own vocation while contributing enthusiastically to a collective vocation. But Wheeler's conclusions in the Auburn Series were a reminder that nothing could be taken for granted. Further, I was convinced that ultimately the collective vocation is discerned from *within*. When joining a theological faculty, one accepts an appointment on the basis of an appreciation of the school's history and mission statement and perhaps some explicit institutional values. But one only really discerns vocation from within the faculty and within the school. And this of necessity was a central priority to my first year in the role for my own sake, but also for the sake of those I would serve as Dean.

The mission statement is an obvious point of departure. But discerning the vocation of a school is much more than merely reading the mission statement, which probably only represents a focus or direction. The distinctive vocation of a theological school is by its very nature something far more complex, nuanced, and more pervasive than a mission statement can express, for it cannot be comprehended except in the context of the institutional and educational culture, which includes what kind of scholarship is valued and how — what role or value is given to teaching and to research. It incorporates the patterns of community life outside of the formal academic agenda, including decision-making processes and formal and informal governance procedures. It includes "the way things are done here," as well as those underlying dreams and longings within the community that represent both individual and collective hopes and aspirations. Discerning the vocation and character of a school includes appreciating the school's history and its patterns of institutional life and decision-making, which means that we recognize and affirm both distinctive strengths and limitations, which in some cases are probably institutional pathologies or at the least negative propensities. Discerning the culture and vocation of the school also means appreciating the way that the mission of the school is lived out in its spaces, particularly those places where people gather for worship, learning, conversation, or business. In other words, vocation is lived out in a set of practices, patterns of behavior, and attitudes.

But most of all, the vocation of the theological school is found in the unique interplay of two realities: the founding charisma of the school and how that founding vision is to be adapted and lived out in the current context. It requires that the collective understand its *present* position and possibilities, and how the original founding vision or charisma will find expression today. Invariably in this debate there will be some who would just as soon shed the original founding vision or charisma. There are many schools, for example, that have concluded that their original purpose is not relevant and that have intentionally distanced themselves from that heritage (for example: schools that have distanced themselves from their original church or religious foundations). On the other hand, there are just as many whose posture is one of resisting change, contending that faithfulness to the original vision requires no adaptation or adjustment to contemporary realities. The end of the matter invariably is one in which the collective is able, doubtless with many internal tensions, to come to clarity about the meaning of the original vision and its implications for the life of the theological school today.

What makes this a unique challenge is that, just as an individual's vocation evolves over time, so does an institution's vocation. Even a relatively young school like Regent College, founded in the late 1960s, will live out its vocation differently in the different chapters of the school's history. Further, many times we find ourselves in institutions in transition where the character or focus of a vocation may well be in flux.

The Vocation of Regent College

In some cases, discerning the vocation of a school is a matter of institutional survival. In a recent visit to an Anglo-Catholic episcopalian school I was impressed with both board members and faculty who recognized that in keeping to the original founding vision they were clinging to an impossible ideal, one that had died decades ago, and that their only possibility of thriving (let alone surviving) was to determine how the distinctive Anglo-Catholic vision and ideal would find unique and dynamic expression today. They recognized that it would necessarily mean letting go of some cherished structures and patterns of life and embracing with innovation and creativity some new possibilities. But this takes special discernment: the capacity to determine what lies at the heart of the original vision or charisma and how that founding dynamic can animate the current collective vision and vocation, so that any necessary changes do not so alter the contours of the school that it no longer is faithful to its vocation, so that pragmatic concerns do not leave it disconnected from its defining calling.

In the case of Regent College, the original founding vision was to provide *graduate* theological education for the laity. The school was established in 1968 by leaders within the Plymouth Brethren, who out of their unease with clergy and all things associated with a professionalization of the ministry sought to establish a school for the "whole people of God." Consequently, Regent initiated something new for North America: post-baccalaureate academic programs in theology designed for the laity. And while Regent has initiated other programs since then, including the Master of Divinity designed for ministerial formation, this original vision for graduate theological education for people in every walk of life and work continues to be the defining purpose of the college.

However, the original vision also included a particular understanding of scholarship and learning evidenced most fully, perhaps, in the resolve that piety and learning were to be integrated, and that theological education was to be informed by interdisciplinary studies. That original vision or charisma has evolved in a number of ways, and there are many other distinctive features of the Regent educational philosophy. But my read of this school's charisma is that these two elements lie at its heart: (1) the focus on the laity; and (2) the character of scholarship (notably the fact that piety and scholarship are integrally related, and that theological learning is informed by interdisciplinary studies). Whatever Regent College becomes and whatever form or shape it takes in its academic programs, its vocation as a theological school is necessarily defined by these two elements.

First, Regent College will only be faithful to our original defining vision if we sustain a resolve and capacity to provide theological education for the whole people of God — theological education for women and men whose vocations will take them into the world and the church. It will likely always be the case (and probably should be the case) that the majority of the students at Regent are those who enroll in degree programs that are not linked to professional religious leadership: they study theology at Regent with a view to being bankers, lawyers, carpenters, school teachers, artists, and politicians. They take their undergraduate and perhaps some graduate studies elsewhere that train them professionally; but at Regent College they study theology with a view to integrate their faith with their God-given vocations. In other words, at the heart of the Regent College vision for theological education is this commitment to provide graduate theological education not for professional religious leadership, but for the empowerment of all of God's people as they seek to serve Christ in the world.

However, Regent College also has a Master of Divinity (M.Div.) program, and many come to Regent with the anticipation that they will from here seek ordination and become, in effect, professional religious leaders within congregations. Given the defining vision of the college it is no surprise that there has been ambivalence about the program throughout the twenty years that it has been offered. However, there is no inherent reason why Regent should *not* have a strong M.Div. program, with the imperative proviso that it be defined in the light of the college's original vision and charisma: the formation, equipping, and empowerment of the laity. This will have many potential implications, but at the very least we can hope that a student who graduates with an M.Div. appreciates that as she enters into the ministry, she does so as one who has come to appreciate that in all of her theological studies she has learned side by side *with* lay persons, so that while in ministry she is never the only "learned" one, but rather one who is learning with her people. Second, I would also deeply hope that while being trained and equipped for the ministry a graduate of Regent who assumes a pastorate knows that he is never taking over a role in which he will "run the church" but rather one in which he is entering into a partnership with lay leaders in his congregation, leaders who will share the ministry with him and lead with him.

Further, just as Regent has always had a commitment to "the whole people of God," the defining charisma of the college has also included a distinctive understanding of scholarship and learning. Regent College is a school with a strong academic reputation, with a remarkable number of students who have gone on to postgraduate studies. But Regent has never allowed its notion of scholarship and learning to be defined by or limited by the disciplinary guilds. It has through its history appointed full professors in one discipline whose actual doctoral training was in a completely different discipline rather than a cognate one (i.e., Spiritual Theology and Geography); it has appointed full professors whose expertise lay as much in the quality of their devotional writing and the depth of their piety, as in their academic credentials. It has fostered an environment in which scholarship for students includes academic assignments that would seem anything but "academic," including aesthetic projects, or journal-writing or devotional reflections, all of which pushed the boundaries in such a way that one could easily wonder if academic integrity was jeopardized. But while there is no doubt that the boundary was indeed crossed at times, and scholarship was compromised by this kind of flexibility, it has been an inherent part of Regent's identity to push these boundaries. And it would be a fair observation to say that despite this, the school has never lost credibility as a venue for serious theological scholarship. Just the opposite: Regent is looked to as a school where piety and scholarship are (finally) integrated, and where learning is never bound by the strictures of the academic or disciplinary guilds.

In the case of the first element of the defining vision, there is always a threat that the college would on the one hand exclude those who wish to train for religious leadership in the church (at times they have felt like second-class students here), and the threat on the other hand that the college would succumb to the professionalization of the ministry and fall prey to clericalism. With respect to the second vision, we will always struggle with compromised scholarship on the one hand, or on the other hand the threat of overreacting and falling prey to a narrow definition of scholarship. These tensions will likely never go away; they are, somehow, inherent in the vocation of the college. That is, if my reading of the college is right, whatever shape or form or expression the school takes, it will only be faithful to its vocation if it allows its original defining vision to continue to shape the heart and center of its character and purpose.

This is offered as one example, and only as one person's reading of that example (and I am very conscious that as a relative newcomer to the college, I am still listening and learning and seeking to discern what it will take for Regent to fulfill its vocation), but nevertheless as an example of the attempt to discern the school's vocation by attending to both the original founding vision and its contemporary potential. It is also an attempt to address the reality that a theological school does not need to be all things to all people; rather, it is "called" to fulfill a particular agenda, which at root is something that is viewed as a "vocation": a calling and purpose that ultimately derive from God. Discerning vocation also means that we affirm and accept that there will be many potential faculty members who would not thrive at Regent College; they would not find a vocational "fit" if they came.

GORDON T. SMITH

The Challenge of Shared Governance

The vocation of the theological teacher is necessarily fulfilled within the context of a collective vocation, the calling of the theological school where one teaches. Ideally, of course, we would find ourselves in schools where there is a high degree of congruence between our individual vocations and the collective vocation. Working in tandem with a collective vocation is a matter not only of discerning that vocation, together; it also requires that we find a way to fulfill the vocation. And increasingly it is apparent to those in theological education that the context most conducive to this end is one in which we work with a model of *shared governance*. The Association of Theological Schools (ATS) actually identifies this as an essential standard for a good theological school, specifying that "Shared governance follows from the collegial nature of theological education."[4] This follows from the fundamental assumption behind the ATS standard on authority and governance that "Institutional stewardship is the responsibility of all, not just the governing board."[5]

The matter of shared governance is made all that more complex because of the changing character of theological education, and the inevitable need for an effective response to these changes. Theological schools are facing a bewildering number of environmental changes, changes that are in many ways threats to the potential of theological schools, threats that for some schools may place in question their viability, especially if they are dependent on tuition income. Higher education is changing in a manner that is fundamental and permanent; and, further, change itself has become a permanent feature of the landscape of theological schools. Student demographics are changing with an ever increasing number of part-time students. All theological schools are attempting to make sense of information technology, and respond to the demands and the opportunities of these new technologies in ways that are congruent with their philosophy of education. Denominational schools are facing the reality of declining denominational loyalty and the demand that the locus of biblical and theological scholarship shift from the academy to the church. And through and

---

4. *Bulletin 43* of the Association of Theological Schools in the United States and Canada, Part 1, specifies standards of accreditation, including Standard 8, Authority and Governance; for this reference, see Standard 8.2.2.

5. ATS Standards of Accreditation, Standard 8 (Introduction).

in the midst of all of this, those of us in theological schools — whether we serve on the faculty, the administration, or the trustees — will find that our schools will not thrive, let alone survive, unless we develop the capacity to respond with innovation and courage to these changes. We will not thrive in the midst of the changes unless we come to see that while many of these changes are threats to the viability and credibility of theological education, they are also opportunities for renewal within our schools.

William A. Barry has made the observation that:

> A burning question for our day . . . is how to make those institutions [in which we work and worship] and structures more attuned to God's will. . . . There is, perhaps, no greater challenge to religion today than to foster the conditions that make communal discernment possible.[6]

While there are many factors that would foster effective communal discernment, our capacity to discern and respond well to the changing environment in which we work will be in direct proportion to (1) clarity about our collective vocation and (2) the capacity to work with a model of shared governance. Without the first, we will always be driven by the "market" and the pragmatics of mere survival — legitimate to a point, but hardly the basis for a collective identity and purpose. The commodification of theological education threatens some of the most fundamental values of good theological learning. And the only way we will be able to respond effectively to the changing character of the environment of our work is if we have a clear sense of the vocation of the theological teacher — its character and essential practices; and if we have a clear sense of the distinctive vocation of the theological school. We need to *think* vocationally and ask the question: What is the inherent and essential calling of this school at this time and place in response to these circumstances and in the light of our essential defining charisma or vision?

But without the second, shared governance, even if we agree on our vocation, we will lack a means by which we can fulfill that vocation together. In other words, even if we were able to come to clarity about our "vocation," we would be incapable of implementing it. Without a model of shared governance, we will lose our capacity to draw on the wisdom of

6. William Barry, "Toward a Theology of Discernment," *The Way, Supplement:* The Place of Discernment, 64 (Spring 1989): 129-40.

many and we will alienate key constituencies as we respond to the inevitable changes. A model of shared governance empowers a school to draw on the wisdom and expertise of all while also, as much as possible, assuring a high degree of ownership of the actions that are taken to respond to these changes. We must respond proactively to the changes in our environment; without an empowering model of shared governance we will either be left to a hierarchical model wherein those "at the top" make the decisions, or we will find ourselves in a perpetually conflicted state that makes effective decision-making impossible. Only with a model of shared governance will we genuinely be able to own together the appropriate response(s) to these changes.

Shared governance also means that everyone is, in some form or another, involved in governance. No one, whether on the faculty or on the board, can with good conscience determine that others will run the school while they go about their work in their "little" corner. The changing character of theological education demands responsible participation from each trustee and each member of the faculty. Faculty in particular need to hear this and realize that we will thrive in our vocations only if we develop organizational expertise — the capacity to live and work with an astute understanding of the culture, patterns of governance, mission, values, and ethos of the school(s) where we are invited to teach. It is from this posture that we have the opportunity to respond to the changes that are inevitable, changes that invariably shape the contours of our work.

In other words, we cannot be naïve about how our institutions, organizations, or schools "work." We must develop the organizational and the political competencies that enable us to be active participants in shaping the culture and character of the schools where we serve. Only then can we engage together in the process by which we determine our collective vocation and assure, together, that our vocation is the primary and fundamental point of reference in the decisions we make about curriculum, resources, and personnel.

Shared Governance Enables Us to Be a Learning Organization

In a consideration of how organizations work effectively and how individuals can thrive within organizations, there are few resources as helpful as those produced by Peter Senge and his associates, most notably, *The Fifth*

Discipline: The Art and Practice of the Learning Organization.[7] Senge and his associates emphasize the need to think *systemically.* We are effective when we see ourselves within a system — a whole and complex network. Senge's work is valuable in large part because it is written for all who work within organizations. So much literature on the quality of organizations and what makes them effective is written for those in leadership and management. And clearly these roles have a critical part to play. But to thrive in our common efforts, all of us need to see what it is that makes for effective organizations.

Senge and company's most distinctive contribution is their call for *learning* organizations. He contends that those organizations that are most effective are those that have developed the capacity to foster continuous learning, not merely in the resource and development department, but throughout the organization. Their work is a reminder that all of us at Regent College, for example, need to be attentive to the changing environment in which we do our work and the changing character of the kinds of students who matriculate with us. We need to bear in mind that the changing character of the church as well as of the economy is the context in which our students will live and work when they complete their studies. And while we may have experts who help us describe and interpret these changes, none can choose a posture of passivity. As it is ably stated in the standards of the Association of Theological Schools, "The collaborative nature of governance provides for institutional learning and self-correction. . . ."[8] At Regent College, for example, we are learning together what it means that the majority of our students enroll in our two-year Master's program rather than being content with our one-year diploma; that the majority of our students are no longer taking a break from their career for eight months of theological study but rather coming for two years and viewing this as a time of vocational discernment; and that all of our students, not only those enrolled in M.Div., must come to terms with the changing character of the church and its mission.

Good learning means that we are able to examine the changes in the environment without always feeling threatened or defensive. It means that

7. Peter M. Senge, *The Fifth Discipline: The Art and Practice of the Learning Organization* (New York: Doubleday, 1990); and the sequel, Peter M. Senge et al., *The Fifth Discipline Fieldbook: Strategies and Tools for Building a Learning Organization* (New York: Doubleday, 1994).

8. ATS Standards of Accreditation, 8.2.3.

we accept the wisdom of those who have been with the institution a long time — the wisdom of those who have been with the institution through changes, perhaps many changes, and observed its capacities to respond and adapt well (or not so well). But it also means that we recognize the distinctive contribution of those who are newer to the community: we must not so limit credibility in decision-making that newcomers are marginalized because they "do not know how we do things around here." The reality is that in many cases it is new faculty members and board members who may be best positioned to suggest ways in which the school's vocation can be most effectively sustained and fulfilled.

The Meaning of Shared Governance:
Mutual Respect, Deference, and Accountability

Shared governance requires mutual respect and mutual submission out of a fundamental acceptance of the distinctive roles within the governance process. It means that trustees necessarily appreciate that their role is that of support and encouragement of their most valuable and significant resource: the faculty. It is a contradiction in terms for a board to develop an adversarial relationship with the faculty; their very reason for being is to support the mission of the school by assuring the necessary fiscal and infrastructural system that assures that the faculty can do their work. Conversely, there is probably nothing more insidious to the well-being of a theological school than adversarial posture by board members towards members of the faculty.

Yet just as surely, faculty are highly dependent on the expertise of the trustees. And though it is often the case that the culture of the board is that of the corporate world, so seemingly different from the academic culture of the faculty, it is nevertheless imperative that faculty view the board as their partners, not their adversaries. The same could be said of administrators — presidents, deans, and others who provide administrative support and leadership for both trustees and faculty. They play a necessary and critical role in the capacity of the school to be effective in response to change. Indeed, both trustees and faculty depend heavily on those in administrative roles who as often as not are those who profile and anticipate the environmental changes that call both the trustees and the faculty to a creative and courageous response.

Mutual respect requires us to rely on one another, allowing the other to play his or her rightful role within the institution, out of a deeply held conviction that no one person can be all things to the school. This also includes a gracious acknowledgment that we are accountable to one another for our work — faculty to deans, and deans to faculty. And if we yield to one another, it means that we acknowledge the legitimate authority of the other, authority that is integral to the role of the other in the school. The trustees, for example, have real authority, and they are only responsible in the exercise of their roles if they exercise that authority. And nothing is gained by faculty members who either resent the fact that the board has such authority or resist it. It is a necessary element in the life of a school. But there is also a distinctive sense in which the board recognizes the necessary and inevitable authority of the faculty. While their authority is less hierarchical, it is no less real, and a board that denies the reality of this authority and power fails to understand the power inherent in presence. The faculty are necessarily at the center of the life and work of the college; they embody its mission and values week by week in the classroom and the places where the common life of the school is sustained and practiced.

To stress the need for shared governance, then, is not to suggest that all share equally in every aspect of governance. I might question, for example, a practice of equal representation from both the faculty and the student body on a key committee if that committee is one in which the faculty should have a privileged voice. The common concern that "everyone would have a say" has the unfortunate effect of minimizing the voice or contribution of those who should have the most influence in a particular decision. Shared governance means that we acknowledge the need of many to speak to a matter while reserving the right of some to make a decision when that decision is inherent in their role or responsibility in the school. In other words, in affirming the place of shared governance, we are highlighting not only a participation in decision-making; we are also affirming a distribution of tasks and responsibilities, a distribution essential to the well-being of the school.

This acknowledgment of the rightful place and even authority of the other, and thus the need for mutual accountability, is required for another reason as well. James Fowler has aptly noted that:

> There is likely no area of potential self-knowledge where we are more subject to self-deception and more tempted to resort to self-serving ra-

tionalizations than in accounting for our efforts to influence and determine the social collectivities of which we are a part and the lives of those
involved in them.[9]

Accepting a model of shared governance means that we graciously work
within structures where our own "self-serving rationalizations" can be
challenged.

Finally, mutual respect and accountability also imply a fundamental
hospitality, a hospitality in the process of decision-making that is reflected
in empathic listening, attentiveness to the legitimate concerns of each one
who is affected by the decisions and actions of the collective.

Shared Governance Means We Accept the Reality of Conflict

As soon as we accept the place of divergent voices and perspectives, we assume that conflict will be part of the decision-making process and part of
what it means to govern together. Conflict is an inherent part of a lively
community and a necessary source of strength to a vital organization.
While we will hopefully have a high level of congruence when it comes to
identifying the defining vision, charisma, or vocation of our particular
theological school, we will never likely agree on the way in which that vision is implemented. In their superb study of the nature of effective leadership, Michael Jinkins and Deborah Bradshaw Jinkins argue that:

> Poor leadership attempts to homogenize . . . various and divergent
> voices into a single voice. Good leadership cultivates [a] discordant plu-
> rality for the sake of the good of the society. . . . a society enjoying cre-
> ative conflict will enjoy vitality, will encourage the vigorous participa-
> tion in its life of diverse voices, and will be the stronger for it.[10]

Conflict can, of course, be destructive; some schools can become so conflicted one wonders if there is any possibility of resolution and health with

9. James Fowler, *Becoming Adult, Becoming Christian* (San Francisco: Harper and
Row, 1984), p. 109.
10. Michael Jinkins and Deborah Bradshaw Jinkins, *The Character of Leadership: Political Realism and Public Virtue in Nonprofit Organizations* (San Francisco: Jossey-Bass Publishers, 1998), p. 117.

the current players. The institutional pathologies have become so deep-seated that only through extensive and expert help will some level of harmony be found. But we cannot, regardless of previous experience, so fear conflict that we shrink from disagreements, or subtly or implicitly shut down discordant voices. Conflict and disagreement is an essential element in shared governance.

This being the case, we do not need to hope for the elimination of conflict. Robert Kegan suggests that a postmodern view of organizations calls us to not merely tolerate the reality of conflict, but actually view disputants as parts, necessary parts, of a whole.[11] Rather than viewing the other with whom I differ as an enemy, why not view the other as enabling us all to be complete and whole? The reality of conflict is a reminder that our lives, our work, and the issues we face are anything but simple. And we will not appreciate their complexity unless we have diverse opinions and perspectives on the table.

But it should be stressed: conflict can be insidious. And we will consequently only be able to thrive in a model of shared governance if we sustain strong interpersonal skills and capabilities.

Shared Governance Means Effective Communication

A model of shared governance means that information is not used as a means of control or power. While everyone in a learning community recognizes the need for privacy and confidentiality in matters particular to individuals — whether it is the grade on an assignment or the details that are part of a faculty review and evaluation for performance — the community is served best when it is well informed. As many have noted, there is no such thing as *over*communication.

An essential element of effective communication is good conversation. Good conversation means, among other things, the leisured give and take of empathic listening and honest speech, which in turn form the context for effective communal discernment. It is the conversation that happens before, after, and around the formal business of the faculty and the board, the conversation of the board or faculty when they are on retreat, or the conversa-

11. Robert Kegan, *In Over Our Heads: The Mental Demands of Modern Life* (Cambridge, Mass.: Harvard University Press, 1994), pp. 319-26.

tion that happens in the common room when there is no formal agenda. This is not the conversation of complaint. Rather, it is the honest conversation about the joys and sorrow of our work, the dreams and aspirations we have for our work, and the shared wisdom of learning to live with grace in the midst of it all. This conversation then becomes the essential backdrop for the formal actions taken in a business meeting, the actions that necessarily shape the contours of the expression of our collective vocation.

I often feel that one of my primary responsibilities as a dean is merely that of fostering good conversation — making sure that the faculty have the time and a plentiful supply of good coffee to be able to step back from the harried pace that so easily besets the academy to talk about their work, their goals and aspirations, the challenges they are facing, and what it is going to take for us to be effective together. In this I recognize that presidents and deans have the capacity to either foster an environment of good conversation and communication or they can subtly but essentially "shut it down."

Shared Governance Calls for Trust

Shared governance presumes a posture of trust, a trust that is ultimately nothing more than a resolve to let others make decisions that affect the contours of our common lives. A model of shared governance does not imply that all decisions are made by a committee of the whole; it does not mean that everyone does everything. It rather calls us to accept the legitimate decision-making role of the *other* and then trust the other to act in our best interests and, ultimately, in the best interests of the whole. It means that we accept that others will make choices and decisions that affect the well-being of the institution as a whole; it means that we accept the principle of *delegated* authority.

This posture of trust seems particularly difficult for some in western institutions and organizations. Robert Bellah has made the observation that:

> Americans often think of individuals pitted against institutions. It is hard for us to think of institutions as affording the necessary context within which we become individuals; of institutions as not just restraining but enabling us; of institutions not as an arena of hostility within

which our character is tested but an indispensable source from which character is formed.[12]

And this deeply felt ambivalence about institutions in general is often translated into a conscious or unconscious distrust of institutions in general and of institutional administrators in particular. In some cases people have good reason to be ambivalent about the exercise of authority and power; many faculty have seen trustees and administrators abuse authority; trustees have experienced the disappointment of having a senior administrator not provide them with all the information they need when called upon to govern well. And the consequence is that people are hesitant to trust.

However understandable, the lack of trust undercuts the capacity of the community to govern well together, to be confident in each other as we serve one another and as we serve on behalf of one another. The irony is that a spirit of mistrust actually fosters a hierarchical climate in which distrust can only fester. The only alternative is a model of shared governance wherein we *choose* to trust the other — where faculty choose to trust the governing board and where subcommittees of the board and the faculty are able to function without fear that their every move is viewed as suspect, and where administrators are not assumed to have personal agendas. However, this is only possible if there is space for the leisured conversation described above. Further, everything said here presupposes that we need to *gain* trust, build trust, and keep trust; and that when trust is broken it may not be easily restored. It may take considerable time. However, building trust is essential to the well-being of the collective, a critical element in shared governance.

Shared Governance Calls for a Fundamental Posture of Service

Finally, shared governance assumes that we are servants of one another and, ultimately, of our common vocation. Administrators often speak of the calling to serve, perhaps because presidents and deans are in positions in which authority and power can be abused. Regularly, presidents and deans need to stand back and ask the question so ably posed by Jinkins and Jinkins: "How would I behave as a leader in this organization if the organization's purpose had a higher claim on me than my own comfort and secu-

12. Robert Bellah et al., *The Good Society* (New York: Alfred A. Knopf, 1991), p. 6.

rity?"[13] But while it is perhaps doubly imperative that administrators ask this question, surely the posture of service should not be theirs alone. If we are going to fulfill our common vocation, we must choose a posture of self-giving generous service in which personal agendas are secondary to the fundamental commitment to the goals of the collective. It means that we do not enter into a committee meeting with the assumption that as one individual we happen to know what is the best alternative or outcome of our deliberations. Rather, we acknowledge that the outcome will be the fruit of a group process of deliberation and discernment, and we enter into the process without preconceived notions of what the outcome will be. It means that we come to a committee meeting with our own convictions and perspectives, but that our posture is one of attending to the other, of listening so that one knows the mind of the collective and so that one contributes in one's speaking to an outcome that is only possible through the deliberation, an outcome that no one could anticipate because it arose out of the collective, and not merely in the accumulation of majority votes. It means, quite simply, that we choose to give priority to the collective vocation and consistently come back to the resolution that our work, our teaching, our research, and our driving concerns are all understood and incorporated within the vocation that we embrace *together*.

Personal Responsibility and Differentiation

I am making the case that if we are effective within organizations, it is because we have the capacity to discern, together, our collective vocation and that we have the capacity to work with a model of shared governance. A third commitment is equally essential. If there is a strong interplay between the vocation of the individual and that of the collective, we must sustain the capacity for both engagement *and* personal autonomy.

Taking Personal Responsibility

We must take personal responsibility for our lives, our work, and our vocations as theological teachers. We cannot allow ourselves to be victimized

---

13. Jinkins and Jinkins, *The Character of Leadership*, p. 118.

by the inevitable changes that are coming to higher education or by the equally inevitable wrongs that will be committed against us by the institutions in which we serve. It means that we never so lose ourselves within the collective that we are alienated or marginalized from our own vocations.

We will only be able, in the end, to respond well to the schools in which we teach if we assume personal responsibility for our own lives and work. Our lives and our work are our own; they do not belong to these organizations, and we must sustain a critical distinction between our own identity and vocations and those of the schools in which we teach. This does not mean that we are independent contractors. But it does mean that we maintain a fundamental detachment. Our vocation is never synonymous with that of the organization(s) where we are employed. They are, rather, both housed within the theological school, and they are exercised in partnership with the theological school and with one another.

Taking personal responsibility also means that we are attentive to those elements within the collective that have the capacity to undermine our individual vocations. For example, every school has organizational or cultural pathologies. Some can be held at bay and kept from poisoning the well; but some are capable of crippling the school and the individuals who work there. I have found it helpful to be sensitive to the prevailing emotion within the school. I once worked in a situation where the dominant energizing (actually, it was enervating) emotion was anger, and I could not help but conclude that if a person was susceptible to anger, this school would be a highly destructive place to be. But more to the point, I concluded that while it is possible to serve without anger in such a place, it was possible only if one was both conscious of the climate within which one worked and if one consciously chose to sustain a fundamental differentiation from that climate.

People Who Are Differentiated

Personal responsibility, then, is only possible if we are differentiated. Success in the collective vocation requires enculturation and assimilation to the ways and values and vision of the collective. But it also requires that we sustain a healthy autonomy. As a senior dean approaching retirement stressed in his counsel to new, younger deans, "Never let them reduce you to your role as dean." He urged his hearers to not take things personally when they are directed to the dean in the role of dean. To be effective, he stressed, it is imperative to distinguish yourself from the role and constantly strive to be authentic in the role.

The same could be said of trustees and faculty members: our identity is never solely that of one who fulfills a role in the school; neither is our personal vocation continuous and synonymous with that of the school. We work within the collective, but we do so as individuals whose identity and call find expression both within the collective as well as on its own merits, distinct from the collective.

Only with this kind of differentiation can we give ourselves with generosity to our colleagues and to the collective vocation, in a generous service that is given with discernment, courage, and hope. Only then can we say "No," when the dean asks us to do one more thing(!) and we know that to accept is to take on more than we can do with serenity and inner peace. Only as we are differentiated can we truly let go of the collective whole enough to trust another and not demand that we are in on every decision, and every action. And then, of course, only as we are differentiated can we accept with grace that decisions will be made with which we differ, decisions in which we vote in the minority. Such actions, an inevitable aspect of shared governance, will not crush our spirits or leave us dejected or feeling mistreated. We can accept with grace both the times in which the collective agrees with us and chooses not to agree with us, quite simply because we have not linked our personal identities and vocations too closely with that of the collective. Differentiation also means that as faculty members we can call for and encourage change; we can stand "outside" of the collective and call each other to rethink the way we do our work, engage the changing environment, fulfill our common vocation, and teach effectively.

Then also, only as we are differentiated, can we let go with grace when it is time to resign or retire. Retirement is essentially a call to "let go," and accept that the school, the collective vocation, continues and is held in trust by others.

The Individual Within the Collective

Finally, the call for personal responsibility assumes the reality of communal responsibility. It is essential that we think in terms of the collective vocation, and that as faculty and trustees we work together toward a common mission, sustained by a common vision and set of values. But this common identity and commitment never so override the individual that we lose touch, individually, with our own call, our own sense of vocation. Indeed, in many respects the very calling of the trustees is to sustain and maintain an environment in which the vocation of the theological teacher can thrive. They are stewards of an extraordinary resource: the teachers of the Church. And their commitment to the school's mission, viability, and financial well-being can never be so defined that they lose a sense of their stewardship of the vocations of those who are called to teach. The trustees, in this regard, do not merely react to the changing environment but also act as a buffer to those changes, insofar as the changes threaten the elements that are essential to the viability and integrity of good theological education. Further, they can never think of their faculty as commodities to be retained or dispensed with in response to the whims of a "market." The very character of theological education demands that trustees view their role as one of sustaining the very environment that makes good teaching possible, an environment in which a student can be confident of a strong residential faculty who are sufficiently protected from the whims of the environment that they can fulfill their vocations with courage and grace.

Ultimately, though, we are each personally responsible for our lives and our work. Even though we have received an appointment to a job, it is *our* job. We are not owned by the school. We ultimately and finally work for ourselves, "as unto the Lord" (Col. 3:23, KJV), and we are ultimately and finally responsible for our own professional development, our own mental, emotional, and spiritual health, and our own capacity to be effective in our work. But all this is immensely easier when trustees and presidents and deans view their work as enabling faculty to be all that they are called to be.

On the other hand, effective trustees work with faculty to assure that there is an effective response to a changing environment, challenging faculty to think in terms of a changing student body, changes in information technology, and changes in the economy that of necessity affect the contours of theological education and call theological teachers, individually and collectively, to rethink and adapt and adjust and thereby be faithful to their vocation. And the ideal, of course, is that this is all the fruit of good conversation: good conversation that sustains a common awareness of the collective vocation, of what makes for good theological education, and of the discernment that is needed for a courageous, creative response to the changing environment in which we fulfill that vocation.

Contributors

Michael Battle is Assistant Professor of Spirituality and Black Church Studies at Duke Divinity School.

W. Clark Gilpin is Professor of the History of Christianity and of Theology at the University of Chicago Divinity School.

Paul J. Griffiths is the Schmitt Professor of Catholic Studies at the University of Illinois at Chicago.

L. Gregory Jones is Dean and Professor of Theology at Duke Divinity School.

Rosemary Skinner Keller is Dean and Professor of Church History at Union Theological Seminary in New York City.

Lois Malcolm is Associate Professor of Systematic Theology at Luther Seminary.

Claire Mathews McGinnis is Associate Professor of Hebrew Bible at Loyola College in Maryland.

Bonnie J. Miller-McLemore is Professor of Pastoral Theology and Counseling at Vanderbilt Divinity School.

Frederick W. Norris is Dean E. Walker Professor of Church History and Professor of World Mission/Evangelism at Emmanuel School of Religion.

STEPHANIE PAULSELL is Visiting Lecturer in Ministry at Harvard Divinity School.

SUSAN M. SIMONAITIS is Assistant Professor of Theology at Fordham University.

GORDON T. SMITH is Vice President, Dean, and Associate Professor of Spiritual Theology at Regent College in Vancouver, British Columbia.

LEANNE VAN DYK is Professor of Reformed Theology at Western Theological Seminary.

PAUL J. WADELL is Associate Professor of Religious Studies at St. Norbert College.